planning and providing for excellence in education

Edgar L. Morphet, *Director*
David L. Jesser, *Associate Director*
Arthur P. Ludka, *Assistant Director*

Improving State Leadership in Education Project,
Denver, Colorado

CITATION PRESS   NEW YORK   1972

ACKNOWLEDGEMENTS

The staff of the project, *Improving State Leadership in Education,* is deeply indebted to many individuals and to representatives of several organizations who have made valuable contributions relating not only to this publication, but to other aspects of the project. These include: the members of the Policy Board and Project Committee, who have provided perceptive and insightful guidance; representatives from the U. S. Office of Education, who have been most cooperative and helpful in assisting the project staff to improve both procedures and product; and to Don Dafoe, Donald Grote and Wendell Pierce who, as members of the Policy Board, reviewed the manuscript and made numerous suggestions that have been incorporated in the final draft.

Specific mention and grateful acknowledgement should be made of the contributions by those who assembled and prepared basic materials relating to planning and change processes in education. These include: Robert S. Fisk, Professor of Educational Studies, State University of New York at Buffalo; Bernarr S. Furse, Administrative Assistant for Special Projects, Utah State Board of Education; Ronald Hildebrand, School of Education, University of Colorado; Walt LeBaron, Planning Consultant, Washington, D. C.; Charles Jung, Northwest Regional Educational Laboratory, Portland, Oregon; Michael J. Koetting, Research Assistant, Improving State Leadership in Education; Henry Toy, Jr., President, Nu-Toy, Inc., Washington, D. C.; and Lyle O. Wright, North Bay PACE Center, Corte Madera, California.

The inputs provided by these consultants have been very helpful in the process of preparing the manuscript. Responsibility for the final draft, however, was assumed by the project staff: Edgar L. Morphet, Project Director—Chapters 3, 9, 10; David L. Jesser, Associate Director (with special assistance of Michael J. Koetting for Chapters 6 and 7)—Chapters 2, 6, 7, 8; Arthur P. Ludka, Assistant Director—Chapters 1, 4, 5.

Special appreciation should also be expressed for the dedicated efforts of Maridee Sensel and Lana Capra, who patiently typed and retyped the numerous manuscript versions, and at the same time, handled effectively the many other demanding matters associated with the project office.

The Improving State Leadership in Education Project was financed by funds provided under the Elementary and Secondary Education Act of 1965 (Public Law 89-10, Title V, Section 505) and the participating states.

PREFACE

For more than a decade the words "excellence" and "quality" have figured prominently in educational literature. In quest of excellence a wide range of innovative changes that seemed to hold promise have been tried. Most of these, sad to say, have contributed little to the goal. For example, some fifteen years ago a prominent educational psychologist predicted that by 1965 the hardcover textbook would have vanished from the classroom, having been replaced by programed materials. Five years ago another student of educational change listed the trends that he believed would lead to excellence: (1) psychological testing, (2) educational television, (3) homogeneous grouping, (4) teaching machines, and (5) team teaching. We see now how often faith has been pinned on false hopes.

It is time to look at educational change from a different perspective. *Planning and Providing for Excellence in Education* assumes that certain conditions are basic to educational progress. These include a clear definition of purposes, involvement of the people who are concerned with education, the exercise of appropriate roles by organizations and agencies, and the intelligent use of communication and problem-solving.

In education purposes come first. Unless we can fix our sights on the goals to be achieved, there is not much use in talking about the means. For example, if we agree that education is concerned with the growth and the fulfillment of the individual, his own personal process of becoming, as well as the great human issues that everybody must help to solve, then we have the beginnings of a basis for planning an educational program. But people must make the decisions.

Education is in a time of testing. Basic beliefs such as the philosophy of compulsory universal education are now being questioned. The people must consider how they want their educational systems to serve them and their posterity. To assist in the thinking, deciding, and doing that the times require is the basic aim of *Planning and Providing for Excellence in Education.*

MELVIN W. BARNES
Vice-President, Professional Relations
Scholastic Magazines, Inc., April 1972

IMPROVING STATE LEADERSHIP IN EDUCATION

POLICY BOARD

Don M. Dafoe, *Council of Chief State School Officers,* Executive Secretary, Washington, D.C.

Lawrence G. Derthick, *National Education Association,* Assistant Executive Secretary, Washington, D. C.

Russell T. Gregg, *University Council for Educational Administration,* Professor of Educational Administration, University of Wisconsin, Madison

Donald V. Grote, *American Association of School Administrators,* Superintendent of Public Schools, Wilmette, Illinois

Byron W. Hansford (Chairman), *Council of Chief State School Officers,* Colorado* Commissioner of Education, Denver

Emil A. Koehn, *National Association of State Boards of Education,* Past President, Parker, South Dakota

Wendell H. Pierce, *Education Commission of the States,* Executive Director, Denver

Mrs. Leon Price, *National Congress of Parents and Teachers,* President, Chicago

Harold V. Webb, *National School Boards Association,* Executive Secretary, Chicago

---

*Administering State for the Project

PROJECT COMMITTEE

B. Dean Bowles, Associate Professor, Department of Educational Administration, University of Wisconsin, Madison

Roald F. Campbell, Fawcett Professor of Educational Administration, The Ohio State University, Columbus

Jack Culbertson, Executive Director, University Council for Educational Administration, Columbus

Harry L. Phillips, Director, Division of State Agency Cooperation, U. S. Office of Education, Washington, D. C.

J. Graham Sullivan, Deputy Superintendent, Los Angeles City School District, Los Angeles

PROJECT STAFF

Edgar L. Morphet	David L. Jesser	Arthur P. Ludka
Director	*Associate Director*	*Assistant Director*

INTRODUCTION

Some writers and speakers have attracted considerable attention during recent years by stating that "public education in this country has failed." With equal ease and invalidity others similarly may get attention by claiming that nonpublic education has also failed. Such unwarranted generalizations tend to create confusion and dissension—to divert attention from the basic issues that must be faced if significant progress is to be made in resolving some of the major problems of modern society.

Actually, as most authorities recognize, education not only has contributed significantly to the progress of the nation but also has been improved in many important respects in most communities and states. It has recognized and is attempting to deal with important problems which were ignored for many generations, including the provision of appropriate opportunities for under-privileged and disadvantaged children and youth, for slow learners and dropouts, for those who do not expect to attend institutions of higher learning, for adults who need continuing education, and even for college and university students who have received little benefit from traditional programs and procedures.

But in most states the changes made in education have been relatively uncoordinated and poorly planned, and are not adequate to meet the needs of a rapidly changing society. Lay citizens and educators in every state and community and all agencies of government at every level urgently need to find more effective ways of cooperating in planning systematically and continuously for achieving excellence in all aspects and levels of education, for effecting needed improvements, and for developing and implementing appropriate provisions for appraising and reporting on progress.

A major purpose of the project, *Improving State Leadership in Education,* is to encourage and assist the citizens of each state to seek and utilize the most appropriate and effective ways to improve all levels and aspects of education throughout the state—to become seriously and meaningfully involved in a continuing quest for excellence in education. Fortunately some people are already deeply involved in this important quest and considerable progress is being made in some areas, but much more rapid progress is urgently needed in every state.

In this country, each state is primarily responsible for the kind and quality of education provided for its residents. But the role of the states and their relations to local school systems and to the federal government have changed considerably during recent years and urgently need further modifications. Because of the crucial and increasingly significant role of the states in improving education, the first publication sponsored by this project was concerned with *Emerging State Responsibilities for Education,* which, in an effort to facilitate communication and cooperation, was supplemented by the monograph, *Directions to Better Education,* and by elaborate multimedia materials for utilization at regional and state conferences.

The present volume is concerned primarily with the state role and relations in *Planning and Providing for Excellence in Education.* This volume, likewise, will be suplemented by a monograph entitled *Directions to Excellence in Education,* and by related multimedia materials for use at conferences and by study groups throughout the nation.

If the citizens of every state seriously plan for excellence in education, they can greatly improve the quality of education for everyone involved and at least closely approach the goal of excellence. This is the urgent challenge that must be faced realistically by everyone seriously concerned with a better future for every citizen in the nation.

Byron W. Hansford, *Chairman, Policy Board,* and

Edgar L. Morphet, *Project Director*

CONTENTS

PART ONE

PROVIDING FOR EDUCATION IN A DYNAMIC SOCIETY

PART TWO

STATE LEADERSHIP IN PLANNING IMPROVEMENTS IN EDUCATION

PART THREE

State Leadership in Effecting Needed Changes in Education

PART FOUR

State Role in Improving Major Aspects of Education

PROVIDING FOR EDUCATION IN A DYNAMIC SOCIETY

Chapter 1

The Quest for Quality

In every society the members of each new generation need to learn at least enough to have a reasonable opportunity to survive and to help their society to survive and improve. Human infants have no basis for distinguishing between forces and conditions that are dangerous or harmful and those that are beneficial. What they learn or do not learn—even whether they survive—is determined at first primarily by their parents or others who may be concerned. *The informal process of education* begins at birth and continues in some form as long as the individual survives, but does not suffice to meet the needs either of the person or of society. All societies have found it necessary to provide some more *formal kind of education* in order to help individual members to contribute to the progress as well as to the survival of the group. As knowledge and understanding have increased, even greater emphasis has been placed on formal education in an effort to help everyone become well enough informed and develop sufficient understanding to deal or cooperate in dealing effectively with problems that continue to arise.

But both informal and formal education have often been used, through ignorance or design, to transmit harmful misinformation or to prevent some members of the group from becoming self-realizing and self-actualizing human beings. In fact, the evidence available seems to indicate that a number of earlier civilizations that were well in advance of their time in many respects gradually disintegrated primarily because something serious went wrong with their values or their system of education or both. The Aztec, Greek, Roman, Mayan, Incan and other civilizations represent historical examples from which modern society can learn and profit.[1]*

*Footnote references are given at end of the chapter.

1

The population and knowledge explosions, rapid advances in the development and utilization of technology, growing pollution, increases in crime and major disturbances, rapidly expanding slum areas and many other similar developments in this country during recent years have led to serious and searching questions by many people. Some have become convinced that the traditional system of education that has placed considerable emphasis on "intellectual learning" and given little attention to modern problems is no longer meeting the needs. They are also concerned that the informal education provided for children in many homes is inadequate and results in serious handicaps. There are many demands that education be redesigned to meet present and emerging needs but apparently there is little agreement thus far on how this can best be accomplished.

It should be apparent that possession of knowledge alone is insufficient for the resolution of the problems facing mankind. Available knowledge must be interpreted, analyzed, applied and utilized to be effective. Knowledge for the sake of knowledge is inadequate. Perhaps some of the absurdities and meaninglessness many people perceive in modern society, in reality, are a result of our failure to be aware of, to integrate, and to utilize effectively the value implication of the knowledge that is transmitted.

Much confusion exists in present-day society as to what can and should be done through education. Moreover there are conflicting attitudes as to what directions should be taken in problem resolution. As Lippman has said, "The supreme question is how men will be willing and able to make themselves willing and able to save themselves."[2] Weingartner has observed, "Our present educational system is an intellectual Maginot Line. It rests on assumptions that were at best marginal 40 years ago; today they are fatal."[3]

SOME DILEMMAS FACING SOCIETY

The members of modern society have enormous power to influence the direction of change. This capacity creates problems, however, for along with this power goes the need to make choices and value judgments about how to utilize it. *Probably the most fundamental and crucial problem currently facing man is how he should utilize this greatly increased power to improve his social and physical environment.* Man is just beginning to realize the magnitude of his power for effecting constructive or destructive change. Neither his cultural and social heritage nor his educational experiences have adequately prepared him for this role.

Another major problem facing humanity is equally serious: *Twentieth century man understands much less about his fellow human beings and his social environment than about the selfishness, greed, inequities and injustices which are still part of the social scene.* Unfortunately, under the guise of progress, the exploitation of man and his environment has been and, to a large degree, still is a factor deemed essential by some people in effecting what they consider to be improvements.

Most major issues—such as how to eliminate international conflict, to provide responsible government, to ensure law and order, and to avoid racial tension, poverty, drug addiction and pollution—are related to these two fundamental problems. Interestingly, and perhaps significantly, groups vitally concerned about these issues inevitably look to the education system to provide a major basis and means for the resolution of such problems. There are some encouraging signs indicating that an aroused social conscience is beginning to demand the eradication of some of the causes of inequality and frustration. More and more though, it appears that education is being called upon to play a major role in helping to provide the basis for alleviating or resolving current social, political, economic and environmental problems.

The evidence also indicates that present day needs are not being met through the traditional education system. Generally, *the education system has failed to adjust to the needs of a rapidly changing dynamic society*. There is little agreement on purpose, on leadership roles, on the need for long-range planning, and on ways of cooperating effectively to modernize institutions, their organization, programs and practices.

Significant changes must be made in education if society is to meet its responsibilities to the general populace and, especially, to the students of today who will be the adult citizens of tomorrow. Neglect of these responsibilities adds to the confusion that exists and serves to limit the opportunities to capitalize on the inherent capabilities of the society. *A major practical and realistic goal for the education system* in a world marked by frustration, conflict and violence *is to educate for human excellence* of which intellectual development is a central but only a partial feature. As Reich has said:

> . . . today's emerging consciousness seeks a new knowledge of what it means to be human, in order that the machine, having been built, may now be turned to human ends; in order that man once more can become a creative force, renewing and creating his own life and thus giving life back to his society.[4]

THE SEARCH FOR EXCELLENCE IN EDUCATION

Often the terms "excellence" and "quality" are used interchangeably. However, excellence is a reflection of the standards of quality that permeate the various aspects and elements of a given condition, situation or product. Quality is an essential ingredient in the search for excellence that can be approached only as there is movement away from low or mediocre to higher quality in any aspect of life.

The term "excellence" is a curiously powerful word—a word about which people have strong feelings. Each person reacts to the idea of excellence in reference to his own aspirations, his own interpretation of what constitutes high standards, and his own hope for improvement. Excellence, thus, is viewed from different vantage points. The search for excellence should be the goal of all endeavors, public and otherwise, and should constitute a guiding concept in all efforts to bring about improvements. As man makes progress in his understanding of himself, his fellow man and his environment, the criteria for what may be interpreted as excellence should turn increasingly toward *the full development of the human potential for all people at all levels.*

Gardner maintains that "in our true democratic tradition, the society must provide each youngster with the particular kind of education that will benefit *him* in the best manner."[5] He also points out that the concept of excellence in education should emanate from two beliefs that are basic in our society:

1. *A pluralistic approach to values.* American society has always leaned toward such pluralism. We need only be true to our deepest inclinations to honor the many facets and depths and dimensions of human experience and to seek the many kinds of excellence of which the human spirit is capable.

2. *A universally honored philosophy of individual fulfillment.* We have such a philosophy, deeply imbedded in our tradition. Whether we have given it the prominence it deserves is a question we must explore.[6]

FORCES AND FACTORS THAT FACILITATE LEARNING

The implications of the search for excellence call for both a society and an education system that are organized and dedicated to the needs of the individual and related to the current and emerging changes in society. For excellence to be achieved, we must strive for the highest standards in every phase of life—in the home, in the community, in education, in government, in industry and in all other aspects of the society as discussed further in Chapter 9. The American point of view should demand that *all learners in the education system be equally entitled to an appropriate education of high quality that will enable them to achieve to the maximum of their potential.* This is every student's entitlement on the basis of his claim to first-class citizenship. Likewise, this point of view should demand that the elements in our society that facilitate learning and human development be re-emphasized and strengthened to ensure that continuous progress is made toward excellence.

THE INDIVIDUAL

Although the uniqueness of each individual is well documented, we need to question whether this concept seems to be fully accepted or reflected thus far in society and its institutions. In the search for excellence, the individual and how well his needs are met should always be a central concern. On the basis of what is known about the needs of an individual, it should be apparent that *every child* should have the opportunity to:

• *Receive the best pre-natal care feasible in order to ensure an optimum opportunity for a normal life;*

- *Have adequate nourishment and care from the beginning and live in an environment that is conductive to physical and mental health;*

- *Be regarded as a responsible person of value and importance at every age;*

- *Have individuality preserved while learning broad standards of responsible behavior;*

- *Understand himself and others and act in accord with that understanding;*

- *Develop the insights and skills essential to creative living;*

- *Experience beauty and express himself creatively; and*

- *Learn to live with change.*

Animal and human studies are providing ample evidence about the impact and significance of the environment on the development of human potential. These studies seem to confirm the needs listed above. The evidence available suggests that early infancy is a critical period for proper mental development and functioning. The negative effects of malnutrition on growth during pre-natal periods are well documented in numerous studies.[7] Nutritional inadequacy, for example, interferes with many aspects of the development of the brain, of the body, and of behavior. Likewise emotional deprivation during childhood can result in severe retardation in growth and development of the total organism.[8] Environmental studies for the last two decades at the University of California at Berkeley[9] have demonstrated that in order for a growing animal to develop a robust, healthy and metabolically active brain it is crucial that it live in a psychological environment permeated by love, kindness, acceptance, stimulation and diverse learning experiences. These observations have implications for all aspects of both informal and formal education for people.

"As the twig is bent so grows the tree" has long been part of Western folklore. Scientific data tend to support this view in relation to human development. *The deprivation suffered by children can never be made up.* It can have negative consequences for learning, for maturation and for interpersonal relations and can result in significant retardation in the performance of complex learning tasks. The implications of the importance of quality in informal as well as formal education should be evident to all who are concerned with human development.

THE FAMILY AND HOME

The significance of the family and the home cannot be overestimated. It is within this setting that the "life style" of a person normally is developed. *If parents accept the challenge of regarding each child as unique, individuality and wholesome human relations can be fostered and encouraged while responsibility is developed.* An analysis of the basic needs

of a person, especially while he is young, indicates that the prime assets
of human development are acceptance, love and affection. Parental attitudes and actions, thus, have lifelong impacts. A much greater emphasis
on increasing the positive influence of the family and home appears to
be needed in modern society in order to provide a more lasting foundation for progress toward excellence. This need, together with the frustrations of some of the youth in America and in the world, is exemplified
in the following poem[10] by Ann de Montluzin, a high school senior in
Baton Rouge, Louisiana:

THE SEESAW

"Respect, respect,"
   our parents demand.
"Earn, earn our respect,,"
   we reply.
"Bow down, bow low,"
   they order.
"Why, why?"
   we ask.
"Ideals, ideals,"
   they preach.
"Examples, examples,"
   we beg.
And the seesaw tilts again.

THE NEIGHBORHOOD AND COMMUNITY

The environment in the neighborhood and the community in which
an individual lives can facilitate or perhaps even prevent the development of his potential. Coordinated efforts by government, business, industry, home, community service agencies, church and school can serve
to assure maximum availability of individual opportunity for personal
development. Learning needs can be more nearly met when the neighborhood and the community:

- Seek expressions, responses and reactions from all social, ethnic,
  racial, religious and economic groups and utilize the results from
  such involvement in planning and implementing programs for local
  improvement;

- Support the educational enterprise by providing appropriate programs ranging from early childhood education to continuing education for senior citizens;

- Invite the involvement of youth in discussions, decisions and efforts
  directed toward community improvement;

- Strive to promote an esthetic quality in the physical and cultural
  aspects of the community; and

- Continually seek to create an environment that constitutes an in-

viting and wholesome place for all members of the community to
live, learn, worship, work and play.

The Enlarged Environment

Likewise, the influence of the "enlarged or extended" environment—
state, nation and world—cannot be underestimated in terms of its impact
on learning. The living room of today opens on a window to the world
with real and simulated informational inputs bombarding its inhabitants
via the printed page, radio and television. Unfortunately, this exposure
does not portray an environment that is greatly concerned about the
welfare and progress of people or about justice for all. What generally
is reflected are evidences of man's inhumanity to man, poverty, hunger,
violence and a rather general disregard for man as a human being. This
"real" world should become part of the subject matter for discussion in
the home, the community, the church and the school. Basic issues should
be debated and analyzed as part of the process of enlarging the perspectives of each person and of assisting him in the development of an understanding, a point of view, and an appropriate attitude about the problems
facing man in his total environment. In this process there should be maximum concern about the provisions developed to ensure the welfare and
progress of people, and procedures for seeking justice as well as for
continuously improving education.

Forces and Factors That Handicap Learning

The forces and factors that tend to handicap learning and progress
are almost the opposite of those discussed above. Ironically, when individuals are denied, or do not have opportunities, for their human potential
to develop constructively, the tendency to be concerned only about "self"
is reinforced. According to Abraham Maslow,[11] this kind of person strives
to meet his physiological needs—the imperative requirements for food,
clothing, shelter and rest—and to keep and protect what he has. In the
process of satisfying these needs, selfishness and greed can become the
dominant themes in his particular way of life. As a corollary to the life
style of these individuals, injustice tends to become characteristic of a
society when excessive materialism, overt economic efficiency and centralized authority and power are regarded as measures of progress for
and in the society. It is unfortunate that generally "in a free enterprise
system, *survival depends on the ability to compete aggressively,* and those
who are able to do so most effectively and with the fewest compunctions
are likely to be rewarded with the greatest material success, as well as
prestige and power." (Italics supplied)[12]

The report of a recent study by the General Electric Company[13] concluded that shifts in people's basic values may be the most important single element in forecasting the environment in which organizations and
people will operate in the future. With increasing affluence bringing pos-

session of material goods more easily within reach and with education inducing a greater regard for self development, materialism and aggression progressively lose much of their appeal as prime motivating factors. Under these conditions, *the trend toward a new concern for quality and the human dimension in a technological world appears likely to continue.* As society provides more opportunities to meet human needs, the ranking of economic efficiency tends to be reduced to nearer a parity with social values such as justice, equality and individual dignity. As this happens, organizational values conceivably can then be modified in favor of individual and social values. Likewise a higher standard of efficiency in terms of *social accountability* can be expected. *There also appears to be a definite trend in our society from authority by position and power to authority on the basis of knowledge and greater participation in decision making.* Hardin has stated, "What we need is a structure of responsibility that will enable us to live contently in the cornucopia we in fact inhabit."[14]

All members of society are faced with the task of making difficult choices in determining what their future will be. Decisions have to be made and, perhaps, attitudes more than other factors will determine which choices are made. In order to make public life more acceptable, the society may have to accept a decreasing emphasis on affluence in private living. The price tag may include a new national attitude toward all kinds of government, public and private, and a recognition that present-day institutions were designed for a simpler past and cannot be expected to serve well tomorrow's complex and sophisticated needs. The challenge appears to be to shift away from the current emphasis on private consumable goods to improved provisions for a better public life. As Miller has emphasized:

> The real price of the American future is our willingness to grow up and become an adult people. It is a matter of spirit. . . . We have to do some national choosing. This is the price of the future. The mature adult understands the world of choice . . . when he then chooses the better and not the worse—the better for his long term happiness, not his immediate delight; the better for his whole community and nation and not the appearance of better for his family or his group—and when he decides to pay for these choices by giving up those alternatives on which he places less value, then he has bought and paid for his good future.[15]

SOME IMPLICATIONS FOR EDUCATION

What then should become the thrust of education—the direction toward which the educational system should move? What aspects of man's development should be reflected in the school system's philosophy, in its goals and its perceived actions? What kind of output or product should the system help to produce?

James E. Russell, Secretary of the Educational Policies Commission, has succinctly stated:

> We need men who are . . . free. The free man is aware of himself and his

environment and the forces shaping that environment. He is aware of his own passions and how they affect what he perceives. He knows that he perceives the world through the screen of his own personality, that the person he is colors the things he sees. He has considered his own values, the values of others, and the consequences to which these values lead. He is free in sum, not because he is without passion, but because he has examined his life and mastered it with his mind. He is slave to no man, to no doctrine, to no ignorance. He is free because his mind has set him free. To give every man a chance to become this man—this is the central challenge of education in our time.[16]

GAINING A PERSPECTIVE ABOUT THE EDUCATION SYSTEM

Significant questions are being raised in this society in an attempt to gain a perspective about the education system. These include:

- Does and should the education system have a specific and carefully defined purpose and a set of goals that are *relevant to the current and emerging needs of its students?*

- Does and should the education system have a *defensible listing of priorities* that are developed objectively and are based on sound criteria?

- How are the goals and priorities effectively *translated into policy, into procedure and into practice?* How should they be?

- To what extent does and should the education system serve as a *vehicle of social, economic and even perhaps political action* while retaining its intellectual objectivity and integrity?

- To whom and for whom is and should the educational system be *responsible and accountable?*

Some of the important questions increasingly being asked about the traditional education system by parents and others revolves around "why?" These include:

- *Why* does the school day usually have the same number of hours for all students?

- *Why* does the school year consist of a certain number of days?

- *Why* are classes of a standard number of students considered appropriate?

- *Why* is the cut-off date for entry into school so definite?

- *Why* are grade levels set up so rigidly?

In trying to find answers to such questions, m̲
concluded that the reasons for many traditic
since vanished and that many school patterns h̲
except "That's the way it has always been."

Inquiry into the education system based on
above undoubtedly would bring about respons
degree of inconsistency and confusion comparabl

other segments of the society. *The interdependence of society and education is well established.* Zigler has stated:

> Unquestionably the school is the handmaiden of society, but society today is extremely unclear in its charge to the schools. One cause of ambiguity might be assigned to the view that American society is not a monolithic and homogeneous entity but rather a spirited and sometimes freewheeling conglomeration of social forces frequently in conflict. The school that attempts to satisfy all of these forces usually succeeds in satisfying none and is thereby branded a failure. But a failure at what? Who shall ever know whether the school is a success or failure until the goals of the school are clearly delineated and agreed upon by [all] segments of society?[17]

The educational system has been reasonably successful in assisting persons to *learn how to do the "right" things, how to perform, and how to act,* but it has not been very successful in assisting persons to *learn how to think, how to value and judge, how to balance,* and *how to perceive.* Implied in the foregoing statement is the need for the educational system to emphasize individual creativeness and leadership as opposed to "followership."

Individual differences can be nurtured as the schools fulfill their important function as a reservoir, synthesizer and transmitter of man's thoughts, knowledge, culture and heritage. This perhaps can be best accomplished in a learning environment that:

- Avoids labelling, by *accepting* and *knowing* each student and working toward developing the potential represented in each individual;

- Assists students in *acquiring basic skills* that are vital in learning;

- Employs techniques that enable *a more individualized approach* to be used, thus allowing students to progress at a pace commensurate with their own ability;

- Builds learning experiences that bring a *sense of realism* to the student as opposed to the "knowledge for knowledge's sake" approach;

- Arranges for the students to have opportunities *to participate in decision making, in assuming personal responsibility* and *in the use of their own creativeness;*

- Utilizes a *problem-solving approach* whenever applicable to build self-reliance within the student;

- Provides experiences that enable each student to increase *understanding of himself and others* by attending schools with individuals of varied racial, social, economic and ethnic backgrounds;

- Acquaints each student with his social and physical environment, the related expectations and pressures of the environment and the *individual's role as a contributor* through work and effort for personal as well as group improvement; and

- Encourages and assists *parents and others to become active participants* in the educational enterprise.

In one of the numerous points of view being expressed about the challenges facing the education system and the need to encourage new structures and procedures, Schrag has pointed out:

> What the ideal system would do—not in rhetoric nor with slogans from the principal, but in practice—would be to declare itself unequivocally to be the ally of difference, of individuals, and of the tolerant against the invidious; *it would recognize its own limitations in choosing for people and recognize their ability to choose for themselves,* and it would, in all cases, stand at their side against the imperious collective demands of crowds, machines, and bureaucrats. (Italics supplied)[18]

MEANINGFUL LEARNING ENVIRONMENTS IN THE SCHOOLS

In helping students to learn how to form and test better ways to deal with change—as well as with the conflicts that may be associated with it—and to develop more stable values, *it is essential that students encounter meaningful problems in which the probability that a difference in values will occur is very high.* School attendance units, for example, should become genuine functional and responsive educational communities in which *problem resolution is a prime growth experience for each student.* Unfortunately, too many schools today are authoritarian and suppress student initiative and activity, thus inducing negativism, frustration or passivity.

Students need structure, rules and leaders but they also need to have experience in learning how a group establishes its own rules and expectations and how to participate responsibly in those decisions that affect the educational growth of their peers as well as of themselves. The educational community should be small enough, or organized in such fashion, to enable such student participation to occur. In isolation, academic information and intellectual skill are insufficient in preparing youth for life in a rapidly changing society and world.

Students should become active participants in the process of their own education: active participants in the making of vital decisions about school life—particularly those that affect their privacy and their constitutional rights. Equally important is the participation of the students in the decisions that affect the rights of others. Responsibility grows out of respect for one's self and an understanding of the meaning of responsibility and personal freedom. *Responsibility cannot develop prior to the granting of freedom.*

If students are to participate in determining their own destiny in school-related matters, they should have opportunities to choose ways to use their talents and interests and to express their feelings. A school environment that recognizes the dignity and worth of students can be organized so that:

- Students have a voice in planning, deciding upon, implementing, and evaluating experiences in which they participate.

- Students have opportunities to work with other young people and adults in a variety of situations and relationships.

- Students share with teachers and other adults the responsibility for selecting and participating constructively in appropriate activities.

- Students are encouraged to originate plans and ideas for enhancing their role and participation in school and community activities.

What is implied in the foregoing is an emerging realization that the educational system must be regarded more as a *people enterprise* than primarily as a *knowledge factory*. Greater attention should be directed toward assisting each person in the development of his full potential. Combs has appropriately stated that:

> The new stress must not be so much on producing an educated person as on producing an educable person who can learn and adapt himself efficiently all through his life to an environment that is ceaselessly changing. If the educational system is not adaptable to changing environmental conditions, how can it expect to produce people who are?[19]

Today's students will spend most of their productive years in the twenty-first century: a century, according to many authorities, that will be significantly different in its demands for *human* competence. Bennetta B. Washington has stressed that, "If our society is to continue as one that truly values the individual and seeks to benefit from the richness of diversity, we must seek greater understanding of ourselves as individuals. Only then can we be sufficiently supportive of the uniqueness of the individuals we seek to teach."[20]

RESOLVING DILEMMAS FACED BY THE EDUCATION SYSTEM

The involvement of the education system in helping to provide a better basis for the resolution of complex social problems is a relatively new concern. As previously indicated, the interdependence of society and education is well established with each having considerable effect on the other. *Cooperative interaction by all national, state and local agencies legally and morally charged with responsibility for education is needed.* Heretofore, such cooperation has been of a minimal nature because each agency has tended to go its own way in developing its own plans for improvement and serving basically as a separate entity for service. The mandate from the environment for change must be acknowledged and respected; relevant information, energy and resources must be identified, acquired, allocated and utilized in a cooperative effort to resolve priority problems.

There is a growing awareness of the need to cooperate on matters of common concern in education. Hansen and Ludka have pointed out that:

> It is most encouraging to note the many improvements that are actually taking place in the relationships of many state education agencies both 'upward' to the federal level and 'downward' to the local level. Federal-state [and state-local] cooperation is now an operating reality to a degree that would have seemed impossible a few years ago.[21]

New patterns of involvement, of cooperation, and new methods of in-creasing productivity are beginning to be developed to overcome the traditional boundaries that have tended to stifle flexibility and the sharing of resources for the common good. Interstate compacts, projects, commissions and the like have proven to be quite instrumental in this effort.

The need for systematic continuous long-range planning for effecting improvements in all aspects of life, and especially in education, is receiving greater consideration, attention and acceptance throughout the nation. Although change will take place whether or not we prepare for it, *appropriate planning can help to offset many of the difficulties that are encountered in society*. Through planning, "blue sky" and "top of the head" decisions can be minimized, thus often enabling adjustments to be made before serious problems arise.

Planning and effecting educational change is not an easy process. Educational decisions in a state, for example, may be made by the Governor, the legislature, the voters, the state board of education, the chief state school officer and the governing boards and administrative officers of the local education agencies. The involvement of students, parents, other concerned laymen, teachers and local and state agencies and institutions is important in this process.

Primarily because many of the major environmental, social and other problems that society faces extend beyond established boundaries in jurisdiction, scope and responsibility, it is not possible for a single individual, group, institution or agency to provide the needed expertise or resources to successfully cope with these problems. *Educational planning, therefore, cannot be isolated from other developments in the cultural, economic and political aspects of the social system.*

There are many definitions and models of planning. But however it is defined, and however the model is structured, planning—properly interpreted—is basically a systematic process wherein it is possible to ascertain *where we are, where we want to go* and *how we might get there*. It is a process—a means of achieving some desired goal or goals.

A meaningful set of guidelines for planning and effecting improvements should include the following: (1) *develop committed leadership*—without which any planning is doomed to failure; (2) *critically review the literature* to identify related concepts and pertinent bodies of knowledge; (3) *evolve a philosophy* that is consistent with modern concepts about improvement; (4) *create dissatisfaction with the inappropriate*—an awareness of and concern about the situation; (5) *overcome the barriers* —analyze the supportive and non-supportive factors and take strategic action; (6) *arrange for appropriate models*—the kind to be determined by the situation; (7) *consider the budget*—whether needed time and financing are feasible and possible; (8) *select an alternative*—the best and most suitable "path" to be followed; (9) *provide on-going evaluation*— by ascertaining the impact of the decisions and actions taken; and (10) *interpret developments and plan further improvements*—utilize extensive communication in "accentuating the positive" and make a conscientious effort to "eliminate the negative."

The above general guidelines for planning and effecting improvements need to be consistently observed and utilized before substantial progress can be realized. Each of the steps should provide for representation from, and deep involvement of, the various groups concerned about and affected by the action to be taken. *Planning by experts or that which is done by one group for another is usually doomed to failure.* Appropriate educational planning can make it possible to avoid the perpetuation of outmoded policies and practices on one hand and "band wagon" changes on the other, and help to ensure that education will meet the needs of a changing society.

THE CHALLENGE TO SOCIETY AND EDUCATION

At the 1970 White House Conference on Children, the delegates directed considerable attention to some major deficiencies in modern society. In the discussions and the content of position statements, the nation was criticized for its vast neglect of children and youth. As indicated in a report on the conference:

> We like to think of America as a child-oriented society, but our institutions and way of life reveal that our national priorities lie elsewhere. The pursuit of affluence, the worship of material things, the hard sell and the soft, the willingness to accept technology as a substitute for human relationships, and the readiness to blame the victims of evil for the evil itself have brought us to a point where a broken television set or a broken computer provokes more indignation and more action than a broken family or a broken child. Our national rhetoric notwithstanding, the actual patterns of life in America are such that children and families [appear to] come last.[22]

Constructive proposals emerging from the conference included:

- The development of a national health care program to assure comprehensive care for all children;

- The enforcement of legislation ending racism and discrimination in all walks of life;

- The reform of the justice system to emphasize prevention and protection; and

- The replacement of large institutions with small home-like facilities.

The education system, a reflection of the society, was criticized at the conference for its failure to interact with and to exert a positive influence on the society. The participants noted that *it is one thing to cram the minds of youth with knowledge but it is something else to teach a person to apply what is learned to human welfare.* Any design for the education system should focus on an appropriate response to the needs of individual learners—child-oriented learning—through personalized evaluation, individualized learning and individualized preparation of all persons involved in education. Freedom of the individual, respect for the rights of others, duties along with rights and justice before privilege represent the balance wheels of civilization that are applicable in any attempts to redesign the education system.

COMPREHENSIVE, SYSTEMATIC AND CONTINUOUS LONG-RANGE EDUCATIONAL PLANNING

There is a need at all levels of public education for systematic continuous long-range education planning based upon a defensible rationale for educational improvement. *As the tempo of change increases and there is an escalation in the societal demand for a better future, the need for order and good judgment likewise increases.* The education system represents a special mechanism for developing the human capabilities that are demanded by these changes. Through education the future can become to a great extent what we want it to be. Planned change in education will require that more attention and more effort be devoted to planning, programming, budgeting for, evaluating and managing the educational process.

Educational planning is enhanced by an understanding of alternative futures: forecasts of alternative possible configurations of the society in the future. Such understanding provides educational policy makers with a basis for designing education for an evolving future to the extent that it can be forecast. *The interrelationship between educational planning and futures-forecasting is implicit: each affects the other.* The Educational Policy Research Center at the Stanford Research Institute has amplified this contention in the following manner:

> Forecasts help identify problem areas and hence stimulate thinking about remedial measures; they indicate the expected magnitude and nature of technical, economic, and social shifts and hence suggest the urgency of political action; they aid in pinpointing fulcral decision areas upon which the future directions of change will turn and hence isolate the key concerns with which policy must deal; they help define the constraints that the present places on possible futures and hence aid policy makers to temper ideals with realism.[23]

Little progress toward the attainment of excellence in all aspects of the society will be made unless there is an emphasis on continuous planning. *A society capable of continuous renewal has to be one that systematically develops its human resources, removes obstacles to individual fulfillment and emphasizes education, lifelong learning and self-discovery.* Toward these ends, the emerging emphasis on planning should accept the concept that there is a vast difference between a *planned* society and a *planning* society and, thus, encourage decisions to be made by the people or their representatives who have the responsibility for determining basic policies in society.

IMPLICATIONS FOR THE STATE ROLE IN PLANNING FOR EDUCATION

Whenever planning is discussed, the questions ultimately arise, "Who should do the planning?" and "How should it be done?" We need to recognize that *planning is not an exclusive franchise granted to any specific agency or level of government—local, state or federal.* Planning is a collective and cooperative effort with each representative group contributing to and supporting agreement on the identification and procedures for the attainment of goals which represent the conceptual framework or design that permeates the thinking of the persons who are involved. "Planning is a *process* that is utilized: it is not a *recipe* [and] should result in determining objectives and guides—not in a blueprint."[24]

Who Should Do the Planning? The logic of viewing the states as having a major responsibility for providing leadership and services in planning, effecting changes and evaluating progress in education extends beyond legal considerations. The state systems of education are a result of, and have been developed from, cultural needs and the demands for services. These systems represent an "outgrowth of the beliefs, values, and aspirations of the people [and have] an evolving design . . . affected by changes in society that have implications for education and by new ideas and concepts regarding education."[25] Nyquist has pointed to the unique role of the state in educational planning:

> The state provides a broader base for educational leadership and planning than is possible at the local level, yet one which is far closer to the local school . . . than the federal government. It makes possible a continuity of leadership and breadth of perspective directly responsive to regional variations, conditions and needs. The state is uniquely equipped to provide leadership, formulate policies, make decisions—and take action on a scale not so limited as to be fragmentary, transient and localized—nor so vast as to be remote, impersonal and conducive to the development of a bland, monolithic conformity.[26]

A resolution recently adopted by the Education Committee of the Chamber of Commerce of the United States[27] proposed that:

• The National Chamber should advocate participation of business and professional leaders on boards, committees and advisory committees to improve state school systems; and

• The National Chamber should encourage consortiums of states to effectively research and plan for needed changes in the legal structure, the organization, the administration, the evaluative process and the inter-relations of state school systems.

How Should the Planning Be Done? New dimensions in educational planning are necessary if present and future needs are to be met in a more effective manner. The planning that is done in a state should be based on a broad outlook and be related to a realistic assessment of the needs of the community, the state, and the nation. Nyquist[28] has noted for example, that in view of the unmet needs of young children, states should take several steps such as the following in planning for early childhood education: (1) develop stated positions that spell out clearly goals and directions; (2) set guidelines and standards; (3) provide professional guidance and supervision of the best leadership quality available; (4) establish certification credentials, or provide for a strong specialization in early childhood education within the preparation for an elementary certificate; (5) develop and assume forceful leadership to make nursery schools and kindergartens an integral part of the elementary schools; and (6) include prekindergarten and kindergarten education in the foundation program of state school support.

Status of State Educational Planning. The Fourth Annual Report of the Advisory Council on State Departments of Education[29] indicates that state education agencies are developing an awareness of the need, and are beginning to take steps to provide leadership in educational planning. With the assistance of federal funds and by utilizing limited state funds, some state education agencies are developing a bona fide planning competence. The progress achieved in Colorado, Florida, Nevada, Texas, Vermont, and Virginia, for example, is reported in several case studies sponsored by the *Improving State Leadership in Education* project. Other states have made comparable progress. Regional Interstate Project Programs, funded by Section 505, Title V, Elementary and Secondary Education Act of 1965 (ESEA), are providing opportunities for state education agencies to cooperate in developing state plans for certain federally-supported programs and in exploring the advantages to be gained from consolidating the administrative funds available to states from various federal programs. These examples and other developments reinforce the point of view that *the state is the logical entity to coordinate the piecemeal and compartmentalized planning that is prevalent in much of education.*

In Summary

Education seems to have been moving from crisis to crisis without adequately adjusting to modern needs. Although in the tradition of the nation there is a vague but well-tested framework of values, *a major problem seems to be one of being faithful to those values in which we profess to believe and of making these values meaningful throughout the society and in its institutions.* The improvements needed in education will require periodic re-examination and redesigning of the system to support the values agreed-upon in the society. Appropriate and effective planning can help to bring about improvements designed to strengthen and nourish the potential of each person the system is supposed to serve.

Adequate state leadership in planning for excellence in education can serve to provide more appropriate procedures for the analysis of alternative courses of action including the selection of appropriate goals; determining immediate and long-range implications of alternative provisions; and the development of program objectives that can be utilized for increased guidance and control of the system. Properly conducted and implemented, such leadership can help to provide some of the answers to complex questions and establish a basis for shaping sound public policy in education. As Gardner has emphasized:

> The years ahead will test this nation as seriously as any we have known in our history. We have plenty of debators, blamers, provocateurs. We don't have plenty of problem-solvers. A relevant call to action would address itself to that complacent lump of Americans who fatten on the yield of society but never bestir themselves to solve its problems, to powerful men who rest complacently with outworn institutions, and to Americans still uncommitted to the values we profess to cherish as a people.[30]

The students of today and tomorrow are stepping into an unbelievingly exciting and new kind of world. *Their world will demand a new kind of person*: a person with genuine flexibility and freedom, a person who thrives on sensing and solving subtle and complex problems. Helping to prepare students for *that* world is undoubtedly the biggest challenge to which all educational effort should be directed.

Footnote References

[1]See, for example, the film, "Primitive Man in a Modern World" (Whittier, California: Moody Institute of Science).

[2]"Thoughts," *Think*, September-October, 1969, p. 26.

[3]Charles Weingartner, "Recommendations for Legislation: Education and Survival," in *Needs of Elementary and Secondary Education for the Seventies* (Printed for the use of the Committee on Education and Labor, Carl D. Perkins, Chairman, Washington, D. C.: U. S. Government Printing Office, 1970), p. 803.

[4]Charles A. Reich, *The Greening of America* (New York, New York: Random House, Inc., 1970), p. 5.

[5]John W. Gardner, *Excellence: Can We Be Equal and Excellent Too?* (New York, New York: Harper and Brothers, Publishers, 1961), pp. 74-75.

[6]*Ibid.*, p. 134.

[7]Rita Bakan, "Malnutrition and Learning," *Phi Delta Kappan*, June, 1970, pp. 527-30.

[8]Ashley Montagu, "A Scientist Looks at Love," *Phi Delta Kappan*, May, 1970, pp. 463-67.

[9]David Krech, "Brain Research, Some Recent Developments and Some Speculations for the Future," in *Toward Century 21: Technology, Society and Human Values*, C. S. Walla, ed. (New York/London: Basic Book Publishers, 1970), pp. 22-23.

[10]Mary Hair, "Students Write," *Educational Leadership*, February, 1970, p. 453.

[11]Ian H. Wilson, "How Our Values Are Changing," *The Futurist*, February, 1970, p. 6.

[12]Judd Marmor, "Psychiatry and the Survival of Man," *Saturday Review*, May 22, 1971, p. 19.

[13]*Our Future Business Environment: A Re-Evaluation* (New York, New York: Business Environment Section, General Electric Company, July 1969), pp. 33-42.

[14]Garret Hardin, "Making Error Creative," in *Toward Century 21: Technology, Society and Human Values, op. cit.*, p. 77.

[15]J. Irwin Miller, "Changing Priorities: Hard Choices, New Price Tags," *Saturday Review,* January 23, 1971, p. 78.

[16]James E. Russell, *Change and Challenge in American Education* (Boston, Massachusetts: Houghton Mifflin Company, 1965), pp. 47-48.

[17]Edward Zigler, "Report of the Yale Conference on Learning," in *Needs of Elementary and Secondary Education for the Seventies, op. cit.,* p. 812.

[18]Peter Schrag, "End of the Impossible Dream," *Saturday Review,* September 19, 1970, p. 96.

[19]Philip H. Coombs, *The World Educational Crisis* (New York, New York: Oxford University Press, 1968), pp. 104-5.

[20]Bennetta B. Washington, "A Social Imperative: Respect for the Individual," in *To Nuture Humaneness: Commitment for the '70's,* Mary Margaret Scobey and Grace Graham, eds. (Washington, D. C.: Association for Supervision and Curriculum Development, NEA, 1970), p. 201.

[21]Kenneth H. Hansen and Arthur P. Ludka, "Persistent Problems and New Dilemmas," in *Emerging State Responsibilities for Education,* Edgar L. Morphet, David L. Jesser and Arthur P. Ludka, eds. (Denver, Colorado: Improving State Leadership in Education, 1970), pp. 32-33.

[22]"Conference Indicts American Society," *Education U.S.A., Washington Monitor,* December 14, 1970, p. 89.

[23]Arnold Mitchell, "Alternative Futures: An Exploration of a Humanistic Approach to Social Forecasting," (A Research Note from the Educational Policy Research Center at the Stanford Research Institute, Menlo Park, California: November, 1967), p. 1.

[24]David L. Jesser, "Systematic Planning: An Answer to Educational Dilemmas?" *The Science Teacher,* May 1969, p. 35.

[25]Edgar L. Morphet, Roe L. Johns, and Theodore L. Reller, *Educational Organization and Administration,* 2nd ed. (Englewood Cliffs, New Jersey: Prentice-Hall Inc., 1967), p. 36.

[26]Ewald B. Nyquist, "State Organization and Responsibilities for Education," in *Emerging Designs for Education,* Edgar L. Morphet and David L. Jesser, eds. (Denver, Colorado: Designing Education for the Future, May 1968), p. 146. Republished by Citation Press, Scholastic Magazines, Inc., New York, N. Y.

[27]Excerpts from Minutes of the Education Committee, Chamber of Commerce of the United States, the Fairmont Hotel, San Francisco, California, October 16-17, 1969.

[28]Ewald B. Nyquist, *ECS Bulletin,* November, 1970, p. 4.

[29]U. S. Department of Health, Education, and Welfare, *The State of State Departments of Education: Fourth Annual Report of the Advisory Committee on State Departments of Education* (Washington, D. C.: U. S. Office of Education U. S. Printing Office, 1969).

[30]John Gardner, "Toward a Self-Renewing Society," *Time,* April 11, 1969, p. 41.

Chapter 2

Effecting Improvements in Provisions for Education

Formal education—participation in the organized educational process —was provided for only a relatively small proportion of the population in most societies until recently. In the more primitive societies, usually only the male youth, upon the attainment of puberty, became eligible to take part in the established educational program. In some of these societies the criteria for determining who should (or would) benefit were quite harsh. For example, the leaders of ancient Sparta developed a method for determining participation in the educational program that was based almost entirely on physical fitness. Plutarch described it thus:

> It was not left to the father to rear what children he pleased, but he was obliged to carry the child to a place called *Lesche,* to be examined by the most ancient men of the tribe who were assembled there. If it was strong and well proportioned, they gave orders for its education . . .; but if it was weakly and deformed, they ordered it thrown into the place called *Apothetae* . . . concluding that its life could be no advantage either to itself or to the public.[1]*

Contrary to popular belief, some selective processes are still utilized in virtually every nation. Most modern nations, including the United States, profess to believe in the principle of equality of educational opportunity—that every person has the right to benefit, to the limit of his capacity, from the educational program. Yet many are denied the opportunity to benefit fully from the educational process and, consequently, society is denied the positive contributions that might have been made by those who do not have an adequate education.

In totalitarian nations, the goals of education usually differ in important respects from those in the democracies. In the former, a primary goal of education is likely to relate to the maintenance and perpetuation of established political structure and dogma. Where this is the case, there is no place in the educational system for anyone who develops the ability or skill to ask troublesome questions concerning the established system. In democratic nations, however, a primary goal of education relates to the development of the individual to his fullest potential, and presumably is to encourage the process of rational inquiry. Yet even in these nations, equality of educational opportunity for all does not exist. Many people are still denied:

• Equal access to appropriate educational opportunities because of

*Footnote references are given at end of the chapter.

20

sex, race, place of residence, social class, economic circumstance or other irrelevant criteria; or

• Equal opportunity to develop their talents and abilities.

Why, in a modern and so-called "enlightened" age, has such slow progress been made toward the goal of equal opportunity for an adequate education? A rather fundamental reason for the lack of suitable progress relates directly to the question: Who should be educated, how, and to what extent? Nations—and people—need to come to grips with this question and answer it satisfactorily before adequate provisions can be made for education.

The evidence available, supplemented by common sense, should make the need for meaningful education for all abundantly clear to everyone. Numerous economists have pointed out the importance of an educated citizenry for economic progress, and have calculated the value of education as contrasted with the cost of non-education. From an economic point of view, there should be no question about the need for every member of a society to have the opportunity to develop to the maximum of his potential. Moreover, as discussed in Chapter 1, when human needs are met through various components of the educational system, the potential societal benefits are likely to be greater than the economic returns.

If a society is to receive maximum benefits from the provisions it makes for education, these provisions must ensure that equal and adequate educational opportunities exist for *every* member of the society. It should be apparent that efforts must be made by educational and lay leaders to assure a *relatively high degree of agreement between what we,* as a people, *say we believe about education,* and *what we actually do to provide adequate educational opportunities for all who can benefit from education.*

GROWING DISSATISFACTIONS AND CONCERNS

Since every society makes some provisions for education, the basic question is *What kind of provisions should be made?* More and more, those with an "inquiring mind"—a product of extended education, improved communications, increased leisure time, and numerous other phenomena—have been questioning the adequacy of existing provisions for education. There have been open revolts against what is commonly referred to as "the system." There have been demonstrations against those educational and other provisions perceived to be inadequate or irrelevant (and, by some, even detrimental) in terms of societal needs; there have been rebellions against rules, regulations and requirements set and rigidly adhered to by the national and other governments; and there have been innumerable demands for changes.

During recent years there have been increasingly strong reactions against outmoded systems of education that are failing to meet either the perceived needs of the students or of the society in which they function. These reactions against the "outmoded system" have resulted in many suggestions, plans, and even proposed programs designed to bring about needed improvements. More and more concerned citizens are convinced that there is a crisis in education. One writer has commented:

> Within the next decade [education] will be changed. It will be changed, first, because it is headed straight into a major economic crisis, is indeed deep in it. *It is not that we cannot afford the high costs of education; we cannot afford its low productivity.* (Italics supplied)[2]

The above observations are indicative of the concerns of many people about education, and are given support—in the United States at least—by the report of a recent study of the attitudes of the public about education:

> People continue to have a high regard for the schools of their community and they believe firmly that education is the royal road to success in America. Yet there is undeniably a *new mood* in the nation with which education must reckon. (Italics supplied)[3]

RECURRING AND EMERGING PROBLEMS

Throughout the modern world, the educational enterprise is confronted with problems and concerns relating to both the investment needed for education and the "new mood" of the people. James Allen, former U. S. Commissioner of Education, pointed out that in this country:

- Some children are going through school without learning to read.

- Teachers are restless in many parts of the country, largely over economic issues, and some teacher strikes are in progress or threatened.

- School finances are in an inflationary squeeze. Financing education is a nationwide problem of mounting urgency.

- Not enough of the educational effort is being directed toward children who need it most—the poor and the disadvantaged.

- Parents are seeking greater say in the operation of the schools.

- More student demands for changes are expected.[4]

In a similar vein, and in an even more urgent sense, Terrell H. Bell, recently Acting U. S. Commissioner of Education, observed that "the biggest issue confronting [education] is the need to restore public confidence in our schools."[5] Bell posed a series of questions to which educators and others should seek answers:

- Are we really doing an effective job of helping the disadvantaged shake off their educational deficit?

- Is the cost of education being equitably shared?

- Are we teaching things that people will really need to know in the last quarter of the twentieth century . . . and the first quarter of the twenty-first?

- Are we teaching as well as we really know how?

- Are we plowing enough dollars into educational research to meet the problems of the future?

- Have we really accepted the philosophy that as teachers we must be accountable for results, or are we still concentrating on what *we say,* and not what *they learn?*

- Have we really accepted the philosophy that what happens in the school room is *so important* to the community that we must involve the community more in the classroom . . . even, maybe, when the individuals in each community who can contribute most to education are reluctant to get involved and the individuals who can contribute least are not reluctant enough?

SOME UNDERLYING FACTORS

As meaningful attempts are made to improve provisions for the operation and organization of education, those responsible—educators and lay citizens alike—must be cognizant of the factors and forces that underlie and emphasize the need for improved provisions.

Societal Changes. Changes have occurred in every society and will undoubtedly continue to occur in future societies. Most people apparently can readily accept such a premise. But many seem to have difficulty in recognizing the *increasing rapidity* with which societal changes are occurring in the modern world. As Farson observed:

> . . . we live in a world which is continually changing. Whether we are talking about skyscrapers or family life, scientific facts or religious values, all are highly temporary and becoming more so. . . . Changes are coming faster and faster—in a sense, change has become a way of life.[6]

When an educational system in a rapidly changing society fails to adjust to the changes that are occurring, the concerns about education are certain to increase. To understand the implications of changes in society for adjustments in the educational system, one need only consider the fact that many of the present jobs or work assignments will not exist even a decade from now, and that some of those that will exist have not yet been defined. Not only people—including some highly skilled specialists—who find themselves out of work because of job obsolescence or changes in priorities, but also many others will undoubtedly have grave concerns about an educational system that has failed to prepare them and many others to live and cope effectively with change.

Both educators and lay citizens urgently need to re-examine the present educational system, and make every effort to modify those aspects that are no longer defensible in terms of the needs of a rapidly changing society. Educational and other leaders must seriously consider the concept suggested by Farson; that "the only people who will live successfully in tomorrow's world are those who can accept and enjoy temporary systems."[7]

Institutionalization of Institutions. If the needs of a society are to be met, institutions of a social nature—including schools, universities, hospitals, post offices, police and fire departments—are essential. The fundamental purposes of these and similar institutions are closely related to societal needs and to an orderly functioning of society. Since societal needs are always in a state of flux—always changing—many of the needs for which certain institutions were created no longer exist. The institutions themselves, however, usually continue to function without major changes and, in many instances, tend to become resistant to any significant change.

Unfortunately, when social institutions, such as those responsible for education, become more concerned with self-perpetuation than with meeting societal needs, a serious imbalance exists, and if allowed to remain uncorrected, will result in chaos. *The ultimate test of any society and its institutions* is not merely whether the society and its institutions are changing, but *whether they are adequate in terms of the needs of the present and of the foreseeable future.*

Environmental Pollution. A college senior recently wrote: "It gets pretty depressing to watch what is going on in your world and realize that your education is not equipping you to do anything about it."[8] Throughout the United States—and in most colleges, universities, high schools, junior high schools and elementary schools—there is an ever-increasing concern about the condition of the world in which we live. The concern relates to the social ills that are prevalent, but in a more basic sense, is related primarily to the environmental conditions of the world in which future generations will live.

The advent of the technological revolution, the population explosion, and the search for the "good life" by an affluent society are but three factors responsible for the pollution of the total environment. In recent years smog apparently has become accepted by many as "something to put up with", at least in our major cities; litter along our highways has become a blight on the landscape; filth and rubbish in our rivers, bays, lakes and estuaries have become a "necessary nuisance" to swimmers, fishermen and many others. Because of uncontrolled disposal of industrial wastes, some rivers have literally become fire as well as health hazards.

Governmental leaders at all levels have become increasingly concerned about the problems of environmental pollution, and some efforts are being made to solve the problems. But if such efforts are to be even moderately successful, political and educational leaders alike will need to recognize that growth, as such, does not necessarily result in progress.

Ways will have to be found to ensure that all growth will ultimately benefit—not harm—*the society in which it occurs.* The educational system and its component institutions need to become much more effective in preparing concerned people to effect the changes needed if the environmental pollution problems are to be solved. In terms of changing societal needs, this is one of the major educational imperatives for the present and foreseeable future.

Technological Breakthroughs. What is commonly called the "explosion of knowledge" is bringing about significant changes in virtually every aspect of life. Computers can work out highly complex problems in a few seconds; new forms of energy are available for the benefit of mankind; new forms of transportation make every area of the world accessible in a matter of hours; and new modes of communication make it possible for people throughout the world to converse with each other in a matter of seconds.

These breakthroughs—in theory, at least—should benefit man and society. But in many instances the educational system has not prepared members of society to make and implement the decisions that are necessary to ensure that the potential benefits are realized.

IMPROVING THE PROVISIONS FOR EDUCATION

As educational leaders, lay citizens, concerned legislators and other officials cooperate to effect urgently needed changes in the provisions for education, they will have to direct their attention to the implications of ever-changing present and future needs. If major improvements are to be made, attitudes toward and about education will have to change. Educators can no longer view themselves primarily as dispensers of knowledge. Lay citizens can no longer view themselves as "exploited taxpayers" who pay all the bills and receive little benefit. And concerned legislators can no longer afford to view themselves primarily as watchdogs of public funds who apportion these funds—often grudgingly—only after crisis situations have become intolerable.

Instead, the educators—teachers, administrators, supervisors, and paraprofessionals—will need to understand and assume the role of facilitators of learning. The lay citizens—the concerned taxpayers—will need to recognize that education is an investment in mankind, in society, and in the overall well-being of the nation. And the legislators—who have as their primary responsibility the wise allocation and utilization of public funds—must recognize that only through adequate planning and appropriate procedures for effecting improvements may crisis situations be minimized, real progress occur, and appropriate returns on investments ensured.

In short, everyone concerned with or about education will need to cooperate if the improved provisions for education that are so urgently needed are to be made. The provisions that are recommended and approved by educators, lay citizens and legislators must be based on the best available knowledge, know-how and insights if the educational system is to make the desired and necessary contributions.

ELIMINATING OR MODIFYING OUTMODED TRADITIONS

Past recommendations relating to provisions for education have in too many instances been based upon, or well-rooted in, some respectable but outdated traditions. The financial base for education in most states, for example, consists primarily of revenue derived from property taxes. This practice—some implications of which are discussed in Chapter 10— illustrates how tradition-based concepts can be perpetuated. It should be obvious that such traditions, when no longer relevant, should be abandoned, and that other, more feasible and relevant alternatives to existing patterns and practices of educational financing need to be identified and implemented if the educational system in future years is to be responsive to emerging needs.

Another example of an outmoded tradition that has been continued in most communities is the length of the school year. Typically, the school year begins about the first of September, and ends during the first or second week in June. The concept of an eight- or nine-month school year was valid and meaningful in an agrarian culture—one in which the services of young people were vital to the harvesting of crops and the tilling of the soil. But in a society in which only five to ten percent of the population can be classified as *rural-farm,* it is obvious that realistic changes should be made.

Numerous alternatives to existing educational policies and practices have been identified, and many should be seriously considered by educators and concerned citizens. Concepts such as differentiated staffing, flexible scheduling, the extended school year and individualized instruction are but a few examples of alternatives to organizational and instructional programs that are available for consideration.

Educators—especially those in universities and positions of state leadership—must assist local school systems to become aware of the fact that there are promising alternatives to many present practices. However, identification of feasible alternatives is only one preliminary step. Much more crucial is the *manner* in which the alternatives are selected. It is in the latter area that the educational leaders of a state can provide the help most needed. Every society must continually assess its traditions, and seek to modify them as necessary in terms of feasible and desirable alternatives. Education and educators must do likewise.

"Better" ways are likely to be "different" ways. But if the end product—an enlightened society—is to be rapidly and effectively attained, the "different" ways will have to be carefully selected and effectively implemented. It should not be assumed, however, that if a proposed future policy or practice is to be considered as "better," the previous practice was necessarily "bad." Harvesting of grain, at one point in time, was accomplished with a scythe and winnowing basket. When this method was commonplace, there was nothing "wrong" with it. Since that time, however, there have been many developments and inventions that have resulted in better methods for the harvesting of grain.

In similar fashion, the educational methods employed in the early 20th century were not "bad". They met the needs of society as perceived by its members at that time. But do such methods meet the needs of the society as the 21st century nears? The evidence overwhelmingly suggests that they do not, and that, in too many instances, the old methods tend to continue. All concerned with change, however, should seriously consider the concept expressed by a contemporary philosopher-priest:

> Whenever you become an agent of social change, you should either retain the old values with new forms which still employ and protect those values. Or you might possibly introduce new values with new forms. *But nothing should be simply destroyed without being replaced with something of value.* (Italics supplied)[9]

Values that are held by a society and the established traditions constitute a vital and essential component of the society. The concept of "freedom of choice," for example, must be viable in a democratic society. But while some of the older values may still be important and necessary, effective educational leadership will have to illuminate and help everyone understand the *context* in which the important older values should operate.

PROVIDING OPTIMUM OPPORTUNITIES FOR LEARNING

Because the existing educational system is not meeting the needs of many learners, it should be modified. New procedures that facilitate learning and understanding are available in useable and tested form. Yet the memorization and recitation of unrelated facts still seems to be the goal of many educators. Hutchins has drawn attention to this problem by suggesting that "If training and the transmission of information should cease to be the central concerns of educational systems, what will be left for them is understanding."[10]

As new and better provisions for education are made, schools and school systems will need to find optimum ways of helping learners to develop a better understanding of themselves and the society in which they will live—to recognize that *learning,* rather than *teaching,* is the primary function of education.

IMPORTANT CONCEPTS RELATING TO LEARNING

Important concepts and guidelines that should be utilized by those charged with the responsibility for developing and maintaining a viable system of education include:

- *Normal children continuously seek to explore, to learn about, and to understand their environment.*

As new and more meaningful provisions for improving learning opportunities are developed, this concept should be considered seriously by every educator, regardless of his specific area of interest or specialization. Provisions designed to minimize the detrimental aspects of unwholesome environments will have to be developed if the potential benefits of a wholesome, healthy environment are to be realized. One of the most urgent needs of education in the emerging society is that the learner be helped to gain an understanding of the many interrelationships between himself and his environment.

- *In a changing society the need for learning and understanding extends far beyond the time span and physical facilities normally associated with schools.*

Many educational leaders are aware of the fact that *learning* occurs in many ways and places other than within the splendid isolation of the school building or school day. Yet few, if any, provisions for education are designed (1) to capitalize on the fact that learning takes place in and out of school for persons in all age brackets, or (2) to make meaningful learning opportunities available for every person in society, regardless of age, occupation, or situation.

Some citizens, including educators, legislators and parents, still are prone to think of learning as primarily the acquisition of a collection of facts—a process in which knowledge is somehow transmitted from the notebook of the teacher to the notebook of the student without passing through the heads of either. *In a basic sense, education, or learning, occurs when the learner senses a need to learn.* Educational leaders must identify or devise procedures that will facilitate learning for all individuals as the need occurs, regardless of age, time of day, or the specific location.

- *Individuals learn in different ways and at different rates.*

Educators—administrators and teachers alike—have long professed belief in the concept of differences among and between individuals, but few realistic efforts to implement this belief have been made. If educators really believe that individual differences exist among learners, their actions should certainly be consistent with that belief. Unfortunately, in too many instances, this is not the case.

Suitable provisions that will facilitate needed improvements in learning opportunities will need to include effective techniques or modes of instruction. Commingled with this concept, however, are the *attitudes* of teachers and other educators toward learning. The provisions should take both into account, and focus upon, modifications that should be made in teacher education programs and in the schools.

- *The educational program should be judged on the basis of how effectively the information gained by learners is utilized—not on the basis of nebulous norms or other irrelevant data.*

As already indicated, the concept of learning implies the ability to *understand and utilize the information or knowledge* that is gained. Unless the learner develops the ability to relate what he has learned to present and future situations, the skills, knowledge and information gained will have little meaning. Educators and others will need to devise means for evaluating education that are in keeping with this concept. It is imperative, however, that everyone concerned avoid the pitfall of holding schools—and the entire educational process—accountable primarily for irrelevant or relatively meaningless educational outcomes.

ORGANIZATION AND RESPONSIBILITIES FOR EDUCATION

It apparently is difficult for many people, including educators and lay citizens, to conceive of any pattern or provisions for the organization of education which differs to any marked extent from that which has existed in the past. As a consequence, new functions of and for education are assigned and accepted, but educators often attempt to make such functions fit into the existing organizational pattern. When this happens educational leaders demonstrate what might be described as the "add-on syndrome" as they seek solutions to problems. Basic patterns and structures of educational organizations, for example, never seem to change: new elements are simply added to the existing structure. This procedure has not worked well in the past, and certainly will not suffice to meet future needs.

Educators—and especially educational administrators—need to recognize and utilize pertinent management concepts, including the idea that structure (organization) *follows* function (purpose), and that the organization must change as goals and objectives are changed. The *functions* of education must be identified and the implications understood before meaningful organizational patterns can be established for education and educational systems. For example, if one of the accepted major functions of education is to facilitate appropriate learning for all students, the educational system must be organized accordingly. If a valid function of education is perceived to be the development of procedures that will enable learners to cope more adequately with changing needs, the educational system will need to be organized to facilitate the implementation of that function.

But regardless of how well the functions of education are defined, or of how well the system and its components might be organized, *unless the responsibilities for education are better defined, more equitably assigned and more commonly accepted, it is doubtful that the necessary provisions for meaningful learning* (bona fide education) *will ever be made.*

At one time, during the formative stages of this country, the family, in cooperation with other families, was primarily responsible for any formal education that was provided. Few would now advocate such an assignment, primarily because it would tend to perpetuate and even increase the gross disparities that already exist in many states and communities.

Some people, including some educators, believe that most of the responsibility for education should be assigned to sectarian religious organizations, as it still done in some societies. This concept, however, is not in harmony with the concept of public education as it has evolved in the United States. Neither is it compatible with the constitutional principle of separation between church and state. Assignment of the responsibility for education to sectarian organizations has led, in some instances, to the development of almost unbridgeable chasms between segments of society. For example, Reller, who studied education in Holland, observed:

> Since many of the leaders of the society find it extremely difficult (in their thoughts and actions) to separate the welfare of the nation from the welfare of their groups, action is taken in the interest of the groups, with too little regard for the national interest.[11]

Some people in this country apparently have become convinced that much of the responsibility for education should be assigned to private industry, even though there is little evidence to indicate that the private sector can do a "better" job than the public sector. One application of this alternative would be the "voucher system," which is receiving considerable consideration; another is the concept of "performance contracting," which has been tried out in several educational settings. Both approaches imply the utilization of private industry to achieve educational ends. Either or both may have some merit for certain groups in some special situations, but neither should be accepted as a panacea.

Nyquist has observed that "education is too important to be left solely in the hands of educators."[12] It should also be apparent that education is far too important to be left in the hands of any single group—and especially in the hands of a group that may have obvious vested interests. Neither education nor the educational system exists primarily for the purpose of allowing business, industry or individuals to gain financial profit. As has been aptly stated: "Schools are for kids."

Both the learner and society should profit from education. If this is to occur, it is imperative that the educational system be organized—with appropriate assignment of responsibility—in a manner that will not only *facilitate* the accrual of benefits to the learner and to society, but will *ensure* that these benefits occur.

State governments, and agencies created for the state-wide governance of education, appear to be the logical focus of responsibility for education within a state. But because education does not take place in a vacuum, *no single agency or institution should assume that it has the sole responsibility for every aspect of education* within a state or community. If learners and society are to derive the benefits that should accrue to them, close cooperation and coordination among all aspects of education will be essential in all levels of governance and all segments of society. Better and much more comprehensive planning will be necessary in and among all segments and levels of education if this is to be accomplished.

THE NATURE AND PURPOSE OF PLANNING

One writer has been observed that, while "educational change is *bound* to happen, needed educational change [on which there is general agreement] must be *made* to happen."[13] This observation underscores the concept that through *appropriate planning* needed changes can better be identified and implemented. It also serves to emphasize a major purpose of planning: *that of effecting, implementing, or bringing about some needed and agreed upon changes that are designed to correct and improve in some fashion the existing situation.* The following concepts merit consideration:

- *Appropriate planning provides procedures by which pertinent information may be gathered and the data analyzed.*

In many instances what is purported to be planning is undertaken primarily as a result of someone's hunches or wishful thinking, and without any serious consideration of the importance or need. In such instances— where the basic problems have not been clearly identified—there is no real need or basis for planning; the important concept, *"planning for what?"* obviously is missing. At the same time, it should be clear that *need* can only be determined by a comprehensive analysis of "what is" and "what might be." Planning, as a total process, must include provisions for the determination of need.

- *Appropriate planning makes possible an orderly and systematic procedure for achieving needed changes.*

Within the framework of education, it is difficult to identify anyone who does not plan in some way. Everyone plans—but in many instances such planning consists of speculative or emotional attempts to "reach the unreachable star." In other instances, planning efforts are haphazard in nature, and have no logical or enduring base. Neither of these approaches constitutes bona fide *planning*—neither recognizes the need for an extensive or comprehensive examination of long-range needs or probabilities. Planning, in terms of a total process, must be systematic; it must be based upon and related to predetermined policies.

- *Appropriate planning includes procedures for identification of goals, objectives, and priorities.*

Planning, as a process, should always be considered only a *means* to achieve appropriate ends. Conscious efforts, therefore, must be made to ensure against the possibility that planning becomes *the end*. It is essential that the end—the "for what"—be positively identified and clearly stated. When this is done, the goals or objectives become tangible and the proper relationship between planning and change can be maintained. Methods can then be devised that will help to determine which of several goals is of critical importance, and consequently should have a high priority.

- *Appropriate planning includes procedures for identification and pro-*

jection of feasible alternative courses of action, based upon established priorities.

Few situations exist in society in which there is only *one* solution to a given problem. Generally speaking, however, it is usually possible to identify one solution that can be described as the "best" solution, or at least as a better solution than others. It must be recognized that such identification can only be made after a careful appraisal of several feasible alternatives. In order for something to be "best," it must be *better* than something else. If only one procedure for effecting a desired change is proposed and considered, there can be no defensible way in which it could be described as the "best."

- *Appropriate planning includes provisions and procedures for implementation, evaluation and needed modification.*

In any planning effort, there must be some way to determine (1) how well the purposes (of the plan) are being achieved, and (2) how the plan might be modified so as to better achieve the purposes. Such a process, obviously, implies that implementation and evaluation must occur so that the effectiveness of anticipated outcomes can be determined. Without such provisions, planning efforts would be little more than academic exercises.

Collectively, the preceding concepts relating to planning comprise the components of what has in recent years become known as systematic planning. Various alternatives in approaches to systematic planning are discussed in Chapter 5. But regardless of variations in the approach, the basic purposes of systematic planning remain the same: the achievement or attainment, to the highest degree possible, of defensible goals that relate to all aspects of educational operations. The goals or objectives of a school district can theoretically be achieved in a multitude of ways— some of which are more effective than others. Everyone concerned should recognize that:

- The productivity of a school district can be increased by the organization of learning activities and supporting services into programs specifically directed toward achieving previously defined goals and objectives.

- Better decisions regarding selection of program plans and greater benefits from their operation result when the costs thereof are considered on a long-term (multi-year) basis.

- Better decisions regarding selection of program plans and greater benefits from their application result when outcomes are methodically related to objectives.[14]

ROLES AND RELATIONSHIPS IN EFFECTING IMPROVEMENTS IN EDUCATION

As systematic attempts are made to strengthen or improve provisions for education, leaders in every segment and level of education need to recognize and accept two fundamental concepts:

- *Educational leaders must be aware of the fact that every educational agency or institution,* regardless of level or scope, *has certain unique and appropriate roles that must be assumed if efforts to improve provisions for education are to be successful.* All too often some necessary roles of educational agencies or institutions are either ignored or unrecognized by those in positions of leadership. As a consequence, many educational needs remain unmet.

- While educational leaders need to be cognizant of the roles and responsibilities of the agencies or institutions they serve, they must also be aware of the fact that no such agency or institution is or can be an "island unto itself," and that none can long exist, meaningfully, in "splendid isolation." *Every educational agency or institution,* if it is to have relevance and meaning in a dynamic society, *must exist in relation to every other segment of education and of society.*

Unless efforts to strengthen provisions for education are made within the context of both frames of reference—that is, the separate and combined roles and relationships—achievement of the needed changes is likely to be delayed or may even become impossible.

IMPROVING PROVISIONS AT THE NATIONAL LEVEL

Although there is no *national system of education* in the United States —no *national agency* that directs educational efforts—there are many federal agencies that are concerned about, and contribute to, the overall educational efforts that are made. The agency that is most directly associated with public elementary and secondary education is the United States Office of Education (USOE).

Until relatively recent years, the primary functions of the USOE were related to (1) collection and dissemination of data, (2) limited educational research, (3) administration of a few federally funded programs, and (4) general support of education (in cooperation with state and local agencies) throughout the nation. The concept of leadership as a function or role of the agency may have existed, but it did not become even a discernible role until about a decade ago.

The major roles or functions of the USOE continue to be those already noted, but with a somewhat increasing emphasis upon leadership. And this leadership, while essential to educational entities, most assuredly cannot be limited or confined to them. Educational leaders at the national level must work closely with leaders of every other segment of the federal government; at the same time, they must be responsive to the needs of state and local governmental entities.

The major role of any educational agency at the national level can only be one of leadership and service if this agency is to function in keeping with the system of education that has been established. This role has been strengthened by legislation such as the National Defense Education Act of 1958 and the Elementary and Secondary Education Act of 1965. Under the leadership of the USOE, and with the help of funds authorized by Congress and administered by that office, state and local educational agencies have made considerable progress in planning for improved educational opportunities.

IMPROVING PROVISIONS AT THE STATE LEVEL

Because public elementary and secondary education is considered to be a responsibility of the individual states, the role of the state education agency (SEA), together with its relationships with other state governmental agencies, is crucial in improving provisions for education. The role of the SEA must be concerned with the governance of the educational system for which it is responsible. But the time is past when the performance of traditional regulatory and perfunctory duties should be perceived as a major function of the SEA. The role of the SEA, with an ever-increasing degree of emphasis, will need to be one of leadership and services in areas such as: (1) planning for the most effective allocation and utilization of human and material resources for the improvement of learning; (2) working with other agencies of state and federal government to ensure the best possible educational opportunities for the children of the state; and (3) helping local school systems to find solutions to the complex problems they face.

Fortunately, most state education agencies have become increasingly aware of the emerging leadership role and functions of that agency. As a result, many SEA's are not only re-examining their traditional roles, but are attempting to determine through comprehensive studies what roles might be most appropriate for the future. In Massachusetts, for example, on the basis of an in-depth study of the Department of Education, the following recommendations were made:

1. The Department must have authority to hire, retain, and promote professional personnel at salary levels that parallel or exceed those of some of the best public schools in the Commonwealth.

2. The Department must undertake a number of reforms with respect to its internal operations, especially in the area of administrative procedures, reducing duplication of effort and programs in certain areas, improving legislative and fiscal processes, organization of specific divisions and bureaus, training of personnel, and planning.

3. Strong efforts should be undertaken to increase the Department's service role to school systems and to minimize the function of the Department as a regulator and enforcement agency with respect to the public schools in the state.

4. Present regional offices of the Department should be strengthened better

to deliver school services of quality directly to school systems; and at least two more regional offices (or service centers) should be created, with one serving the needs of the Greater Boston Area.

5. A program should be launched under the aegis of the Department calling for the establishment of educational goals for Massachusetts students, assessment of student achievement with respect to goals, evaluation of schools, and accountability by educators and educational decision makers to the publics they serve for their performance with respect to students.[15]

Similar studies and recommendations, and, in some instances, proposals for legislation, have been made in other states. Efforts of this nature— to improve provisions for education at the state level—are helping to focus attention on the new and emerging role of the state education agency.

Indicative of the strengthened leadership role of the SEA are the instances in which important legislative changes been enacted. In Florida, for example, the legislature in 1968 gave very specific direction—and necessary support—for the emerging role of the state education agency.

The legislation, in part, prescribed the following:

Sec. 229.053 *General powers of state board.*

(1) The state board of education is the chief policy-making and coordinating body of public education in Florida. . . .

(2) The board has the following duties:

(a) To adopt comprehensive educational objectives for public education;

(b) To adopt comprehensive long-range plans and short-range programs for the development of the state system of public education;

Sec. 229.551 *Plan for effecting constructive educational change.*

(1) The commissioner of education shall as rapidly as feasible expand the capability of the department of education in planning the state's strategy for effecting constructive educational change and providing and coordinating creative services necessary to achieve greater quality in education.

IMPROVING PROVISIONS AT THE LOCAL LEVEL

Because of the nature of the educational system in the United States, it is obvious that new and improved provisions for education should be made at both the national and state levels of education. But, unless new and more suitable roles are identified and actively assumed by the local educational subdivisions of education, the efforts made at the national and state levels are likely to be relatively ineffective.

A key role for local educational units in the changing society is to provide effective leadership and services in improving education. At the local level of education, more than at any other, a basic concern must be for and about *people*—parents, patrons, and, most importantly, students.

The local school system, through its elected board and appointed administrator, should develop and maintain high quality leadership skills, and use those skills to involve people in meaningful study and discussion of important educational problems and issues. Unless the people who are most directly affected by the provisions that should be made for education actively support those provisions, there is little likelihood that effective changes will be made.

STRENGTHENING RELATIONSHIPS

During the past two decades, there has been a marked change in relationships between educational entities at the national, state and local levels of government. The state education agencies, for example, have tended to view, until relatively recently, efforts of any federal educational agency with suspicion. Local education agencies have also tended to view the efforts of state education agencies in similar fashion. Moreover, many activities of both state and local education agencies have been somewhat discounted by many engaged in education at the national level.

In recent years there has been a shift away from the basic suspicion or distrust among the several levels of educational governance. There has been a lessening of competition among the levels, and a growing awareness of the need for effective cooperation.

SUMMARY AND CONCLUSIONS

Improvement of learning opportunities within the educational system is a continuing, on-going, and vital need. Societies change; so do the needs of societies. Because of such changes, it is imperative that opportunities for and procedures in learning also change. But changes within the context of the educational system, however, must not be allowed to merely "happen," or to occur by default. They must be planned—and made to happen—if they are to result in needed improvements.

State educational agencies, by virtue of the responsibilities for education that have been assigned to them, are in the most advantageous position to facilitate planning efforts designed to improve provisions for education and learning. Such planning efforts, however, are not the exclusive responsibility of state education agencies. Other agencies, institutions and organizations must also be actively and cooperatively involved in improving the provisions for learning.

Those involved in planning at all levels of education, including coordinators, technicians and specialists will need to view planning as a means to an end—not as an end in and of itself. When planning is properly perceived as being only a *means,* it is essential that educational planners, or those who assume responsibility for planning, clearly understand the *relationships* that exist between planning (the means) and a needed improvements (the end).

Educational and other leaders must deliberately strive to devise arrangements and procedures through which the planning processes can be interwoven, or at least function in concert with each other. Unless this happens, planning undoubtedly will continue to be a "professed good"—

but a relatively ineffective social force. On the other hand, when these relationships are appropriately recognized and the implications utilized by all concerned, education can become a viable system which recognizes that:

- Nothing is ever taught: it is only learned.

- Some things are learned best by some students independently of the teacher, while other things are learned best through the mediating or facilitating influence of the teacher.

- All normal students are capable of learning; the variables are in terms of the style and rate of learning.

- The content of education (whatever is learned) should always be considered a means—never an end in itself.

- Learning, in order to be effective, must be relevant to perceived needs.

Footnote References

[1]Harry J. Siceluff, ed., *Readings in the History of Education* (Berkeley, California: McCutchan Publishing Corporation, 1970), p. 2.

[2]Peter F. Drucker, "Education: The High Cost of Low Production," *Think,* July-August, 1968, p. 2.

[3]George Gallup, "The Public's Attitude Toward the Public Schools," *Phi Delta Kappan,* October, 1970, p. 100.

[4]*Rocky Mountain News,* Denver, September 2, 1969.

[5]Terrell H. Bell (Remarks prepared for Conference on State Agency Personnel, Washington, D. C., November 25, 1970).

[6]Richard E. Farson, "How Could Anything That Feels So Bad Be So Good?", *Saturday Review,* September 6, 1969, p. 20.

[7]*Ibid.,* p. 20.

[8]John Fischer, "Survival U: Prospectus for a Really Relevant University," *Harpers,* September, 1969, p. 12.

[8]Frank Riley, "Storm Over Micronesia," *Saturday Review,* September 13, 1969, p. 93.

[10]Robert M. Hutchins, *The Learning Society* (New York: F. A. Praeger, 1968), p. 76.

[11]Theodore Reller, "The Netherlands," Chapter 4 in *Comparative Educational Administration,* Theodore Reller and Edgar L. Morphet, eds. (Englewood Cliffs, New Jersey: Prentice-Hall, Inc., 1962), p. 90.

[12]Ewald B. Nyquist, "State Organization and Responsibilities for Education," in *Emerging Designs for Education,* Edgar L. Morphet and David L. Jesser, eds. (Denver, Colorado: Designing Education for the Future, 1968), p. 154.

[13]Kenneth H. Hansen, "Planning for Educational Change" (Unpublished paper, 1968), p. 1.

[14]Adapted from *Report of the Second National Conference on PPBES in Education* (Chicago, Illinois). Conducted by The Research Corporation of the Association of School Business Officials.

[15]John S. Gibson, *The Massachusetts Department of Education: Proposals for Progress in the '70's* (Medford, Massachusetts: Lincoln Filene Center, Tufts University, 1970), pp. 4-5.

PART TWO

STATE LEADERSHIP IN PLANNING
IMPROVEMENTS IN EDUCATION

Chapter 3

Forces and Factors That Affect Planning

Individuals and families have always found it necessary to do some rudimentary kinds of planning in an effort to obtain food and to provide shelter and protection. Some have planned rather wisely in the light of prevailing knowledge and conditions, while others have not even exercised enough foresight to meet their own needs. Most social groups have also found that they had to be concerned to some extent with the future and to do some elementary planning if they hoped to survive. Much of the responsibility for planning was usually delegated to a few competent leaders. But, over the ages, it frequently has been attained through subterfuge or violence by some "strong man" and his trusted supporters, primarily for their own benefit. Thus, in the minds of many people, the idea of planning often has been associated with conniving to ensure and perpetuate special privileges for those who are especially clever or ruthless. These tendencies to exploit the masses—that were widespread during the colonial and early industrial periods—persist in some nations and always constitute a danger even in modern democracies.

Many of the present problems in this country have developed and continue because some people, as individuals or members of an organization, accept and support indefensible traditions that give them unfair advantages, or continue to seek ways of exploiting for their own benefit the natural and human resources of the nation. Norman Cousins has observed that the brains of the nation are constantly being developed and mobilized on a large scale for purposes connected with exploitation, confrontation or destruction, but there is no comparable mobilization of human intellect and conscience on the level of man's greatest needs. He notes, however, that there is a sound basis for anticipating significant improvements in society:

> The capacity for hope is the greatest fact in life. *Hope is the beginning of plans.* It gives man a destination, a sense of direction for getting there, and the energy to get started. . . . It gives proper value to feelings as well as to facts.[1]* (Italics supplied)

---

*Footnote references are given at end of the chapter.

The public sector of society—and especially education—has been slow to accept and utilize systematic planning as an important means of dealing with current educational and social problems. Perhaps a major reason for this slow acceptance has been the belief and concern by many that planning for social change is not democratic but totalitarian. Events and conditions of the past few years, however, make it increasingly clear that: (1) a planning society in which everyone has an opportunity to contribute differs significantly from a planned society in which the experts plan for the people; (2) a patchwork way of doing things for education will tend to perpetuate or increase chaos; and (3) it is essential that the concept of long-range planning be understood, accepted and implemented.

Fortunately, most people now understand that there is a significant difference between the kind of activities that are primarily concerned with obtaining or perpetuating special advantages or making expedient changes, and the constructive and necessary process of planning for a better future for humanity. There is also a significant difference between the limited, often wishful-thinking kind of planning that was acceptable when little information was available, and the systematic comprehensive planning that is feasible and necessary under modern conditions. *Because adequate and relevant education constitutes the soundest basis for progress under modern conditions, planning for the improvement of education must have high priority in any society.* But planning for better education needs to be closely related and contribute to the process of planning for the improvement of all aspects of society, and must involve the active participation of substantial numbers of well informed and competent citizens who are deeply interested in and concerned about developing a better and more humane civilization.

SOCIETAL PRESSURES FOR CHANGE

Perhaps never in its history has this nation been beset with such deep-seated and widespread agitations for changes in its institutions and organizations as have occurred during recent years. All social, political, and economic areas are affected by movements involving dissent, disruption, and occasional violence. These movements may have been stimulated to some extent by technological advances that stagger the imagination and a body of unassimilated knowledge that is increasing dramatically. Values are being questioned and even changed radically in the minds of many. Nothing in the current culture is held sufficiently sacred to be inviolate from attack by those who "feel" a compelling need for change. In fact, substantial numbers of people seem to believe that any existing institution of value should be challenged simply because it is a part of the current "establishment."

Societal institutions are generally noted for their slowness to change. Augmenting this general conservativeness is the modern phenomenon of huge bureaucracies that have become so complex as to make them virtually impregnable to any significant modification. The extreme difficulties which a president, a governor or any other leader faces in trying to bring about changes which seriously affect bureaucracies provide excellent illustrations of this problem. But people are no longer content to accept the unresponsiveness of their institutions and other organizations. As the aspirations and expectations of people expand, they see various institutions and organizations as either blocking the path they wish to follow or as holding the key to a door to the future they would like to enter.

Although neither the idea of planning nor some of the basic concepts and procedures are new, *many recent and prospective developments have resulted in a new sense of urgency and a growing conviction that unless we can proceed promptly to plan and effect needed improvements in education and in other aspects of society, the future of humanity may be in jeopardy.* Pertinent background conditions and factors in addition to those already noted, include:

- The rapidly accumulating evidence concerning the continuing ruthless exploitation and waste of the natural resources and the increasing pollution of the environment in which people must live.

- The obvious waste, underdevelopment and exploitation of a significant proportion of the human resources.

- A growing awareness of the increasing pace of change and a strong belief that some prospective changes may be harmful to civilization.

- The assumption—and hope—that some of the potentially undesirable changes can best be avoided through systematic long-range planning.

- A strong conviction that major problems must be solved—or at least significantly ameliorated—as promptly as possible, and that better provisions for, and procedures in, education can contribute significantly to their solution.

There are more and stronger demands for systematic long-range planning for improvements in this country, in many other nations, and in the world society than at any previous time. These demands apparently have increased and are likely to continue primarily because: (1) an increasing proportion of the population is better educated and informed; (2) the rapidly accumulating evidence about pollution and other developments has dramatized the growing threats to humanity as well as to the environment; (3) most people are increasingly concerned about the weaknesses or inadequacies in many existing agencies and institutions, as well as about the injustices and inequities for a substantial proportion of the population; (4) most students and many other people apparently have become convinced that, in many respects, the present provisions for education are neither relevant nor adequate in terms of modern needs; and (5) as a result of many recent developments, it has become possible—and even essential—to plan for and effect needed changes in society and in the institutions and agencies it has established.

DEVELOPMENT OF POLICIES AND
STRATEGIES FOR EDUCATIONAL PLANNING

Most of the basic *theories, strategies and technologies* for planning and effecting changes under modern conditions have been developed during the past three decades by agencies such as the Department of Defense and by business and industry. Many of these have had to be *adapted*—not just *adopted*—for use in education and have made important contributions to the improvement of planning in and for education.[2] However, most of the important *concepts and policies* relating to *educational planning* have been developed by educators who have kept in close touch with developments in other areas. For example, the policies and criteria quoted below (that were adopted by the Council of Chief State School Officers in 1944) are still appropriate and should continue to be used for *general guidance* in all comprehensive planning efforts concerned with education.[3]

1. The responsibility for leadership in planning the educational program properly belongs to and should be assumed by the regularly constituted educational agencies and authorities at the proper level.

2. The planning procedure and process should be carefully formulated, unified, and systematically carried out.

3. Educational planning should be recognized and carried out as an integral aspect of community, state, and national planning.

4. Definite provision for planning must be made in educational organizations in order that planning may proceed satisfactorily and attain tangible results.

5. One phase of educational planning should provide the basis for organized research. Another phase should be built on and utilize fully the results of research.

6. Educational planning must be thought of and established as a continuous process requiring constant adaptation of plans to emerging needs.

7. Educational planning to be functional must be realistic and practical but should not be needlessly limited by existing situations.

8. All educational planning should involve the active and continuing participation of interested groups and organizations.

9. The planning program should result in specific recommendations which are understood and accepted by those who are participating in the program.

10. Provision for continuing evaluation of the planning process is basic to the program.

About the same time, some 150 representatives from the 14 states in the Southern Region served on committees that were organized to cooperate in studies of all aspects of education in the area and in developing plans and proposals for effecting improvements. In the introduction to its report, the group stated:

A better world, a better nation, and a better Southern Region can be built through education. But that must be an education which is geared to change. It must be an education which is deliberately designed to meet the needs of the people . . . which recognizes and accepts the challenges of the past, the demands of the present, and the opportunities of the future.[4]

This report proposed a number of important supplementary policies and procedures relating to state planning, including the following:

- Planning should be projected in terms of the aims [and goals] of education and of society and therefore must take into consideration the [needs and interests of all] groups in the planning area.

- Planning committees should be fair and open-minded and should . . . recognize and accept valid suggestions for the betterment of school programs.

- The state planning committee should differentiate between plans for possible immediate attainment, plans that might be implemented in the near future, and plans that may require several years for accomplishment. [It] should always seek to encourage public understanding of the periods for possible accomplishment of plans.

- It is assumed that one of the functions of a state planning agency is to assist in correlating the planning of the different state agencies . . . including education.

- Unless one educational board or authority is established in a state . . . it is suggested that a central advisory committee be created . . . to coordinate educational planning.

During the past few years, several projects in this country have been concerned with the role of the states in planning and effecting improvements in education, and with helping the participating states as well as others to plan more effectively. These include, especially, the eight-state project *Designing Education for the Future* and the seven-state project *Comprehensive Planning in State Education Agencies.*[5] Also appropriate and helpful are materials prepared by The Education Commission of the States and by groups concerned with planning in other areas, including the American Institute for Planners and the American Society of Planning Officials.

An important source of information concerning planning throughout the world and at the international level is the International Institute for Educational Planning, created by UNESCO in 1963 for research and advanced training in educational planning. This Institute has commented perceptively that:

In the past decade a new kind of educational planning has become necessary to cope with the sweeping changes in education's environment and with the vastly accelerated pace of change and growth in education itself. This new educational planning differs from the old in five main respects:

1. A longer time perspective—which looks five, ten and fifteen years ahead so that actions can be initiated now to meet tomorrow's anticipated needs, allowing for education's long "promotion cycle."

2. Broader coverage—not simply piecemeal planning, but comprehensive coordination of the *whole* educational enterprise, including nonformal education —so that its various levels and parts will grow in balance, thereby avoiding serious wastes and maximizing education's contribution to national development.

3. Closer integration . . . of educational development plans with manpower needs and other requirements of economic and social development, taking realistic account also of the nation's resource limitations.

4. Accent on innovation—the fostering of research and experimentation to achieve the changes needed in educational structures, content and methods in order to keep education up to date and to match its performance to the nation's needs and resource limitations.

5. Modern educational management—improved organization and administration that will ensure not only the formulation of sound and feasible plans but their effective implementation.[6]

Other Important Concepts Relating to Planning

If the purposes and goals of education are to be articulated, understood, achieved, evaluated, and changed as needed, then no level, agency, group, or program can be considered in isolation. All of these need to be organized to facilitate coordination and strengthen the whole. After all, the total impact of formal and informal education upon the individual is a reflection of his entire educational experience. The best hope for avoiding chaos and possible disaster is through a process of enlightened, systematic, comprehensive and continuous planning (putting together and utilizing all appropriate tools, techniques and processes in an integrated approach to problem solving) for improvements that are demanded and vigorously supported by a majority of the citizens in each state and community.

Changes in one level or aspect of education often have implications for changes in other levels or aspects. Ideally, long-range planning should be concerned with education as a major system within the entire social system. Actually, planning for improvements in elementary and secondary education often cannot be postponed until the stage has been set for planning improvements in higher education and in related public services, or the reverse. But at some time and in some appropriate way these plans will need to be coordinated.

Planning can and should become a major instrument for effecting improvements (changes) in education that should be utilized creatively and effectively by all leaders. As perceptively pointed out by Culbertson[7] and others, there are two major kinds of planning which have different purposes: strategic planning and management planning. *Strategic planning,* which fosters and requires productive relations and linkages with public agencies and groups other than those directly responsible for education, should receive major emphasis because it *involves the determination of policies and the establishment of new goals and objectives.* *Management planning* is also important because it *is concerned with the efficient attainment of objectives that have already been established,* and should be utilized in every state and local school system and educational institution.

Future Orientation Essential

Everyone interested or involved in planning and effecting improvements in education should be concerned not only with present problems and needs, but also with the implications for education of prospective changes in society. All planning for education in a changing society must not only be *future-oriented,* but also be concerned with the identification and resolution of present problems as one basis for preparing to meet emerging needs. Moreover, everyone involved in the process needs to recognize that students should be prepared through current and continuing educational programs to adapt to, or deal effectively and constructively with, the changes they will encounter during the coming decades, and that the ongoing educational program must, in many fundamental respects, be future-oriented.

Some people seem to be so overwhelmed by the magnitude of existing problems and overawed by the impossibility of predicting future developments that they would be satisfied to settle for a few needed changes. But, while piece-meal adjustments may help to alleviate the situation, they definitely will not meet even present needs and often ignore the changing needs of an increasingly complex society.

Forecasting the Future. Although many aspects of the future cannot be accurately *predicted,* it is possible to utilize appropriate information as a basis for *forecasting* possible alternative developments. For example, the Bureau of the Census periodically issues forecasts of population changes, ranging from low to high with some intermediate possibilities. State and local planning groups will need to supplement such forecasts with any pertinent information that can be obtained and by their own carefully considered judgments in making the alternative estimates they consider most defensible. They will also need to develop tentative plans for each of these possibilities and be prepared to modify these plans in the light of subsequent developments. Similar procedures should be utilized and contingency plans developed for all other prospective changes, including any emerging technologies that should be considered.

Moreover, it is necessary to use reliable forecasts concerning major changes in society itself—that is, attempt to take a macro-view of prospective changes in a dynamic society. For example, Harman[8] has utilized this approach in considering the implications for education if developments during the next few decades result, on the one hand, in merely moving to a later stage of the present industrialized society, or, on the other, if they result in a society that becomes increasingly concerned with individuals and their development. Fortunately several studies and reports during recent years have been concerned with prospective changes in society[9] and many others are in progress.

LONG- SHORT-RANGE PLANNING

Most of the educational planning in the past—except for population projections, goals and housing—has been for one-or two-year periods and often has been closely related to the traditional annual or biennial budgets. Such short-range planning will continue to be essential, but will not suffice under modern conditions. Even this limited planning can be greatly improved if it is intimately related to longer-range plans.

Authorities agree that most long-range plans for education should be developed and projected for at least a ten year period. These plans need not be developed in detail but should include consideration of one or more feasible alternatives—with the most appropriate to be identified and necessary details developed as more reliable information becomes available.

Middle-range plans for five to ten years should be developed in somewhat greater detail in order to provide a better perspective for short-range plans. The latter should be developed in full and defensible detail—especially those for the first two or three years.

USE OF PLANNING TECHNOLOGIES IN EDUCATION

Perhaps the most important single factor in determining the capability of a state education agency to provide the leadership and services needed in planning is the development of systematic planning technologies and their subsequent application to educational problem solving. Although generally not new in their basic concepts, these technologies are new in the way they formalize and build upon these concepts. *Their use necessitates thorough consideration of those elements which should be considered in planning.* They also encourage utilization of the best procedural steps and effective involvement mechanisms. One of the their greatest contri-, butions is in bringing about attitude changes by helping educators and others to recognize the importance of improving the methods and procedures utilized in planning.

A basic component of virtually all systematic planning techniques is the development of performance objectives—a clear concise description of each desired outcome. Each such objective should be expressed, insofar as feasible, in terms which are so specific that everyone involved can interpret them in essentially the same way. The performance described or the product of any such performance, or both, are observable, hence the achievement of a performance objective can be readily measured and evaluated, and the person or persons to whom the responsibility has been assigned can be held accountable for the outcome. The three essential components of any well-constructed performance objective are:

1. The product to be produced and/or the action to be performed;

2. The conditions under which the action *must* be performed, particularly noting any special aids required or any limitations in availability of aids; and

3. The criteria, or specifications, which describe how well the desired outcome is expected to be performed.

There is nothing mysterious about the systems approach to planning that, as explained in Chapter 5, includes basic problem-solving steps such as the identification of needs and problems, analysis of problems, development of solutions, implementation of the planned solutions, evaluation of results, and feedback to provide a basis for modifications or other pertinent decision making. Essentially this approach is designed to ensure that, insofar as practicable, all procedures will be logical, systematic and defensible, and to provide safeguards against irrational or ineffective procedures and unwise or indefensible decisions.

DATA AND VALUE JUDGMENTS

Some people seem to be convinced that if enough "hard facts" are available and are appropriately analyzed and interpreted, defensible decisions can be reached on all matters without having to depend on or utilize value judgments. Adequate information is essential and should constitute the basis for all decision making. But seldom can all pertinent information be obtained, and even if it could, it would be impossible to avoid value judgments in some of the interpretations and conclusions.

Value judgments can always be challenged on the basis of possible culture-conditioned or other unrecognized biases or misinterpretations. For example, let us assume that leading citizens throughout a state or in the nation were asked to respond to one of the crucial modern-day question: *What priority should be assigned to the development of provisions and procedures that, insofar as practicable, would ensure excellence in education for everyone in the state or nation?* If the responses were based on actual convictions and beliefs and the willingness, or lack of willingness, to help with the implementation there would almost certainly be a wide range of reactions because of the value judgments involved.

In any planning process, as in many other aspects of life, *some value judgments are essential.* These should, however, always be carefully examined, and every effort made to ensure that they are the most defensible that can be made in the light of the best information that can be obtained.

RECOGNIZING AND AVOIDING PITFALLS

Under present conditions, everyone needs to recognize that there are grave dangers and pitfalls ahead which, unless identified and dealt with promptly and realistically, could result in increasing confusion and even disaster. These include: (1) the tendency of many people to challenge and attempt to discredit or destroy existing agencies, institutions and values merely or primarily because they have been developed or accepted by "the establishment"; (2) a strong belief or "feeling" on the part of some people that changes are so essential that they should be made by "any necessary means," without seriously considering the implications or alternatives; (3) attempts that will undoubtedly be made by some people and groups to control or manipulate the planning and change processes for their own benefit; and (4) some complacent groups, institutions and agencies that do not see any need for major changes and will tend to resist any bona fide planning efforts.

Howsam[10] has discussed some other hazards and pitfalls relating to planning and change processes in education that should be clearly recognized by everyone concerned. These include:

1. Underestimating the need and pressure for changes and failing to become seriously involved in the process of planning for the future;

2. Being swept along by the pressures with little or no opportunity to choose the best alternative or the most appropriate course; and

3. Becoming so involved in or concerned about one aspect of the comprehensive problems of education that we fail to consider the implications for, or relations to, the other aspects.

He has also cautioned against the danger of: (1) planning for a world that no longer exists; and (2) assuming that a problem is the same as one encountered in the past but merely bigger, or that all that is required is a larger "dose" of the remedies previously utilized.

Largely because the kind and quality of education provided for present and future generations will have significant implications for the destiny of any nation and of society, many of the controversies relating to planning and change purposes and procedures will tend to center around, or focus on, this vital area. This tendency can and should be utilized to help people understand better the role and importance of education in providing the basis for improving all aspects of society. Unless wisely directed, however, it could result in such sharply polarized controversies that the progress of the nation would be jeopardized.

Some influential people and groups have been insisting recently that the system of education established in this country has failed and should be replaced by new provisions. Although the evidence indicates that the present system is not meeting the needs of many students and has not adjusted effectively to the requirements of a rapidly changing society, there are many equally valid indications that it has adjusted in many important respects and is making many significant contributions to the progress of the nation. Controversies along these lines tend to divert attention from the basic issue: *What kind and quality of education is essential to meet present and emerging needs, and how can it best and most effectively be provided?* This issue can best be resolved by bona fide and systematic long-range planning *with* rather than *for* people that is encouraged and supported by the citizens in each community, state and in the nation —rather than by polemics, arguments and controversies that tend to confuse basic issues.

THE POLITICS OF PLANNING

The statements above should not be interpreted to imply that controversies about some issues relating to education can or should be avoided through the process of systematic planning for improvements. Indeed they cannot, but *long-range planning can provide an opportunity to consider most issues and controversies from a broader and more appropriate perspective or frame of reference than might otherwise be feasible.*

. Those who advocate systematic planning as well as those who provide leadership in the planning process must bear in mind that politics will continue to play a significant role in determining what is to be accomplished. This is a necessary process in a democracy and educational planners and leaders must be knowledgeably involved in the process or fail to accomplish their major objectives.

The effect that greater knowledge concerning options and costs will have upon the use of traditional means—compromise and private bargaining—has not yet been determined. It is probable that there will be considerable change in the power of, and the relationships among, officeholders, lobbyists, and private citizens. Each will have to be sufficiently flexible to accomodate to change. No group or person can expect to go on doing business as usual in the face of the changes that are almost certain to occur in society.

In many important respects, planning is, or should be, primarily a *non-partisan* political process. For example, there must be substantial agreement among the citizens of a community, a state and in the nation that systematic long-range planning is essential—or at least is appropriate —before adequate resources can or will be provided or utilized for that purpose. Moreover, no proposal for a major change in the purposes, scope, organization, procedures, or provisions for support of education is likely to be implemented unless it is considered necessary or at least desirable by a substantial number of the citizens who are concerned.

In other respects, however, planning is, or should be a technical and non-political process. Assuming that the criteria are agreed upon (partly a political process), the pertinent information should be assembled and analyzed by competent experts (a non-political process, except perhaps when alternative interpretations can be made). The fact that the planning process provides for the careful study of all pertinent information before any recommendations are made, should make it possible to avoid some controversies and consider others from a more defensible perspective. When value judgments must be made, the values can or should be identified and discussed on their merits.

DEMANDS FOR INVOLVEMENT

As society and education have become increasingly complex during the current century, relatively few people directly concerned with education—board members, administrators, principals or teachers—have shown much interest in encouraging lay citizens to become involved in, or concerned about, many issues directly relating to education. The public generally seems to have been oriented toward non-participation unless motivated by some controversial issue. Many people now believe that present and emerging demands on the educational enterprise are of such character and magnitude that they cannot be met unless more citizens, including students, "become active participants in reordering educational goals and priorities."[11]

Recently, substantial numbers of individuals and groups have become increasingly interested in and concerned about participating in many aspects of the public decision-making process. Some of these, at present, seem be more interested in enhancing their own power and prestige than in improving major aspects of society, but the potential should not be ignored. *Effective ways of channeling these interests and efforts constructively are being, and should continue to be, sought and increasingly utilized.*

A number of community groups, with or without the encouragement of educators, have broken through the "apathy barrier" and are seeking—in some cases, even demanding—a voice in determining the policies and even the procedures of the school system or of the schools their children attend and for whose support they pay increasing amounts through taxes. Some of these groups are convinced that the schools have changed too slowly to meet the needs; others object to some of the more recent changes. Still other groups seem to think most of the decision-making responsibilities should be turned over to them.

Students and teachers, likewise, are insisting on—and, in many cases, demanding—a voice in the educational planning and decision-making processes. Understandably many students and teachers are no longer satisfied to have the program and procedures that affect them in vital ways determined and imposed without consulting them. The basis for many of these and similar developments is the understandable and commendable desire of most people to participate in important decisions that may significantly affect their lives and welfare. *One of the most important but commonly neglected responsibilities of education is to find and utilize appropriate ways of helping students as well as adults to learn how to participate constructively and effectively in planning and in decision making relating to important issues.*

In some states, there seems to be a tendency for the governor or certain members of the legislature to develop and want to impose their own solutions for education problems. This attitude can be understood in states in which the state education agency has neglected or failed to provide the leadership and services that are essential to plan needed improvements in education, but should be considered indefensible if recommendations submitted by any state education agency on the basis of carefully developed plans are ignored.

All state education agencies should expect and be expected to involve competent and representative citizens and local educators, as well as appropriate technicians and other experts in the planning process. If they fail to do so they ignore the growing demands for participation in decision making on the one hand, and invite challenges and confrontations on the other.

In summary, *both state education agencies and local school systems should encourage responsible participation in decision making pertaining to educational problems and issues.* One of the best ways to do so—and to avoid expedient decisions on pressing problems—would seem to be for state and local education agencies to provide the leadership and services needed to encourage and facilitate continuing comprehensive and systematic long-range planning for the improvement of education.

THE ECONOMICS OF PLANNING

Operation of the educational system, including the policy decisions which affect priorities, is made possible primarily through the use of public funds—the major source of all educational financing. The availability of public funds for education in general, as well as for the various levels and aspects within education, is controlled by the health of the economy, the political strength of the competing forces that are seeking support from public tax funds, and the many other forces and factors that relate to, or have implications for, the economics of planning. The current stresses and strains in society and within the educational system could result in a considerable shift in public priorities. *Whether such a shift would be beneficial or detrimental would probably depend largely upon whether the pressures are based on knowledge and understanding or on self-interest or irrational approaches.*

Many people, including state and local officials, have become greatly concerned during recent years about the rapidly increasing costs of education—and especially about the growing burden on the property taxes that constitute the major source of revenue for support of public schools in most states. There is a strong and defensible insistence that costs be more closely related to outcomes—to the quality of the education provided and the returns on the investment. Many of these demands, if properly recognized and utilized, can and should provide considerable impetus for better planning including the use of any new technologies that can help to resolve these concerns on a rational and constructive basis. The identification of needs and the analysis of benefits constitute valuable tools or procedures that are applicable in resolving problems of relevance, cost and resource allocation.

Relatively few local school systems or state education agencies, thus far, have become seriously involved in, or attempted bona fide comprehensive and systematic long-range planning. Many have been so involved with pressing problems, crisis-generated situations, and the planning related to annual or biennial budgets that little attention has been given to longer-range objectives and needs. Under modern conditions, such procedures should be considered economically indefensible.

Long-range planning requires funds and other resources that have seldom been available in adequate amounts to local school systems or state education agencies for that purpose. Yet, if such resources were available and utilized wisely, the long-term gains in student learning and in the effective utilization of staff and other resources should more than counterbalance the funds required for effective planning. Moreover, the *meaningful involvement of competent citizens in the planning and decision-making processes can and should result in a broader base for the support of education and probably even in more adequate financial provisions.*

RESPONSIBILITY FOR PLANNING AND EFFECTING IMPROVEMENTS IN EDUCATION

Everyone, including students and teachers, should be interested and seek opportunities to help in planning improvements in education as well as in effecting needed changes and evaluating the results of these changes. However, *in every state there must be a plan for educational planning that should be agreed upon* in order to avoid needless conflicts and confusion. The essentials include:

The kind and scope of planning to be done at each level of government. Each state, as emphasized in other chapters, should provide the leadership and services needed to plan and effect improvements in education throughout the state, provide guidance and assistance to local school systems and educational institutions, and seek to facilitate the coordination of federal, state and local planning activities and recommendations. But each level of government and agency must be continuously involved in planning improvements in its own functions and services.

The kinds of services needed for the technical aspects of planning. Defensible planning requires the services of many kinds of competent experts and technicians. These include systems analysts, computer programmers, information management specialists, cost-effectiveness experts, and many others. Some of these may be employees of the agency primarily involved in the planning, while others may be borrowed or employed on a part-time basis. Above all, it should be understood by everyone concerned that *these people are not to do the planning or make the basic policy decisions,* but are to obtain the pertinent information, make the necessary analyses and present the findings and tentative conclusions for consideration by such policy or decision-making groups as a policy committee, a board of education or the legislature.

The policy decisions and recommendations. Everyone also needs to recognize that the basic policy decisions and recommendations should be made by the sponsoring committee or agency—but only after thorough study of all pertinent information, including the recommendations of special study committees and the suggestions submitted by interested and informed groups and individuals. Moreover, everyone should understand that some of these recommendations cannot be implemented without the support of a majority of the citizens and perhaps approval by the board of education, or even by the legislature.

INITIATING THE PLANNING

When there is an awareness of the need for change and improvement in education, and when those having responsibility for education are convinced that planning should precede change, there should be no further delay in organizing for a cooperative planning endeavor. At this point it is only natural for people to ask: "Who should take the initiative?" In this country, the right to provide leadership in planning and implementing improvements in education has not been reserved to any particular person or group, official or otherwise. Throughout the history of American education, groups of all kinds have emerged to make their "feelings" about schools known. Most of these groups have been constructive and helpful; others, formed with a selfish "axe to grind," have been harmful. Few would question the potential value of such groups. No advocate of democracy would contest their right to exist.

The complexity of the problems emerging in this society makes it necessary that leadership be provided to bring all public agencies and institutions—and insofar as practicable, all groups—together in a coordinated effort to meet the challenges. Education will no longer be able to afford the luxury of permitting the universities, the colleges and teacher-training institutions, vocational schools, schools for adults, schools for the handicapped, community colleges, and local schools—elementary and secondary—to continue in an uncoordinated manner. They must be brought together in behalf of the interests of society as a whole.

State Planning. Initiation of a state planning project involving education can start with any individual or group. The impetus may be provided by the governor, the legislature, the state education agency, some other state agency, lay organizations, or a self-starting group of individual citizens. Each has advantages and disadvantages. The key factors, however, are personalities, objectives, and relationships. The question, "Who should initiate the sponsorship of the project?" has almost as many answers as there are states. The decision as to what is the best for a given state depends largely on conditions, timing, and people.

A project authorized by governmental authority—the governor or legislature—has official prestige. It has direct access to special information, possible mandatory cooperation from all governmental agencies, and perhaps financial help. The formation of a group with this sanction often encourages immediate action, because people are apt to feel that such a step would not have been taken by the authorities unless the problems were acute. On the other hand, some people may believe that such a project has an implied obligation to maintain the status quo or to make certain changes, that it is likely to be political, or that the recommendations may be shelved and, as a result, the group would be powerless to move into the implementation stage.

Almost the same possible advantages or disadvantages pertain to projects initiated by a state education agency, except there may be less danger of partisan political influence in many states. However, because of its responsibility for providing the leadership and services needed for the improvement of education in a state, each state education agency should be intimately and continuously involved in every state project that is concerned with, or has important implications for, education.

Local Planning. Local school systems that are interested in long-range planning have three major options:

1. *Reassign or employ and provide inservice training for staff members who are to assume the responsibility for directing, coordinating and providing the planning services needed.* But, funds may not be adequate to make this possible; there may not be any staff members who are competent in planning; or, if the planning is done by the staff without involving representatives from the community, the proposals resulting from the planning may not be accepted by the citizens.

2. *Employ a competent consultant or consultants, or obtain the services of consultants from the state department of education to help to direct or coordinate the planning.* But, funds may not be available to employ consultants and the state department may not be in a position to provide the needed services; or the consultants may not be able to work constructively with the staff or know how to work effectively with representatives from the community.

3. *Contract with a consulting firm to develop the plans.* But, while this procedure may seem to be an easy solution to the problem, the employment of a consulting firm is usually expensive; some firms may not be competent or willing to make the effort to develop the kind of plans needed; or the plans proposed may not be accepted by the staff or the citizens in the school system because they have been developed by "outsiders," are not considered practicable, or because neither the members of the staff nor the citizens have been involved in the process. Moreover the persons most concerned probably will have had little or no opportunity to learn much about planning which must be a continuous process.

But local school systems, regardless of the problems and difficulties, must become seriously involved in systematic and continuous long-range planning. They can no longer expect to meet the educational needs of the community by attempting to develop expedient solutions for basic problems highlighted by a series of crisis-generated situations. They can and must arrange for the necessary training of competent staff members who can provide the essential leadership and services, and find ways of obtaining appropriate assistance, as needed, from the state education agency or other sources. Moreover, they urgently need to develop defensible policies for involving competent community representatives in appropriate aspects of the planning process as a basis for helping to ensure that the plans will be adopted and result in significant improvements in the provisions for education, in learning opportunities, and in progress for all students.

ROLE OF STATE EDUCATION AGENCIES

State education agencies that should be expected to provide the leadership and services needed to plan and effect improvements in education in the state, to evaluate progress and to assist local school systems in planning, are confronted with similar dilemmas. However, a number of states, at least partly as a result of the stimulation and assistance provided through federal funds and projects, have made significant progress and important contributions. Providing leadership and services in planning has been recognized as a major responsibility—a way of life—by some state agencies. This important responsibility, discussed in general terms earlier in this chapter and in greater detail in other chapters, urgently needs to be recognized and accepted by all states and vigorously supported by all citizens.

IN SUMMARY

Change is now a certainty, but the unanswered questions are: What changes should be made in education? How should they be made? How soon? At what cost? Impatience with delays is clearly evident among growing numbers of citizens, primarily as a result of major changes in society and the slow progress in bringing our ideals, policies and practices into harmony. The extent and direction of social unrest, the dramatic pace of technological change and other disturbing developments emphasize the necessity for education to be more responsive to societal and individual needs. The growing demands for relevance, the resistance to rising costs, and the competition traditional educational institutions are receiving from industry and new agencies in the field of education clearly point to the need for education to be more effective and efficient, to relate costs to effectiveness, and to make the relationships known to all who are concerned.

The state education agency in each state should provide the leadership and services needed to facilitate comprehensive long-range planning for the improvement of education in each state. One purpose of such planning is to bring about beneficial change and help to avoid the perpetuation of outmoded policies and practices. This concept implies that planning is to be followed by implementation and evaluation. It is assumed, therefore, that those who are involved in the details of planning will be closely related to decision makers at all levels—school boards, legislatures, the voters, and so on. It would not be safe to assume that good planning will necessarily result in quick decisions that support the recommendations of the planners. It would be more logical to expect that the presence of planning—with the resulting increase in the quantity and quality of information with which to make decisions—is almost certain to create some new problems and require some important adjustments.

Many state, municipal, regional and county governments now employ specialists, frequently referred to as "planners," and a number of universities presumably are preparing planning experts in a number of areas. There is currently a great demand for planning in all aspects of society, but there seems to be considerable confusion about the role of those who are commonly referred to as *planners* as well as about the planning process itself.

In education, as well as in other aspects of society, planning has become increasingly important. But, many citizens in most communities and states want to participate in the process of planning improvements in education, and tend to be suspicious of any person or group that might seem, by implication, to want to plan the kind of education to be provided for them or their children. For this and other reasons, the terms "planning coordinators," "planning specialists," or "planning experts" would seem more acceptable to many people, at least for the present, than the term "educational planners."

Under modern conditions, the services of experts or specialists should be considered essential to help to guide educational planning which, if it is to be adequate and meaningful, must be a systematic process that utilizes all the available knowledge, insights and technologies as a basis for identifying and effecting needed improvements. Planning has advanced beyond the stage of deciding impulsively on proposals because they sound promising or have influential advocates, or of suggesting minor changes that might meet with popular approval but would not provide for some of the basic needs.

Planning is a systematic process for identifying existing and prospective problems of the entire educational system and proposing solutions relating to long- and short-range priorities that, when implemented, will result in adequate provisions for, and progress of, all students in learning. Goals must be clearly identified, needs ascertained, performance objectives specified, and appropriate procedures for measuring progress determined and properly utilized. One of the basic components is the development of pertinent performance objectives—clear, concise descriptions of desired outcomes—for the system, for all personnel and for all students.

But everyone involved in the process should recognize that systematic planning is only one essential step in the continuing process of improving, and evaluating progress in improving, all aspects of education. The best plans that can be devised will be relatively meaningless unless they are implemented and the results continuously monitored. Moreover, they should be considered unrealistic or inadequate unless the implementation results in better and more adequate education for all students.

Footnote References

[1]Norman Cousins, "The Case for Hope," *Saturday Review,* December 26, 1970, p. 18.

[2]See Jack Culbertson, "State Planning for Education," in *Planning and Effecting Needed Changes in Education,* Edgar L. Morphet and Charles O. Ryan, eds. (Denver, Colorado: Designing Education for the Future, 1967), Chap. 12. Republished by Citation Press, Scholastic Magazines, Inc., New York, N. Y.

[3]From report on *Planning and Developing an Adequate State Program of Education* by the Study Commission on State Educational Problems, as approved by the National Council of Chief State School Officers. Published in *Education for Victory,* December 20, 1944, pp. 15-16.

[4]*Building a Better Southern Region Through Education* (Tallahassee, Florida: Southern States Work-conference on Educational Problems, Edgar L. Morphet, Executive Secretary and Editor, 1945), pp. 57-60.

[5]Especially pertinent are the publications: *Planning and Effecting Needed Improvements in Education,* Edgar L. Morphet and Charles O. Ryan, eds. (Denver, Colorado: Designing Education for the Future, 1967). Republished by Citation Press, Scholastic Magazines, Inc., New York, N.Y.; *Comprehensive Planning in State Education Agencies,* Bernarr S. Furse and Lyle O. Wright, eds. (Salt Lake City: Utah State Board of Education, 1968); and the numerous references cited in each publication.

[6]*Progress Reports,* International Institute for Educational Planning, *1963-1967,* (Paris, France: UNESCO, 1967).

[7]Jack A. Culbertson, "Simulation of Educational Planning Problems," June, 1971, pp. 3-4. Unpublished paper available through The University Council for Educational Administration, Columbus, Ohio.

[8]Willis W. Harman, "The Nature of Our Changing Society: Implications for Schools." (Prepared for the ERIC Clearinghouse on Educational Administration, Eugene, Oregon, October 1969).

[9]For example, see discussion by Richard C. Lonsdale in *Preparing Educators to Meet Emerging Needs,* Edgar L. Morphet and David L. Jesser, eds. (Denver, Colorado: Designing Education for the Future, 1969), pp. 19-31, and the footnote references at end of the chapter. Republished by Citation Press, Scholastic Magazines, Inc., New York, N.Y.

[10]Robert B. Howsam, "Problems, Procedures and Practices in Designing Education for the Future," in *Cooperative Planning for Education in 1980,* Edgar L. Morphet and David L. Jesser, eds. (Denver, Colorado: Designing Education for the Future, 1968). Republished by Citation Press, Scholastic Magazines, Inc., New York, N.Y.

[11]See, for example, Donald J. McCarty and Charles E. Ramsey, *The School Managers: Power and Conflict in American Public Education* (Westport, Connecticut: Greenwood Publishing Corporation, 1971).

Chapter 4

State Responsibilities for Planning

Planning for educational change has been considered desirable for some years; today it is essential. The current mandate for planning comes from the people: they want better education and this tends to be interpreted as a "different" education. An education system that does not meet present and emerging needs soon loses the confidence and support of the people. This appears to have happened in recent years. Planning should mean *planning for needed changes in education*—not for the preservation and maintenance of the status quo, nor merely for greater economy or efficiency—but *"to provide appropriate learning experiences for all citizens* of every age and social background, to offer diversified programs to meet individual needs, develop individual potentialities, and furnish the common experience-background which gives unity and direction to our society."[1]*

A systematic analysis of educational needs and a judicious assessment of state educational priorities should be regarded as the basis for the kind of planning that is: (1) comprehensive in scope; (2) long-range in projection; and (3) statewide in involvement and participation not only of educators, but also of other groups including those concerned with health, welfare, recreation, business and industry. Barrett has stated:

> . . . our new society believes that participation is a right that is desirable and that it dignifies man. The output from such participation [in planning] is assumed and expected to be change, new ideals, new goals and new creative thrusts.[2]

The dissatisfactions in modern society with educational change that just happens—random reactions to the forces that affect education—or with planning that does not lead to improvements, amplifies the need for more rational planning to bring about desired changes. The whole purpose of planning should be to identify and achieve desired goals in each state through a rational approach that considers feasible alternatives as a vital element in the process.

STATE RESPONSIBILITIES

Within limits prescribed in the United States Constitution, federal court decisions and laws, each state is responsible for attempting to meet the needs of its residents. This responsibility implies that the states should

---

*Footnote references are given at end of the chapter.

consider prospective changes as well as present needs and that careful planning is essential in each state. In most areas of concern, piecemeal or expedient action does not bring about effective resolution of problems and, in the long run, tends to aggravate existing conditions. *Systematic comprehensive planning is inherent in the state's responsibility* as consideration is given to the general welfare of the state's residents in matters of health, justice, welfare, transportation, the environment, consumer protection and other areas and, especially, for the education of children and youth as prospective citizens and voters.

The citizens of each state, through their representatives in the legislature and state officials, will decide—hopefully after considering alternatives—how much emphasis is to be placed on planning, for what purposes, and how it is to be conducted. The possibilities range from highly *centralized planning* for most state functions to *limited planning* for a few aspects and delegation of responsibility to local units for others. The policies accepted in a state determine the kind, role and major functions of the organization for planning that will be established or the modifications that will be made in the organization that has already been established. Because of contemporary and emerging developments and needs, additional states are almost certain to place increasing emphasis on systematic planning in all aspects of government.

STATE ORGANIZATION FOR PLANNING

Three major alternatives are available in organizing a state to engage continuously in planning, but whether the choice from among them is (or will be) influenced primarily by educational considerations is subject to question. Planning normally will be under the supervision and control of the executive or legislative branches of state government or both. Nevertheless, the following possibilities in organizing for planning warrant careful attention:

1. The responsibility for planning in a state can be assigned to a *centrally controlled planning agency or body.* This agency becomes an adjunct to the executive or legislative branch of government and, conceivably, tends to be concerned primarily with matters of importance to state authority or of significance to the people. Its tasks are *centrally determined* and do not specifically reflect the interest of any one agency of state government—the state education agency, for example.

2. A variation from this pattern of organization would be a structure that includes a centrally controlled planning body, but relies heavily upon the divisions and agencies of state government to carry the initiative for planning in their respective areas of concern. The central agency's major responsibility would be *communication, consideration of state priorities and coordination.* This pattern might be interpreted as *coordinated state planning* within which, for example, the state education agency's planning effort would be directed to its own operations and priorities as well as to statewide educational policies and programs.

3. Another pattern of organization would provide for *each state agency to be responsible for planning* its own role, functions and activities. The degree of coordination in this arrangement would depend upon state laws and appropriations by the legislature, or would be voluntary on the part of each agency. Effectiveness in planning would be directly related to the leadership perceptions of the agency and the degree to which planning is regarded as an integral aspect of the agency's function.

CENTRALIZED PLANNING FOR ALL FUNCTIONS AND SERVICES

Planning as a continuous and all-inclusive responsibility of a single office, agency, or body may find increasing acceptance as constituting the state's most efficient and effective means for guiding broad social and economic developments. With the acceleration of competition by agencies responsible for health, welfare, highways, education and other segments of state service for state funds and the need to assign priorities consistent with the state's overall needs and political considerations, both the governor's office and the legislature may view this form of organization with great favor. The increasing pressure for accountability also tends to support the contention that the responsibility for planning should be placed in an identifiable group within a state's bureaucracy.

Some Possible Advantages

- A balanced approach could be ensured in that the needs of the state could be more clearly identified and optimum resources allocated to meet these needs.

- Overlapping goals and functions and the duplication of efforts could be minimized.

- The standardization of reporting forms, schedules and data analysis would be enhanced.

- Costly and scarce planning talents and technology could be more easily acquired and supported.

Some Possible Disadvantages

- The public usually does not have much confidence or faith in a central authority that could be affected by and reflect partisan political influences, especially in the matter of planning for improvements in education.

- In all probability, the agencies that would be responsible for implementing plans would not be seriously involved in developing plans.

- Some proposals could become unrealistic if various authorities or knowledgeable persons were not continuously consulted and utilized in planning.

- The probable emphasis on measurable outputs in order to demonstrate solid progress could place education in low priority as related to more measurable activities because some of the outcomes are difficult to measure.

- The membership of the central planning body may be responsive to the rise and fall of political fortunes and, thus, be vulnerable to partisan political influences if it is to maintain status and continuity as an entity.

COORDINATION OF STATE PLANNING

Most state education agencies and their constituencies probably would view a coordinated state approach to planning with somewhat greater favor than one where the primary initiative and resources rest in a centralized state planning body. It is difficult to identify any matter of state interest and concern relating to education, health, welfare, natural resources, revenue, labor and commerce that does not reflect a degree of interest or have implications for several state agencies. Each state agency has some unique characteristics that would tend to support the contention that the agency should have the primary role for initiative and follow-through activities on matters within its domain. The coordinated approach to state planning warrants serious consideration as an option that has merit. In harmony with this approach, a subcommittee of a Governors' Conference in the early 1960's prepared a policy statement relative to organizing a state for planning which recommended that each state:

> . . . create a planning unit that can take into account all state development efforts and help coordinate and integrate these into an overall plan [and] . . . re-examine the need for planning units in its major operating units to strengthen existing units or establish new ones where they are considered advisable. . . .[3]

Some Possible Advantages

- The sharing of information in a coordinated planning effort should encourage the development of collaborative planning and ensuring action programs where overlapping concerns exist.

- The effectiveness of a state agency's planning effort could be substantially improved through the resources made available through the state's coordinating mechanism.

- An increasing statewide confidence in the quality of the state's planning endeavors may evolve because of the cooperation, coordination and collaboration embodied in this approach.

Some Possible Disadvantages

- The need to have open communication, mutual respect, and reliance upon an even-handed and fair-minded process in a coordinated approach is subject to human failings (quest for power, authority, jealousy, and the like).

- The uneven distribution of resources, competencies, and planning commitments among the various state agencies may decrease the effectiveness of a cooperative approach to state planning.

- Education and other agencies may be forced to wait for necessary cooperation to evolve in matters that should have top priority.

EACH STATE AGENCY RESPONSIBLE FOR PLANNING

Because of the special interests and abilities that are concentrated in each state agency, some persons would contend that substantial improvements in a state can only be made when the responsibility for planning its own functions and programs is placed in each agency. The complexity of contemporary issues in the society tends to require that experts be involved in the resolution of problems. If this assumption is accepted for guidance, the responsibility for planning in its own areas of concern would be assigned to each agency because of its capacity to utilize its human and other resources to meet a need. This alternative in organizing a state for planning would appear to be the one most favored by most state agency personnel as they could pursue their specialized interests and apply their efforts accordingly. Personnel and other resources could be marshalled to meet the needs of a state in transportation, health, welfare, education or other areas of special concern reflected in the respective state agencies.

Some Possible Advantages

- The effectiveness of an agency in bringing about needed changes in a state can be furthered when responsibility for planning is placed in the agency.

- Each state agency could concentrate its efforts on priority matters that are identified through planning.

- Accountability can be more clearly assigned in relationship to the agency's basic responsibility and purpose.

- Needed interaction of persons who are concerned about a particular issue could be more easily obtained and utilized by each state agency.

Some Possible Disadvantages

- Conceivably state agencies most favored by the governor, state legislature or influential special interest groups might receive greater attention and support in their planning efforts than other agencies.

- The interrelations that are necessary to bring about substantial improvements may be overlooked due to the limited perceptions that may prevail within an individual agency.

- The need for cooperation and coordination tends to be ignored when an agency functions as an entity in isolation from other state agencies.

PLANNING FOR EDUCATION IN A STATE

The organization for educational planning in a state should strongly support the development of an effective affirmative force for leadership in the state's education system. This suggests *a primary but not an isolated role* for the state education agency. Minear has pointed out that, "The state education agency must serve as the chief sensing and planning instrument for local, state, and national educational control through signal interpretation and feedback from each level."[4]

Traditionally, state education agencies have not been perceived as having a major responsibility for leadership in educational planning but this responsibility is now being recognized in most states. Many state education agencies have made considerable progress during recent years in defining the role these agencies should have in planning and effecting improvements in the state's education system.

The alternatives available to a state education agency in organizing for planning depend on the policies established by the state and the perceptions held within the agency itself as to its leadership role. The major alternatives deserving consideration are:

1. *Centralized planning for education in the state* by the agency itself might be regarded as an appropriate activity. Initiative would grow out of state leadership and the state education agency would *order and direct* the flow of improvements in a state. In essence, this arrangement calls for an emphasis in *planning for the people.*

2. In sharp contrast to the first alternative, state education agency *leadership in the coordination of educational planning* suggests a broadly-based endeavor concerned with local and intermediate as well as state educational problems, interests and concerns. The cooperative process built into this approach emphasizes *planning with the people.* "While . . . leadership [is] exercised by the state education agency, the participation of organizations, associations, industry and other governmental agencies that can contribute to the success of such planning is necessary."[5]

CENTRALIZED STATE EDUCATION AGENCY PLANNING FOR EDUCATION

Each state has a fundamental responsibility for all education, public and private, within the state. *Implicit in this responsibility is the planning function.*

The citizens of a state should expect the state education agency to develop and foster a major planning endeavor. This need not and should not be an activity isolated and remote from local and intermediate concerns. Nevertheless, the people of a state might logically assume that centralized planning, at least for elementary and secondary education, should be within the province of the state education agency (as in Hawaii) in view of the state's responsibility. A strong planning capability within the agency is thus implied. The primary initiative and the driving force in planning improvements in the state's education system would rest with the state board of education and its operational arm, the state education agency. Appropriate state reports, recommendations and actions would evolve from such *planning for the state's system.*

Some Possible Advantages

- If the state education agency is to be held responsible for the quality of the education that is provided for the people of the state, it presumably should have the authority to conduct the planning implied by this responsibility.

- Local provincialism in educationally-related matters can be offset through the much broader perspective that should be reflected at the state level.

- The needed special talents and skills for planning would more likely be available to the state than in local education agencies.

Some Possible Disadvantages

- *Planning for people* as contrasted with that of *planning with people* tends to be contrary to the perceived wishes of most members of the American society.

- Centralized planning could lead to the development of a bureaucratic "hold" on education.

- There is much evidence to support the contention that education is too fundamental a concern to be left to the discretion of the state without the necessary continuous interaction between local and state levels of governance and of leadership at both levels.

- The impersonality of the "state" can be envisioned as a factor in the increasing dehumanization trend that is perceived as a threat to the traditions of the American society.

COORDINATED PLANNING FOR EDUCATION

With the growing distrust of the "establishment" and the efforts by many segments of society to challenge authority in its present modes, it becomes increasingly apparent that state leadership and services in the coordination of educational planning may offer much to contribute to the improvement of education within a state. Planning procedures that place local and state representatives in a face-to-face relationship should contribute to the definition of basic issues and to rational agreements on ways to resolve them.

Coordinated planning may be conceived as essentially a *people-based* endeavor. It suggests a broad scale, open and pervasive approach to planning, relying most heavily upon inputs from throughout a state at the "grass-roots" level. It carries the potential of *widespread participation by both lay citizens and professionals at the community level.* Based upon the assumption that education is the concern of all people and that there is a strong desire to retain local decision making as a vital force in education, such planning efforts are often viewed as likely to attract broadly-based political interest and support for necessary decisions at the state level. This approach *led by a state education agency,* as indicated in the Florida legislation in Chapter 2, can provide a sound basis on which to recommend specific legislative programs for improvements in education to the state's elected officials. The involvement of diverse groups and individuals in the process of helping to make decisions and having to live with the consequences helps to increase the understanding of all who are involved.

Some Possible Advantages

- Increased attention to decentralized or "client-centered" approaches develops and maintains the confidence of those for whose welfare the planning process is presumably designed.

- The gap between planning and action can diminish significantly in that the involvement of local leadership in state planning enhances the necessary understanding of the relations between state and local needs and action.

- Coordinated planning should help to develop more positive attitudes throughout the state concerning the need to examine the present and contemplate the future in a systematic fashion and, thus, lead to a greater acceptance of change as a normal fact of life.

- Through their encouragement of and involvement in state planning, state education agencies can enhance the partnership concept implied between the state and local education agencies in educational matters.

Some Possible Disadvantages

- Coordinated planning, unless sensitive to the widely varying concern about commitment to public education from one community setting to another, may well become immersed in all manner of local cross-currents in a given setting or result in non-soluble conflicts between and among localities and regions having their own self-interests.

- Serious confrontations can emerge when, in the difficult areas of decision making, state leadership is challenged by consortiums of local education agencies unable to sense other problems and priorities of statewide concern.

• Wide-spread involvement of local communities in the analysis and projection of needs of a state as a whole could lead to local attempts to interfere with or eliminate the responsibility that can be best assumed by the state.

CONSIDERATIONS IN ORGANIZING A STATE FOR PLANNING

As indicated, each of the alternatives for the planning organization and procedures in a state has its unique characteristics and its advantages and disadvantages. Several or all may exist simultaneously with similar or different foci, priorities and sanctions. Each alternative presents a different set of problems to be resolved in the development of a systematic and effective planning mechanism in a state.

The preceding discussion of the major alternatives and their possible advantages and disadvantages constitutes an attempt to explain several approaches available to states that recognize the need for more effective planning. A variety of state structures for planning are in use throughout the nation with some functioning in a more effective manner than others. In some instances, the political powers are in complete control. In a few others, planning organizations are merely "paper" representations on organizational charts.

The alternatives for planning within a state, especially for education, should receive careful consideration before any decisions are made as to the most appropriate course of action to be taken in order to bring about the improvements needed in the quest for excellence in education. There obviously is an urgent need for each state education agency to: (1) plan its own role, functions and services; (2) provide state leadership and services in planning statewide improvements in education; (3) assist local school systems to learn how to plan and to plan to meet present and emerging needs; and (4) coordinate activities related to education with those of other state agencies.

Many individuals with varying interests and status—together with separate branches of government, educational institutions and other sectors of the formal organizational structure of a state—play roles that are likely to be critical in determining the success or failure of planning activities in a state. Obviously, the patterns and structures may vary widely from state to state at a given time and within any state over a period of time. They will be influenced by traditional roles, legal restrictions, contemporary pressures of all kinds, personalities, partisan political factors and bureaucratic considerations.

ORGANIZATIONAL CONSIDERATIONS

The complexities and issues involved in comprehensive educational planning are so important that any standardized approach to the organization of planning for the improvement of education in the states would

appear inappropriate. The decisions should be made by the states themselves because of the varied organizational, political and legal differences
among the states. However, the following basic objectives appear applicable in every state:

- Establish an appropriate organization in the state to enable planning for
  educational improvement to be conducted in a *systematic and comprehensive
  manner;*

- Relate the planning organization appropriately to *action agencies*—the state
  legislature and executive department—so that statewide, comprehensive plans
  may be translated into action programs mandated by these agencies; to other
  educational institutions—local school districts, colleges and universities, and
  the private sector of education—to influence the future planning of their
  programs; to *concerned agencies and groups*—lay and professional in a state
  —to ensure appropriate involvement in the decision-making process; and

- Build into the planning organization the needed technical competence to enable planning to be based on systematic valid study and evaluation of education.[6]

As Governor Robert E. McNair from South Carolina has emphasized,
"Where the state is willing and capable to undertake this type of coordinating responsibility, a far greater return on the invested dollars
can materialize."[7]

INCREASED STATE AND FEDERAL SUPPORT

The impact of proposals for increased federal support through categorical programs, block grants and, perhaps, some form of revenue
sharing will have a bearing on how a state organizes or adapts its organization for planning to this thrust. Regardless of these developments, the
emphasis in planning in a state should be on needs assessment, the determination of priorities, and the selection of alternative procedures to
meet the priorities. Such an emphasis can help to minimize the struggles
by factions and groups who will attempt to influence the decisions as
to where increased financial support should go. Each state should have its
goals well defined and accepted and its avenues of goal attainment planned
so that piecemeal actions are not needed to comply with the provisions
for increased support whether from the federal or state level. It would
behoove state education agencies to be prepared to be in a position to
influence the decisions that are made at the state level. Future provisions for additional support will almost certainly help to create a greater
awareness of the need for effective state planning. Every state needs to
prepare and plan for this eventuality.

POLICIES AND PROVISIONS FOR PARTICIPATION IN PLANNING

Regardless of where a state determines to place the responsibility for
educational planning, major decisions will need to be made with respect
to the power and authority within the planning structure and the desired
competence of its human components. The involvement of people (dis-

cussed further in Chapter 6) is essential in bringing about improvements. Those who participate in a state's planning effort should be qualified to perform and provide appropriate planning, training, consulting and evaluating services. Each service should utilize a systems approach to ensure the quality and adequacy of the services performed and, thus, contribute to product (output) in relation to the needs and priorities of the state. This approach can and should provide complete, accurate, relevant and timely information for decision making and be sensitive to specific time, cost, value and technical requirements for effectiveness.

THE CLIMATE FOR EDUCATIONAL PLANNING

The emergence of an organization for comprehensive educational planning in a state normally flows from the interaction of professional-educational, partisan-political, social-cultural-ethnic, economic and bureaucratic considerations that stimulate a recognition of the need for planning. Each of the forces leading to this recognition has the potential for affecting both the organization and the process for the planning effort. In turn, these same forces may be altered by the changes brought about through planning. *Major power struggles can and do emerge within a state in the effort to "capture" the planning process by controlling the planning effort.*

It is important for everyone to be aware of the potential for conflict that exists at all stages of any planning activity. For example, a vital financial or idealogical (e.g., church-state) issue can hardly be ignored by a state's major political parties, its governor and its legislature since it will affect major interest groups. If any group views a potential change or plan for change as a threat to its power or particular concern, it will almost certainly attempt to influence the action through the elements in state government most susceptible or sensitive to political pressure.

This adversary kind of relationship needs to be reversed. In education the loser in most conflicts is the student, a victim in every sense who may be powerless to affect his fate. *Consistent attention should be focused on meeting the needs of students in the best possible way and on avoiding getting caught up in defending a traditional position or organization.*

Within the array of states in the nation can be found governors who are deeply interested in education or concerned about the share of state resources—financial and otherwise—devoted to education; legislative leaders who are jealous over their prerogatives in allocating resources as between state functions and local communities; universities with diverse service orientations; state education agencies with varying perceptions of their leadership roles; and local education agencies with diverse points of view as to the leadership role of the state. Each entity tends to view itself as having a primary role in planning for the improvement of education in a state. The validity of these interests cannot be challenged but the critical importance of education for the future welfare of a state as a whole should lead to the acceptance of *rational as contrasted with partisan political or other pressure group considerations* in determining the role in planning of each office, agency or division of government.

The state education agency that is engaged in more than mere regulatory functions will recognize the need for greater involvement of diverse groups in planning in order to obtain guidance in devising criteria for assessing progress, developing new programs and services, solving pressing problems and providing the leadership that is demanded by the public in education. An operating consensus strengthens the decisions that are made in that most people concerned will know in advance that there will be constituencies who support the decisions. The technique of *providing for participation in planning* also helps to modify the stereotype of bureaucracy to which units of civil government are subject and serves to involve knowledgeable people in decisions about the control of education. For these and other compelling reasons reflected in the demands of contemporary society, the coordinated planning approach under the leadership of the state education agency should receive increasing attention in the organizational structure for state planning.

COMPONENTS OF A PLANNING ORGANIZATION

A comprehensive coordinated approach to planning requires an effective organization in order to be successful. If planning is to be a regular and continuing function in a state, the planning organization should be a permanent element in the administration of the state. The structure for this kind of organization should normally include provisions for (1) a planning unit, (2) planning councils or commissions, (3) study committees and/or task forces, and (5) access to consultants or experts.

PLANNING UNIT

The technical arm of a state's planning organization might be regarded as a planning unit. It should be staffed, regardless of its position in the organizational structure, primarily by personnel with expertise in planning technologies. As indicated by Furse:

> The planning unit functions essentially as a catalyst to stimulate technology-based planning and as a facilitator in providing assistance to the planning activities that are undertaken. . . . The planning unit will coordinate planning, provide training in planning technology, conduct certain technological aspects of planning, provide technical assistance to [all persons involved in planning] and organize task forces for specific planning assignments.[8]

Realistically, in an organization for planning that represents a comprehensive coordinated approach, *the planning unit should not be expected to do the planning*. It should be regarded as a service unit and provide assistance in areas such as: systems analysis, information systems, economics, and sociology. Though a core staff is implied, needed services can be acquired on a short-term basis dependent upon the thrust of the planning effort in a state. The effectiveness of a state's organization for planning tends to be related to the funds, manpower and accessible data available to the planning unit.

STATE PLANNING COUNCILS OR COMMISSIONS

Assuming that one of the purposes of state planning is to effect improvements in education, there would appear to be a need for an appropriate state educational planning council or commission. Membership will be dependent on the structure established for planning in a state. This group should be so located—in relationship to the governor's office, the legislature and other agencies—and so constituted, in terms of representation that it will (or can) have a major impact upon the decision-making bodies—the executive and legislative aspects of state government along with the policy-making board for the state education agency.

The council or commission for educational planning may be made up of (1) appropriate state agency officials, (2) representative professional and lay leadership, or (3) some combination of these. By the nature of its role, planning for statewide educational improvements would seem to profit most from the advice, counsel and direction of a competent group that is as representative as possible of all interested parties, governmental and non-governmental, lay and professional. Representation from vested interest group should be avoided insofar as possible.

There are some distinct advantages in having representation from diverse groups on planning councils or commissions for education (as well as for other concerns) in that fresh new ideas and new goals may emerge from such participation. Conceivably, the encrustations of a bureaucratic outlook could be offset by persons who might question the status quo and point to more effective ways of bringing about improvements. If, as many believe, progress is best accomplished under rational considerations that are developed and endorsed by persons widely representative of the public, responsible officials and professional persons, it would seem that the planning council or commission should be representative of the citizens of the state.

A competent executive secretary or study director should be selected to assist the group. This person can be very helpful in bringing about the kind of order and systematic procedure that is vital to the effectiveness of a planning council or commission. Beyond the necessary detail related to such an assignment, this position would call for competence in maintaining effective communications, in working with diverse personalities, and in perceiving and structuring the tasks that must be undertaken by the group.

The decisions that are made as to the scope of power and authority of a planning council or commission have significant implications for the effectiveness of planning in a state. It would appear that this body must perform both an advisory and a policy-making role. It would be policy making with regard to the foci and processes of the planning endeavors themselves and, ultimately, with regard to the priorities it assigns to its recommendations. It would necessarily be advisory in urging the implementation of the recommendations that emerge from its appointed study or task forces, whether at the state or the local levels of government. In either case, however, its role can be significant in determining the smoothness and comprehensiveness of the planning effort.

STUDY COMMITTEES AND/OR TASK FORCES

No planning council or commission, no matter how representative, could expect to possess within itself the varying talents and expertise necessary for effective planning. While this group normally is concerned with basic policies for planning, with the direction and priorities in planning, and with the definition of those areas of study that flow from such priorities and policies, there *is a need and a role for study committees and/or task forces* to work in major areas of identified concern. The work of these groups should be under the general supervision of and be coordinated by the planning council or commission, preferably through the aforementioned executive secretary or study director for the policy group. This person also should have the responsibility to keep the council or commission continually apprised of the progress of the study committees and/or task forces.

Personnel appointed to each of these special study groups should be selected because of their expertise, concern, perspective, and interest in the particular area to be studied. They should, as with the parent group—the council or commission—be as representative of the state as possible and include persons from the state and local levels. State agencies—especially the state education agency—the legislature, citizen groups, community ·and professional organizations, local school systems, institutions of higher learning and business and industry are potential sources for membership. It is important that adequate services be provided for these groups through the state's planning organization in order to ensure maximum input to the planning process. Normally appointed by the planning council or commission for a specific purpose related to a planning need, *the committee and/or task force should be dissolved when its assignment is completed.*

An organizational pattern for participation in planning that was effectively used in the project, *Designing Education for the Future,*[9] is shown in Figure 1 and should serve as a model for consideration in the context discussed above.

Figure 1. *State Organization for Planning*

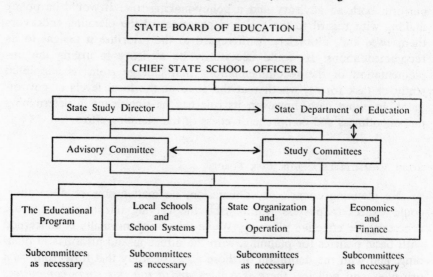

Consultants and Experts

In some instances it may be desirable to seek the insight and objectivity of an expert or a consultant team, particularly in matters where new ventures are contemplated and with which the state has no previous experience. The consultant, expert or team may help with special studies, in gathering and evaluating appropriate evidence, and in developing conclusions, recommendations and/or alternative courses of action with projections of their probable consequences. Such services can be performed for any aspect of the state's planning organization: the planning council or commission—that normally makes the decision to use this kind of service—the planning unit, or the committees and/or task forces—that normally request such help.

Various patterns exist in the use of consultants and each has its advantages and disadvantages. Some of the approaches most commonly used include:

1. *The committee, group or agency may contract with an individual or a consulting organization to make the study and prepare the report, including recommendations.*

Some Possible Advantages

If the individual or organization selected to make the study is capable and conscientious, the report that is prepared probably will be thorough, impressive and defensible and will include recommendations that, if implemented, would result in significant improvements. It may even be better in some respects than a report that could have been prepared by the group responsible for the study.

Some Possible Disadvantages

The person or organization with whom the contract is made may not be in a position to prepare an adequate report, or may overlook some of the facts or factors that should be considered and therefore some of the recommendations may not be defensible. There is always a possibility that the sponsoring group may not agree with some of the proposals and, thus, may find itself in a difficult position. Moreover, even if the report and proposals are defensible, the sponsoring group will have to assume the responsibility for attempting to facilitate their implementation. Finally the cost of such a study will probably be at least as great and may even be greater than if some other alternative had been selected.

2. *The committee, group, or agency responsible for the study obtains the services of competent consultants, works closely with them at all stages, but expects the consultants to conduct the studies and to prepare the report.*

Some Possible Advantages

A competent group utilizing the services of a consultant or consultants in this manner would be in a position to help to build the basis for effecting improvements into the process utilized in making the studies. Moreover, if the consultants work closely with the committee at all stages of the study, the recommendations should be realistic. Finally, a report prepared by competent consultants who know how to work effectively with the committee may be better than any report that could be prepared by the committee without these services.

Some Possible Disadvantages

Unless the members of the group and the consultants understand clearly their respective roles, serious differences of opinion may develop during the course of the study. If the report prepared is recognized as primarily the report of consultants rather than of the committee, implementation may be handicapped.

3. *The committee, group or agency assumes the major responsibility for making the study and for preparing the report and recommendations but utilizes the services of competent consultants to help in designing the study, analyzing data and preparing the report.*

Some Possible Advantages

Perhaps the major advantage is that the people of the state or community will recognize that, while this is basically an indigenous study, the services of competent experts have been used in designing the study and preparing the report. The consultants can provide safeguards against state or local biases and provincialisms.

Some Possible Disadvantages

Unless the roles and functions of all who are involved are clearly delineated and the procedures for making the studies and preparing reports are carefully developed and fully understood, there may be a basis for dissension or confusion. Some aspects of the report when prepared may be less satisfactory than if they had been prepared by consultants.

In *an analysis of the approaches* in the use of consultants, the first approach requires less involvement of knowledgeable people in the state or community than the others and therefore is likely to result in little or no implementation unless special steps are taken. Other things being equal, the second or third alternatives should provide the best opportunity to develop defensible proposals and to ensure effective implementation in most states. The most important conclusion seems to be that the feasible alternatives should be carefully studied by the planning council or commission as a basis for making the wisest possible decisions as to the help that is needed under the circumstances.

In Summary

As the citizens of each state have begun to turn to the state for educational leadership, it has become more and more apparent that planning is vital to this leadership role. Until recently, little attention has been given to discovering where educational efforts are being directed or to the evaluation of results. This is apparent at the local level where many decisions seem to be made on a day-to-day or semester-to-semester basis and at the state level where little attention seems to be directed to developing a long-range comprehensive program for educational improvements in a state. As Hagen has pointed out, "Too often, it appears that the educational planning that is conducted provides little more than hindsight remedies for today's problems."[10]

The need for improvements in education is too critical to the nation's survival and to the welfare of each state to be left to chance or uncoordinated developments. Comprehensive coordinated planning provides a vehicle for orderly and rational progress to be made. Under the leadership of a state that develops an effective organization for planning, all efforts should be directed to the continuous improvement of quality in the effort to ensure excellence in student learning. This procedure can, as Landry has emphasized, provide the state with:

A logical process for making decisions about *why* changes should be made; about *what* changes should be made; about *how, when* and *where* changes should be made; and about *who* should make the change.[11]

To be effective, the planning organization which is or should be established in a state should have the capacity to:

1. *Elicit inputs* from all relevant constituent elements within the state.

2. *Assimilate* appropriate inputs into an integral whole, and to specify goals, priorities, and objectives of the planning.

3. *Translate* these goals, priorities and objectives into alternate courses of action, based on technical study and evaluation.

4. *Feed back* alternatives to constituent elements for reaction and input.

5. *Mediate* reactions as advantages and disadvantages.

6. *Decide* on appropriate, achievable, and defensible comprehensive plans for statewide educational improvement.

7. *Advocate* acceptance of plans by responsible agencies and institutions.[12]

Footnote References

[1]Kenneth H. Hansen, "Planning and Change: Design, Decision, Action," in *Cooperative Planning for Education in 1980*, Edgar L. Morphet and David L. Jesser, eds. (Denver, Colorado: Designing Education for the Future, January 1968), p. 76. Republished by Citation Press, Scholastic Magazines, Inc., New York, N.Y.

[2]F. D. Barrett, "Tomorrow's Management: Creative and Participative," *The Futurist*, February, 1971, p. 13.

[3]Sub-Committee on State Planning, The Governors' Conference, *State Planning: A Policy Statement* (Chicago, Illinois: The Council on State Governments, 1962).

[4]Leon P. Minear, "State Responsibilities, Procedures, and Relationships in Planning," in *Planning for Effective Utilization of Technology in Education*, Edgar L. Morphet and David L. Jesser, eds. (Denver, Colorado: Designing Education for the Future, August, 1968), p. 138. Republished by Citation Press, Scholastic Magazines, Inc., New York, N.Y.

[5]Vitaliano Bernardino, "Planning for State and National Development" (Unpublished paper released through the Office of the Undersecretary of Education, Manila, Philippine Islands, 1967), p. 1.

[6]Adapted from Bernarr S. Furse, "The Organizational Context for Planning," in *Comprehensive•Planning in State Education Agencies*, Bernarr S. Furse and Lyle O. Wright, eds. (Salt Lake City, Utah: Utah State Board of Education, 1968), p. 25.

[7]Robert E. McNair, "A Governor's Perspective of Total State Planning and the Role of Vocational Education," in *Articulation of Vocational Education Planning with Comprehensive State Planning*, Darrell L. Ward and Edward N. Kazarian, eds. (Columbus, Ohio: The Center for Vocational and Technical Education, The Ohio State University, January, 1971), p. 2.

[8]Bernarr S. Furse, *op. cit.*, p. 28.

[9]*Designing Education for the Future: Rationale, Procedures and Appraisal*, Edgar L. Morphet and David L. Jesser, eds. (Denver, Colorado: Designing Education for the Future, June, 1969), p. 15.

[10]Hal E. Hagen, "Development of the Institute," in *Institute for State Educational Planners* (Mankato, Minnesota: Mankato State College, papers presented at the National Conference on Educational Planning, October 17-25, 1968), p. 1.

[11]Leonard Landry, "Educational Planning" (Memorandum from the Colorado Department of Education, Denver, Colorado, July 24, 1969).

[12]Bernarr S. Furse, *op. cit.*, p. 26.

Chapter 5

Policies and Procedures for Planning:
Some Alternatives

The organization for planning that is proposed or utilized in a state is normally a reflection of the perspectives and attitudes of the decision makers—the governor, the legislature, boards, and other people in leadership positions. *General acceptance of the need for leadership in planning for improvements is a first and major step if there is to be much significant planning in any state.* Carefully developed and systematic provisions for developing a planning capability should ultimately yield rich dividends. Inherent in this process (discussed in greater detail later in this chapter) is the need to develop appropriate policies and procedures to maximize the potential of the planning process. Agreement on the general idea of planning may not necessarily imply agreement on the policies and procedures relating to the determination of goals, needs, priorities and other factors that must be considered. Selecting the policies and procedures that are most appropriate and consistent with the resources of a state thus becomes a fundamental matter. Often the choices, from among the options that are available, are difficult to make.

POLICY: A REFLECTION OF LEADERSHIP

Policy is a definite course or method of action selected from among alternatives and in light of given conditions to guide and determine present and future decisions (Webster's Collegiate Dictionary). The nature of the organization for planning is, in itself, a reflection of general state policy or lack of policy relating to planning. The variations among the states reflect, to some extent, the perceptions of the citizens of each state about the importance of planning as an integral element in the state's leadership role. James E. Allen, Jr., formerly U.S. Commissioner of Education, has pointed out:

> The states conduct planning in a variety of ways. In a few, the governor has the legal duty to conduct the statewide planning effort. But in the majority of states, the responsibility is fragmented. Different state agencies are required to develop plans for the different sectors of state operations, and the overall direction of state development is determined by those proposals which happen to receive legislative approval and funding.[1]*

---

*Footnote references are given at end of the chapter.

76

In reality, the organization for planning that is created together with the policies and procedures that are established reflect state leadership that is based on a *reactive* philosophy (responding primarily to problems as they become serious), a *future-oriented* philosophy, or a *blending of both*. In modern society—its institutions, agencies and government—there appears to be considerable movement toward a more initiatory, qualitative effort in providing leadership in comprehensive, long-range planning. Unfortunately, however, a reactive kind of leadership appears to be more commonly found. Neglect or lack of positive action by authorities in areas of societal concern has compounded the crisis faced by modern society to a point where there is an increasing demand for more effective leadership at all levels of government. There seems to be an increasing public readiness to expect and want to become involved in determining *where we are, where we want to go*, and *how we might get there*. This appears to be the case in many areas of concern in modern society. Inevitably many of the concerns seem to focus on *education as a major key* to the improvements needed in the society.

Contemporary planners perceive planning to be a *process* designed *to facilitate the attainment of some predetermined goals* rather than as an end in itself—a paper product that frequently includes proposals destined to gather dust. The analogy of the military adage—*the mere issuance of an order in no way ensures that the order will be carried out*—appears to be pertinent in this context. Appropriate follow-through procedures must be regarded as essential to give "life" to policy and enable implementation to become a vital element in the process of effecting needed change.

The individual states generally organize their planning effort around one of two basic concepts: (1) a *rational-comprehensive approach* that is designed to be future-oriented and all-inclusive; or (2) a *limited-comparsons* approach that is limited to responses to serious problems. Unfortunately, the latter appears to be the kind of planning that normally takes place in many organizations that make any attempt to plan. Within this framework, the organizational and operational policies as well as the procedures utilized in planning in a state can be analyzed to determine its overall leadership policy.

THE RATIONAL-COMPREHENSIVE APPROACH TO PLANNING

Any entity—a state, a state education agency or a local school district—utilizing the rational-comprehensive approach to planning builds on the past only as experience is embodied in theory or in prevailing accepted belief. The characteristics of this approach include:

- Clarification of values or objectives is distinct from and usually prerequisite to the empirical analysis of alternative policies.

- Policy formulation is approached through a means-ends analysis: first the ends are isolated, then the means to achieve them are sought.

- The test of a "good" policy is that it can be shown to be the most appropriate means to a desired end.

- Analysis is comprehensive: every important relevant factor is taken into account.

- Theory or rationally accepted belief is heavily relied upon in the process.

The design for a comprehensive planning process utilizing the rational-comprehensive approach will include aspects of operations research, statistical decision theory and systems analysis. Thus, the results can be clarity of objectives, explicitness of evaluation, a high degree of comprehensiveness of overview, and, when possible, quantification of values for mathematical analysis. Responsibility for funding the designs (educational or otherwise) that emerge from this process rests with the state legislature on the premise that *here are the apparent facts, here is how they are interrelated,* and *this is what they imply* in terms of improving the general welfare and ensuring progress in a state.

The number of variables to be considered may be so numerous and the value problems so complex in comprehensive educational planning that this approach may appear inappropriate to some persons. In a period of crisis, a cross-section of professional, lay and political leaders may find it difficult to apply their energies to the development of an overall policy of design when immediate problems seem to require maximum attention. The unorthodox nature of the times may suggest to some states that it would be better to initiate planning processes through demonstrable achievement in limited or crisis planning in narrow but high priority areas. This appears to be the situation from the point of view of some legislators as well as some educators in relationship to educational matters. Perhaps Hitch identified a major dilemma in comprehensive planning when he stated:

> I would make the empirical generalization . . . that operations research is the art of sub-optimizing, [for example] of solving some lower level problems, and that difficulties increase and our special competence diminishes by the order of magnitude with every level of decision making we attempt to ascend.[2]

The Limited-Comparisons Approach to Planning

Whereas the rational-comprehensive approach utilizes theory or accepted belief as its base, the limited-comparisons approach to planning continually builds from the current situation, step-by-step, and by small degrees. In the latter approach attention in planning is restricted to a few of the most important problems, values and alternatives from among the many that might be considered. As indicated previously, this approach to policy making and planning is commonly used, at present, by most agencies and organizations in society. One could probably refer to this approach as the "art of the possible" as opposed to the "art of the ideal" that is implied in the rational-comprehensive approach.

The characteristics of the limited-comparisons approach would include the following:

- Value goals and the empirical analysis of needed action are not distinct from one another but are deeply intertwined.

- Since means and ends are not distinct, means-end analysis is often inappropriate or limited.

- The test of a "good" policy is one that is based on agreement on the appropriate means to an agreed-upon objective.

- Analysis is limited and normally subjective in that possible outcomes, alternative potential policies and affected values tend to be neglected.

- A succession of comparisons with past experiences greatly reduces or eliminates reliance on theory.

The limited comparison approach to planning is familiar to educational leaders and to administrators in public and private endeavors. It conceivably could be referred to as a "seat of the pants" approach with great reliance on past experience. Inevitably, this method is resorted to in personal problem solving where means and ends are sometimes impossible to separate, where aspirations or objectives are under constant development, and where drastic simplification of the complexities of the real world is urgent if problems are to be solved in the time that can be given to them.

The making of short-term policy under the limited-comparisons approach is somewhat easier than in the rational-comprehensive approach. Past sequences in policy making provide the insights utilized in forecasting the consequences of further similar steps. By moving slowly in effecting changes, there is less apt to be criticism about "rocking the boat" or not having faith in the so-called "tried and true." Also, past error may be corrected more easily than would be possible if policy proceeded through more distinct steps over a longer period of time.

The use of this approach precludes extensive change during a period when radical change may be needed. The organizational status quo tends to be protected because traditional alternatives are regarded as the ones to be relied upon in decision making. In effect, a *survival strategy* is employed and a *survival syndrome* permeates the organization. Some persons view this situation as analogous to that of a dying organism—increasingly irrelevant to the needs to be served in a dynamic society and, especially, in the pursuit of excellence in education.

IMPLICATIONS FOR STATE EDUCATION AGENCIES

It is likely that there will and probably should be some uncertainty within a state education agency about the relative merits of a rational-comprehensive planning process geared to a future-oriented policy as contrasted with the traditional approach to crisis abatement. Although a realization of the need for the broader approach may exist within the agency, serious problems of an urgent nature such as school finance, district reorganization, and desegregation demand a great deal of attention. Ideally, the policies and procedures related to planning should deal with comprehensive educational effort and, yet, make possible concentration upon high priority matters as need is evidenced. *The task,* therefore, in establishing state policy for educational planning and in developing the structure, personnel and other resources to support it, *is to provide enough flexibility to meet pressing and specific needs and have these endeavors fit within and contribute to ongoing comprehensive planning.*

The design for a comprehensive educational planning system can emerge from a highly rational approach; one consistent with contemporary systems theory. It would encourage the development of models for planning that would include a great deal of attention to systematic data gathering, for example, in an effort "to anticipate the wide variety of demands for information upon which to formulate policies and make decisions."[3] In essence, the functions required to serve systematic comprehensive planning are fully as valuable for more specific or limited problems.

A major outcome of systematic comprehensive planning should be the delineation and definition of problems requiring high priority and primary attention. Those who are familiar with systems analysis approaches will recognize that an analysis of sub-systems can make a contribution not only to the solution of problems identified within a given sub-system, but also to an increased understanding of the whole system.

As is the case in any major endeavor in planning there are problems, many of which can be anticipated. Proposals for resources and other means needed to establish or expand a comprehensive statewide planning process in state education agencies, or in some other aspect of state government, may be questioned by funding authorities whose vision of the future is necessarily clouded by political, financial and other imperatives of the present. Of necessity, there should be an attempt to structure the policy-making process in the organization for planning in such a way that the weight of balance in the scale of values is on the side of a future-oriented outlook, but with provisions to meet the urgent crises situations. As stated by Jennings:

> . . . state planning, or the development of the sets of decisions for influencing future action, has developed comprehensive and coordinative dimensions. . . . The real question has become what resources can be brought to bear on a problem or a set of problems once a policy decision has been made. . . . Its [planning] future seems to be that of coordination, the provision of services and an element of overall policy control.[4]

It is necessary to make a clear distinction between policy, planning and implementation. The organization for planning for education in a state must be such that although the separation is maintained, there should be close coordination through contact and communication at appropriate points in the organization.

DEVELOPING A PLANNING CAPABILITY

The development of a planning system that is comprehensive, coordinated and long-range requires extensive effort over a period of time. Leadership at both the state and local levels must first of all be concerned with developing a planning capability—that is, with the means for establishing a planning system that is available and appropriate to the entity and consistent with its resources. Planning certainly cannot be an "overnight" occurrence if it is to be regarded as a positive force in improving education. Decisions made from the "top of the head" based on "seat of the pants" experience are inadequate in the resoluion of current and emerging problems. Careful and systematic attention to the development of a *plan for planning* ultimately makes the entire process much easier when it is implemented. In-service and other training programs are also needed in each state. These programs should be cooperatively planned and developed by state and local school systems and colleges and universities to meet specific needs in planning.

Using Colorado[5] and Texas[6] as examples, initial action to develop a planning capability within their respective state education agencies was initiated several years ago and is currently beginning to produce visible dividends in the improvement of education in both states. In these education agencies there was need to:

- Decide upon appropriate policies that would be accepted by the state board of education to guide the planning thrust.

- Develop a procedure within the state education agency itself for developing and submitting plans for review, approval and subsequent action.

- Provide extensive in-service activities for personnel that moved beyond mere orientation and understanding of the planning process to an intensive examination of the elements and factors that must be considered to make planning effective.

- Clarify and amplify the state's educational needs and priorities in respect to the state's educational goals through the use of internal task forces charged with developing proposals for needed changes and possible reorganization of the state education agency.

- Open channels of communication through institutional, other agency and lay involvement in advisory groups that focused their attention on priority areas of concern.

- Establish a pattern of coordinated effort through interaction in planning with other agencies, institutions and organizations at local, state and federal levels.

- Implement some pilot projects at state and local levels to foster cooperation in planning and better understanding of the planning process.

A flow chart developed by Wright and Furse[7] (Figure 1) that describes the steps in the development of a planning capability is presented as a guide for making a careful analysis of all that is involved in a prudential approach either to comprehensive planning or, for that matter, to the development of a more narrow, specific and limited approach at any level or kind of governance, public or private.

Figure 1. *A Flow Chart of Steps for Developing A Planning Capability*

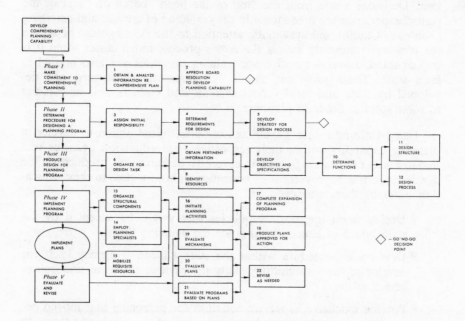

A model of this kind may appear to be so directive and inviolate as to "turn off" many persons who may take what they term a more humanistic approach to policy determination. The mood and tone, however, are set by the context of the planning, by the factors that motivate it, and by the nature of the *broad* supervision and policy-making approach to the planning. In other words, the quality of leadership and the support that leadership receives from the policymakers can largely set the climate for proceeding in a manner consistent with such a model.

COMMUNICATION PROCESSES

Effective communication processes are vital to the success of planned educational change. A rational approach would call for efforts to inform affected groups and the public as to what the planning process is, its focus, its findings and recommendations and ultimately the results of the implementation of whatever has been recommended. To settle for much less would be to invite public suspicion, serious challenge and possible failure.

As in the case of all other aspects of planning, the communications process demands expertise that is sufficiently close to or part of the organization for planning that it can anticipate and prepare for the steps in the process of informing the public. The multimedia approaches that modern communications technology and know-how have made available should certainly be used. Opportunities for feedback from the various audiences and constituencies can both affect the quality of planning and influence its direction and timing. A steady flow of valid information will provide for increased public understanding and acceptance of findings and recommendations. There would seem to be no substitute in modern society for effective communication in breadth and depth.

MONITORING THE PLANNING PROCESS AND ITS OUTCOMES

An essential component of the planning process within any central state planning organization or, for that matter, within a state or local education agency should be a research and evaluation unit. This unit should be charged with the assessment and evaluation of the outcomes of the planning activity; the identification and explication of deficiencies in the planning and its implementation; and proposals for improvements in future planning and/or implementation. Such a procedure, constituting as it does a sort of continuing critique of the functioning of educational system, should be so located in the organizational structure for planning that it has access to all aspects of the educational process and to the decision makers who are involved in that process.

The need for a monitoring system for the planning endeavor has been pointed out by Ziegler:

> Educational planning in the United States has largely ignored the need to make qualitative assessments. It has accepted educational goals as given, then translates these goals in to quantifiable targets. Even the occasional application of more modern "systems" techniques . . . appear to have provided neither a psychological incentive nor an intellectual tool for generating alternative goals, or for expanding the boundaries of conventional wisdom concerning the future directions education might take.[8]

The organization and personnel of such a monitoring office, together with its hardware and resources in the form of computers and other technology, may well constitute an invaluable resource to the planning enterprise. Presumably this office should have data-gathering and analysis facilities, access to data banks and other means for providing information helpful to planning. The continuing studies it makes (or should make) can lead to insights regarding possible next developments in all aspects of educational activities. If this office is related to, but not directly responsible for, the planning and the strategy for planning, it may well be able to suggest improvements in both activities.

GOALS: THE FOCUS OF DECISION MAKING

Planning should be purposeful. Its entire effort should emerge from the *goals* initially defined and revised as the need becomes evident. The task of stating goals and objectives is far from simple. Lonsdale has emphasized that:

> The planning program should make goal formulation the focus of management decision making. The role of top policy makers is to continuously consider the program goals—initially to identify the key questions as a guide to the researcher in developing information useful for decision making; then to re-evaluate the goals to guide the development of preliminary plans; and finally to revise the goals in order to resolve problems uncovered in the planning process and to direct the further refinement of the plan.[9]

Certain basic assumptions—such as those dealing with "what is best for the individual, the school, the state, or the nation"—usually underlie any educational planning effort. These assumptions should be formulated and stated as explicitly as possible as background for developing goals and objectives that can be stated in behavioral or performance terms. The use of broad goals often is confusing as it hinders the decision-making process and limits the effectiveness of planning. As noted by Molinaro:

> Goals must be formulated simply. Goal statements tend to turn off many hard-headed people, because they usually sound like truisms and cliches and we have come to associate them with people and organizations that are powerless to bring them to reality.[10]

DIMENSIONS IN GOAL DETERMINATION IN EDUCATION

It seems apparent that in comprehensive planning for better and more relevant education, the following categories of goals appear to be applicable:

- *Those relating to the scope of present educational endeavors and the determination of new needs viewed feasible within the existing educational design.*

Within this category may emerge specific goals concerning the percentage of youth for whom community colleges should be provided, the nature and support for pre-school programs, the range of opportunities for occupational education needed, and many others that readily suggest themselves.

- *Those primarily concerned with an assessment of present effort and the contemplation or projection of new, more effective approaches.*

Here there may be attention to the concept of accountability as inputs, means and outputs are correlated. Pursuing the goal of effectiveness, for example, may suggest specific objectives dealing with dollar inputs for improved technology and the evaluation of results obtained from such technology.

- *Those which may possibly seriously challenge present assumptions regarding program, organization, contemporary outputs and, indeed, the efficacy—both present and future—of endeavors based on prior assumptions.*

Such goals may have to do with coping with the alienation of youth, intervening in a cycle of poverty, and preparing youth for the challenges and threats of emerging values and information on drug usage, sexual mores or environmental pollution. Here it may be anticipated that planning may need to contemplate designs that differ significantly from present modes of education and include experimentation with and the development of entirely new models.

- *Those which are concerned primarily with helping the state to establish basic priorities in its efforts to improve the education system.*

Assuming limited resources for both planning and implementation, goals should be established that are consistent with the best modern thought concerning the chances for changes that will make a difference. What is implied is the difference between the "possible" and the "impossible" in the expenditure of effort in planning.

REACHING AGREEMENT ON GOALS AND PRIORITIES IN EDUCATION

The determination of the goals or categories of goals that should receive high priority attention within a state may be a delicate matter, the outcomes of which may turn out to be quite unpredictable. The decisions may well, and perhaps appropriately, be political because of the process used. Education is becoming more political particularly as social turmoil, costs, and questions of relevance and accountability become matters of general concern. On the other hand, a state with a strong tradition of relying upon a non-partisan state board of education and able professional leadership in the state education agency may be inclined to depend upon the normal policy-making bodies to set priorities for the educational planning process.

In determining the priorities in state planning, it is both advisable and likely that a wide variety of factors should be taken into account, including:

- Contemporary social developments will probably play a larger role than heretofore because of the crisis mood of present-day society. Concern for human welfare, the reduction of social tensions, and greater educational opportunity flow logically from most analyses of social, economic and political developments.

- The apparent readiness of persons in status positions and of the people generally for planning to move in particular directions will affect decision-making bodies that are increasingly sensitive to the public mood.

- The fiscal and personnel resources available will be highly significant.

- States with good management information systems should be able to obtain reasonably valid information as to areas of possible need, and at least substantiate or challenge goals that have been more subjectively determined.

- The enthusiasm and commitment of leadership in education can hardly be underestimated when selecting or ordering priorities.

- The likelihood for success is an appropriate concern in any venture where continued support depends primarily upon general public understanding and support.

- Perhaps the most important of all considerations, though often based on a combination of hard data and value judgments, is the social value or utility of the likely outcomes. There is little value in pursuing alternatives that have few important foreseeable social implications.

ACHIEVING GOALS THROUGH RECOMMENDED CHANGES

One could conclude that the effectiveness of a coordinated approach to educational planning will, of necessity, be dependent upon the various strategies that are utilized in attaining the goals determined as being important in education. Recommendations that imply changes or adaptations and that are consistent with established state leadership policy normally can be achieved with little or no opposition. These may include recommendations that broaden opportunity through a well-established program, that provide for a consolidation of programs to affect greater economy, or minor organizational shifts that allow for greater efficiency to evolve in the education system.

In contrast with such minor changes or adaptations, major recommendations for change to achieve goals can be facilitated through the use of strategies that permit, encourage and generate the kind of public acceptance and endorsement that provides a wide base of support for the necessary actions that need to follow. The involvement, endorsement and "active" support of professional—educational and other—associations and organizations should not be overlooked in the process. Recommendations involving the reorganization of urban and/or rural school districts; greater community control of schools; major curriculum changes relating to social questions in drug usage, sex education, interracial issues, foreign ideologies and sensitivity training; parochiaid; performance contracting and the use of the voucher system are representative of areas of controversy that are subject to extensive deliberation in view of present cross currents in public attitude and opinion.

Effective planning, thus, is based on an awareness and understanding of change and the change processes discussed in greater detail in Chapters

6, 7 and 8. Appropriate change techniques can be selected and utilized to increase the probability that goals will be attained in accordance with the circumstances and conditions within a given state. An example of an effective procedure for bringing about major changes and the strategies utilized in the process is reflected in the report of a Utah case study[11] prepared for the project, *Improving State Leadership in Education*. The report explains and appraises the state education agency's effort to develop a practical design for improvements in education in Utah. A comprehensive, coordinated, statewide study of the future resulted in valuable goals, pertinent information on costs, time-tables, priorities and guidelines that emerged from the study as a contribution to long-range planning under the leadership provided by the state education agency.

SYSTEMATIC PLANNING PROCEDURES

The emergence and utilization of systematic planning has had a substantial impact in bringing about planned change in modern times. Successes have ranged from the highly dramatic to the simple and relatively commonplace advances that have been made. Most people know about the tremendous achievements in the space program, but only a few have any understanding of the key role that systematic planning has had in these endeavors.

THE SYSTEMS APPROACH TO PLANNING IN EDUCATION

For too long the education system has been viewed by many persons, including educators, as a self-sufficient system that seems to be quite autonomous and independent of other systems. As a result, education has not been especially concerned with the scientific, economic, or human needs of the society in which it operates and to which it contributes. In reality, *the education system interacts with other systems of which it is a part,* for example, the community. The education system produces an effect on the community, while the community, in turn, modifies educational objectives in some dynamic ways. What is implied is that a consideration of the needs of the *total* environment of the educational system, both internal and external, is vital in systematic planning in education.

As indicated previously, there is a pressing need for more rational decision making in education, as well as in other areas of public life. *Rational* in this context should be interpreted as a logical analysis that emphasizes the systematic application of the elements of efficiency and effectiveness in planning as opposed to intuition and experience alone. The task in education appears to be one of combining products and services in such a way as to maximize educational outcomes for a given level of resource input. In essence, it is a continuing attempt to bring about more "output" per unit of "input."

The systems approach to planning can make a significant contribution to local as well as state education agencies as they attempt to deal with many complex institutional and organizational relationships. The approach was developed out of the need for logical analysis and synthesis tools and procedures that could provide for an understanding of complex systems. Basically, the systems approach to planning has, as its central focus, the idea that *functional system components are interrelated and that a complex process can be understood best if it is treated as a "whole."* In practice, this approach includes:

- Attempts to analyze the system in as large a perspective as possible, including the external as well as the internal environments;

- Consideration of the operational system in terms of an "input-output" relationship; and

- Reliance on an effective information system that serves to bind the interacting elements of the system together.

Systematic Planning Technologies. As noted in Chapter 3, a number of problem-solving models have been developed to incorporate the basic principles of a systems approach in planning. Examples of the methods that have become relatively well-known include systems analysis, operations analysis and planning-programming-budgeting systems (PPBS). The Research Corporation of the Association of School Business Officials has attempted to interpret and adapt the PPBS approach to what is referred to as an Educational Resources Management System (ERMS)[12] in order to make it more understandable and applicable to educational problem solving for more effective management of educational resources.

Technologies for Specialized Planning Purposes. Many other technologies are available that can be used for specialized planning purposes. Several processes are available, for example, to assist in scheduling operational activities so that they can be properly integrated and will be completed in appropriate order. Falling generally within a classification of network-based management systems, these include the Program Evaluation and Review Technique (PERT), the Critical Path Method (CPM), the Line of Balance (LOB), operations mapping, and some others.[13] Each is useful, under certain conditions, and the selection for use should be governed by circumstances related to the planning process and to the specific purpose that justifies their use.

Computers can provide an invaluable assistance in the processes for planning. Their availability makes possible the development of highly sophisticated information systems and interrelations to provide the requisite inputs for effective planning and ongoing management activities. Evaluation and research techniques are also improving to match planning technologies used in the various aspects of educational problem solving.

The use of contemporary systematic techniques in planning can result in a rational determination of alternative courses and/or methods of action for accomplishing important objectives in light of relevant situations and conditions, future probabilities and perceptions of consequences to be experienced. Thus, assessment, integration, time-phasing, cost estimates, evaluation and communication can be related to objectives. As Buchner[14] has pointed out, planning can become more effective through systematic approaches used in:

- Analyzing, evaluating and interpreting relevant data in relation to objectives to be achieved;
- Systematically appraising choice-consequence relations;
- Selecting preferred alternatives for the achievement of objectives;
- Simulating and graphically portraying the functions and tasks required to achieve each objective; and
- Determining probability factors for successful and effective achievement.

IN SUMMARY

A state cannot proceed with any degree of effectiveness in its planning for education as well as for all aspects of state concern without defining as clearly as possible what should be the direction and nature of the improvements needed in a state. One might assume, in the final analysis, that the critical judgment of those in leadership roles determines the specific state problems that warrant or receive attention. Presumably these determinations should be made upon some systematic consideration of the feasibility of proceeding in a given direction at a given time with the human and material resources available and in light of social and political factors. Hopefully in education, policy-making bodies at the state and local levels can establish or plan to establish reasonably specific policies from which can flow the procedures needed to effect improvements. In planning, all pertinent factors should be examined and evaluated in determining the best approach to be used in meeting specified needs and goals. From this process, the strategies that offer the greatest potential for success in a state should emerge.

A systems analysis approach to decision making should in no way limit or force a given course of action except through careful consideration of all conceivable factors related to most likely outcomes. Thus, alternatives can be perceived by policy makers and by planning bodies, sorted in terms of feasibility and appropriateness and, then, hopefully, the most promising can be selected as a basis for action. Few persons can challenge the wisdom of examining problems in the context of all related conditions and factors.

Hartley has pointed out that:

There are exciting opportunities, accompanied by risks and dangers, in the application of modern decisional technologies. . . . The new systems analyses mode of thinking is already exerting influence on political structure and style. . . . In assessing the success of planning . . . one should keep in mind that most projects have been characterized by incomplete implementation, institutional resistance, insufficient resources, and inadequately trained personnel.[15]

Bernard Shaw observed that the only trouble with Christianity was that it had never been truly tried. Perhaps a similar thing might be said about systematic comprehensive planning in many states. Through a combination of common sense considerations and the use of the increasing sophistication and expertise in planning, society should be able to resolve present educational and other problems by establishing priorities for action and, at the same time, facing more intelligently the challenges of the future. Each state has a definite responsibility to make contributions toward those ends.

Footnote References

[1]James E. Allen, Jr., "Renovating the Planning Process," *Compact,* February, 1969,

[2]Charles Hitch, "Operations Research and National Planning, A Dissent," *Operations Research,* October 1957, p. 718.

[3]Sam W. Bliss, *The Extent and Utilization of Management Information Systems and Planning, Programming, Budgeting Systems in State Education Agencies* (Denver, Colorado: Improving State Leadership in Education, April 1971), pp.6-7.

[4]Robert E. Jennings, *Alternative Roles and Interagency Relationships of State Education Agencies in Comprehensive Statewide Planning* (Denver Colorado: Improving State Leadership in Education, May 1971), pp. 4-5.

[5]Arthur P. Ludka, *Planning in the Colorado Department of Education to Facilitate Improvements in Education* (Denver, Colorado: Improving State Leadership in Education, September 1970).

[6]Keith L. Cruise, *The Evolution of Planning in the Texas Education Agency* (Denver, Colorado: Improving State Leadership in Education, September 1970).

[7]Lyle O. Wright and Bernarr S. Furse, *Developing Comprehensive Planning Capability in State Education Agencies* (Salt Lake City, Utah: Utah State Board of Education, 1969), p. 6.

[8]Warren Ziegler, "Some Notes on How Education Planning in the United States Looks at the Future," *Notes on the Future of Education,* Volume 1, Issue 3, 1970, p. 14.

[9]Richard C. Lonsdale, "Predicting Future Environments" (Unpublished manuscript prepared for the 1968 National Conference of Professors of Educational Administration).

[10]Leo A. Molinaro, "Truths and Consequences for Older Cities," *Saturday Review,* May 15, 1971, p. 30.

[11]Jay J. Campbell and Afton Forsgren, *The Impact of the Designing Education for the Future Project in Utah* (Denver, Colorado: Improving State Leadership in Education, November 1970).

[12]"Conceptualization of the Educational Resources Management System," Chapter 2 in *Educational Resources Management System* (A working draft of a report of the Second National Conference on PPBES in Education conducted by the Research Corporation of the Association of School Business Officials).

[13]Allen L. Buchner, *Network-Based Management Procedures* (San Mateo County Schools, California: Produced by Operation PEP, Prepare Educational Planners for California, February 1970), 180 pp.

[14]*Ibid.,* p. 3.

[15]Harry J. Hartley, "Politics and Education," *The School Administrator,* April 1971, p. 7.

PART THREE

STATE LEADERSHIP IN EFFECTING NEEDED CHANGES IN EDUCATION

Chapter 6

The Nature and Process of Change in Education

As explained in previous chapters, educational planning should always be considered

> . . . as a total process, in which the 'plan' on paper is but one stage. The accent here is on action and results and planning is seen as an instrument for getting the best results possible in the circumstances. . . .[1]*

Such an approach to planning obviously requires some systematic attention to the way in which action flows from the "plans" into reality. Unless this portion of the process is carefully considered, there is always a possibility that the "plans" that are developed will ultimately have little or no impact on the schools or on the learners.

Change *can* occur with or without planning, and planning can be accomplished and have no tangible results. In such cases, however, the planning that is accomplished and the changes that occur do not lead to an increased ability to deal with future environmental problems. But as educational leaders attempt to develop more effective plans that are designed to bring about needed changes in the educational environment, they will need, to a greater degree than ever before, to understand the *intimate and interdependent relationships that exist between planning and change* and to find ways of capitalizing upon the inherent strengths of these relationships.

Any plan, if it is to be worthy of the designation, must relate to some needed or desired change. By definition, a plan is future-oriented—it is designed to lead to a different situation that, for whatever reason, has been determined to be better than an existing one.

In order to better understand the necessary and vital relationship between planning and change, educational leaders with responsibilities for planning should develop and maintain a functional frame of reference

---

*Footnote references are given at end of the chapter.

91

which will focus on the elements that assist or resist movement *from a "plan" to some meaningful "change."*

This chapter considers the general concepts of social systems that are germane to the focus on action which is a crucial part of the educational planning process. The following chapter (Chapter 7) is devoted to specific forces and factors which impinge upon the change process and, accordingly, upon the process of planning for change. In Chapter 8 various strategies by which "plans" are translated into changes are discussed.

PEOPLE, SOCIAL SYSTEMS AND CHANGE

While many appealing proposals (often referred to as "plans") were developed and numerous attempts made to effect educational change during the 1960's, a recent research report indicates "that many of the highly recommended and publicized educational innovations of the past decade have never reached the classroom."[2] Part of the problem is no doubt a deep-seated, though probably unconscious, hypocrisy in dealing with change. It would be difficult to understand why education is so slow to change if all educators and other citizens who profess to favor changes were indeed change oriented. But that is by no means the whole answer. A considerable amount of good intention—often the kind embodied in the more naive educational "plans"—gets lost between inception and implementation because many would-be innovators lack a frame of reference for making a realistic assessment of the actual impact of their actions. As a result, many "revolutionary new programs" quickly degenerate into "more of the same," only under a new name.

The first step in developing such a frame of reference is to realize that all the formal and many of the informal structures which are intended to facilitate learning cannot be treated as a mere aggregate of unrelated individuals, agencies or institutions. *They must be seen as a social system.* That is, it must be understood that these individuals, agencies and institutions are all dynamically interrelated and, therefore, form an aggregation —a system of mutual interdependence. They are, correspondingly, subject to the laws which govern the behavior of all other social systems. Two general laws are applicable:

- *Social systems tend to resist planned change;* and

- *Social systems tend to spread unplanned change.*

SOCIAL SYSTEMS AND PLANNED CHANGE

More than anything else, the inherent tendency of social systems to resist planned change accounts for the inadequate formal implementation of promising innovations mentioned earlier. Partially this is a natural consequence of the fact that social systems tend toward internal equilibrium— that is, they tend to achieve a balance of all the forces acting on the system. If a change is initiated in one particular subsystem, but not in all subsystems of the original system, there will be certain obvious pressures from the other subsystems to return to doing business in the established way. Usually, some degree of compromise is reached—the adjacent subsystems make some adjustments—and a slightly different order prevails. But the new equilibrium which emerges is rarely as significant as the originators of the change had hoped or imagined it would be.

To describe the fact that the tendency toward internal equilibrium does not necessarily make change impossible, theorists speak of "dynamic equilibrium" as opposed to "static equilibrium."[3] Dynamic equilibrium is achieved to the extent that the interaction among subsystems is flexible enough to allow for some changes. Only a social system in dynamic equilibrium is able to make the necessary adaptations to changing environmental demands. To the degree that a social system is locked into static equilibrium, it is so inflexible that internal pressures prohibit any change, even one which makes the social system more functional in the existing environment. As a result, social systems in static equilibrium eventually deteriorate because they are no longer functional in a changing society.

Another part of the explanation stems from the fact that the social system of education exists in a larger environment—physical and social. This larger environment often exerts pressures which tend to minimize the effects of a desired change, although everyone should recognize that environmental influences are by no means limited to the kind of negative forces implied here; some of them may facilitate changes as well. Nevertheless, environmental forces rarely completely stop a change from being effected, but instead they tend to reduce the impact of any change.

In either case, the net effect is not at all unlike putting a drop or two of food coloring in a batter: there will be *some* change in the overall color of the batter, but the original ingredients of the batter will conspire to dilute the shade of the food coloring almost beyond recognition.

Some Examples. A rather concrete example of resistance to the implementation of one ambitious plan for a major change in education has been described by Richard Colvard.[4] A large grant was offered by a foundation to the various teacher training institutions in Arkansas, on the condition that all would develop and implement a plan for a new five-year teacher education program. The participating institutions were not enthusiastic and for various reasons the program never achieved the state-wide status its designers had anticipated. As a result, it was completely abandoned within a few years.

According to the case study report, the overall reason for the failure of this attempt to effect change was that the sponsoring foundation and other proponents had considered the proposal only in terms of its own merits and demerits, and did not attempt to assess the program in relationship to its environment. A glaring omission was the failure, on the part of the proponents, to consult the students—the people who would have to participate actively in the program. As a result of this omission, the fact that many of the students would not be financially able to afford an extra year of formal education was completely overlooked. The proponents of the plan also failed to perceive and understand the rivalry—for prestige as well as for appropriations—between the smaller institutions and the state university. As a result, the smaller institutions, which had been producing most of the state's teachers, were reluctant to participate. The proponents also overlooked—or failed to recognize—the fact that at the time the proposal was made, Arkansas was experiencing a severe teacher shortage and that many teachers in the field had not even completed a four-year teacher preparation program. As a result, few of the state's educators were interested in a proposal which appeared likely to compound the existing problem by adding to the shortage, at least temporarily.

In summary, the proponents of this program completely overlooked the relationships between teacher education programs and the other components of the Arkansas educational system. They had apparently forgotten that such programs "are affected not only by each other's actions, but by actions undertaken by—or imputed to—a whole host of other organizations in the structure of the larger society."[5]

An example of how the impact of a planned change was diminished by forces from the outside environment may be seen in the case of a large suburban school district. In the interest of experimentation, an elementary school was designed and constructed with few internal partitions, presumably in order to give teachers and students alike a greater degree of flexibility. Unfortunately, the population of the attendance area in which the new school was built grew much more rapidly than had been anticipated. As a result, the enrollment of the new school exceeded the intended capacity when it opened, and within two years it was operating at almost double capacity. Instead of added flexibility, the school was faced with serious difficulties.

Implications for Education. The implications of the tendency of systems to resist planned change should be obvious to those interested in effecting needed educational changes. Unless educational leaders recognize the numerous forces and factors that impinge upon a desired change, and unless counter-balancing measures are developed, *any attempt to make a specific change in one subsystem* (e.g., learning unit, school, school system, state education agency or university) *of education will probably be diluted by pressures from other systems, in and out of education.*[6]

Such dilution will undoubtedly create problems for those who are responsible for achieving the goals of education. If educational and lay leaders believe that education needs major changes in order to reach the goals that have been identified, *they must attempt to effect these changes by revising existing programs or by initiating new ones.* In either instance, the tendency is for those concerned to perceive the change as a change in a *specific element or subsystem of the educational system.* A new curriculum for the humanities, a new set of certification requirements, or an improved formula for distributing funds are examples of the kinds of changes familiar to state education agencies.

Since changes such as the above are not intended to be ends in themselves, but rather are intended to lead to the accomplishment of broader goals, the question is actually one of effectiveness: *Will the specific changes that are brought about in a single subsystem of education, after interaction with other systems in the environment, still be strong enough to move the total educational system closer to its goals?*

This problem is particularly crucial for state education agencies because they are charged with the general responsibility of advancing education toward its goals. Devotion or attention to any one element of the program or programs at the expense of the total overall program can have statewide ramifications. State education agencies must, therefore, be especially aware of the relationship of various subsystems to each other and the relationship of the total educational system to the external environment if the desired educational changes are to be effectively brought about and maintained.

SOCIAL SYSTEMS AND UNPLANNED CHANGE

Although social systems do tend to resist planned change, as indicated earlier, the interrelatedness of many social systems tends to transmit changes in one social system or subsystem to other social systems or subsystems—most often *in unplanned and unanticipated ways.* For example, vast demographic upheavals have changed the composition of many cities since the Second World War. And although these changes have been in the environment external to education, they have nevertheless exerted great pressures on the educational system, and on many other social systems as well. Likewise, a change in one aspect or component of the educational system will place certain pressures on other aspects. As more and more elementary schools, for instance, are established and successfully operated along the lines of the open school model, pressures will be generated that will encourage the educational system to create new and compatible models for secondary schools. The opposite will also be true: as new models are established for secondary schools, they will encourage different kinds of elementary schools.

These are only a few of many possible examples of how change in one system can affect other systems. The point, however, is that *change in any system will create pressure on and tensions in other related systems.* And since the technological revolution, the cultural upheaval and the knowledge explosion combine to ensure that there will be continuing changes in the American social system, the only question which educators can legitimately face is how to deal rationally and realistically with these pressures for change. Whether or not these pressures exist is substantially out of their hands.

Unfortunately, there seems to have been a general tendency for many educators to pretend that outside pressures don't exist—perhaps in the vain hope that they will somehow go away. Such an escapist attitude is not, and never will be, defensible. It certainly will not be suitable in future years. A failure of the educational system to modify itself as changes take place in other social systems generates a dangerous amount of stress both in the educational system itself and the larger social system that is external to education. Consider a cobweb: shake one strand and the entire web moves. But what would happen if one strand were moved vigorously, while someone tried to hold the rest of the web rigid? The cobweb would be torn apart. Failure of a social system (such as education) to adapt to changes in other systems could have the same effect on the entire social system, which, in some respects, is scarcely less fragile than a cobweb.

It is not always easy to recognize when or where a change in an adjacent system of the environment is having an impact on a specific system. In the example given earlier, the population shift had been taking place for some time before it was identified as one of the sources of stress in the school system. The stress, however—as evidenced by the fact that the educational system wasn't functioning properly in some areas—was recognized much earlier.

In view of the probability that any major change in society will create stress or tension points, *educational leaders need to learn to anticipate, identify, and deal realistically with all such situations.* When things in education are not going right, one of the possible problems is that some other system or subsystem has changed, thereby causing stress. Rather than exclusively investigating the educational system itself, educational leaders need to study all related external systems and internal subsystems. If evaluation shows that the educational system is no longer meeting societal needs and goals, it might be necessary to investigate how other systems in the external environment have changed, as well as to attempt to determine what the schools are doing that is not consistent with recognized needs.

CHANGE IN SOCIAL SYSTEMS

In light of this difficult situation—where the interrelatedness of all the systems in the environment creates the need for major changes in education, and at the same time makes it difficult to achieve the educational changes desired—the responsible state education agency has two primary tasks as it attempts to facilitate changes to meet emerging needs: (1) the state education agency must assess in detail the social systems in which any proposed change will take place and ascertain what pressures from external environmental systems and internal subsystems can be useful in the implementation of change, and what pressures will have to be resisted or otherwise dealt with; and (2) it must take appropriate measures to follow up on this assessment.

Assume a specific change has been decided upon by a state education agency or mandated by the legislature. Most likely this change will either be a change within the department (e.g. departmental reorganization) or a change in the department's relationships with local or other educational agencies. A third possibility that should be considered would be a shift in the relationships of the state agency with the U. S. Office of Education or with other federal agencies. In most cases, however, this shift will not depend upon the initiative of state educational agencies, except perhaps for internal change.

In any case, each such change obviously implies a different *target system,* that is, a different specific subsystem in the educational system in which the change will take place. In the first case, the recipient of the desired change would be either the entire department of education or some division or divisions of the department. In the second case, local educational agencies would be the recipient. In many cases, however, the desired change necessitates action in both the state agencies and the local agencies. In such instances, both subsystems can be considered as target systems—recipients of the desired change.

However, to state that a change in a state department of education is the intended goal of a particular change can be misleading. Ultimately, any change in any educational system should be designed to improve the quality of education offered to students. In that sense, improving education for *the student population—the learners—is always the ultimate goal.* A change in a state education agency can be a goal only in an intermediate sense. For this reason it is especially important to keep in mind the broad goals of education when dealing with any specific program.

The Elements of a System. Assuming, however, that a subsystem has been identified in which a change is to take place, the next step is to consider the specific nature of this subsystem. All social systems have at least three dimensions—people, resources and relationships. The *people* in a social system are obviously those who are involved in the system. It is important, however, to realize that the designation "people" includes all aspects of the population—their attitudes, their previous experiences, their expertise, and so on. *Resources* are the resources the system has or can obtain to accomplish its goals, including money, time, materials, and personnel. And *relationships* are the interactions that take place both within the system itself and between the particular subsystem in which the change is intended and other systems. Relationships are frequently the most difficult aspect of a given system to identify or understand. Although many relationships in the educational system are defined by laws or regulations, many others are informal and do not appear either in a personnel file or on a ledger sheet. Nevertheless, understanding the relationships involved within a specific system is crucial because this is the point of greatest interaction with other systems in the environment.

Clearly these distinctions are not at all neat: people can be resources; and relationships—no matter how formally defined—will be influenced by the people involved, their attitudes, biases, modes of communication and so on. Yet, these three dimensions of a system are the framework against which environmental influences can be measured, and, accordingly, constitute the arenas for implementing change.

The Impact of the Elements. The next step in promoting successful change is for the person, division, department or agency planning or encouraging a particular change, to attempt to determine—after there is agreement on the scope or magnitude of the end change desired—what adaptations will have to be made in the three dimensions of the target system (people, resources and relationships) if the change is to be effective. Functionally speaking, this means there must be a realistic appraisal of the adjustments that would have to be made before the minimal conditions for effective change, as listed below, are met:

- System personnel must be willing and able to carry out the change;

- Adequate resources must be available; and

- Structural relationships must be capable of handling the change.

This is where the actual assessment of environmental influences begins. At this point it is necessary to consider the other systems in the environment which relate to each of these dimensions. What systems, for instance, influence the attitudes of the population of the particular subsystem in which the change is intended? And what other systems in the environment determine the resources of the target system?

To facilitate this process, it may be possible to organize each direction of inquiry around the same three dimensions—people, resources and relationships. For example, in attempting to predict the attitudes of teachers concerning a curriculum change considered to be necessary, the people, resources and relationships that come to bear on the teacher from outside the particular subsystem—in this case the schools for which the change is intended—should be carefully considered. In this manner, it is possible to develop a coherent list of the relevant influences on the particular subsystem in which the change is intended.

To summarize, the following steps are necessary to assess environmental influences:

- Identify the specific subsystem in which the change is intended;

- Analyze the components of each dimension of this system—people, resources and relationships; and

- Trace the influence of other systems on each dimension; in practice, this means to ascertain the dimensions—people, resources or relationships—from other systems which come to bear on each dimension of this system.

There is also another way of assessing the environment: compiling a list of factors and determining the significance of these factors for changes in the educational system. Such a list has been prepared by Cooper, Leavitt and Shelly. It covers a wide variety of factors including:

1. Physical aspects of the environment such as: . . . characteristics and location of centers of population, industry, government, education, research, entertainment, recreation, arts.

2. Social aspects of the environment such as occupation and economy, stratification and mobility of the population, political organization and authority, religion and society . . . education; law, the arts, recreation, and entertainment; technology; science, value systems, beliefs, symbolic systems, health and welfare.

   Social and economic states; level of the economy, health, education, crime morality, morale, intergroup tensions, cold war, strikes, disasters, etc.

   Factors defined by locales and geographic setting of the organization: physical and social factors peculiar to locales, remoteness, physical restraints (communication, travel, mobility), parameters of nonmaterial culture, social and economic states applicable to sites and locales of operation.

   Relations wtih other organizations: hierachical relations with parent and subordinate organizations, sources of support, competitive organizations, sources of threat and conflict; relations with unions, clients, regulator agencies, trade associations, community groups, eleemosynary agencies, etc.[7]

However, it is not always clear how such lists relate to a specific situation; nor do they provide a logical scheme for integrating these various factors. Nevertheless, they are a potentially useful tool for analyzing the environment for a proposed change.

But any kind of rigorous thinking about systems that relates to a change will help to determine the possibilities for a specific change to induce the desired general change into the system. And, when a complete grid of the various interacting subsystems is developed, it may become obvious that there are other, and perhaps superior, specific alternatives for achieving a broad goal. For this effect to accrue, however, it is necessary that those interested in change understand the relationships between the specific change and the ultimate goals.

Offsetting Dysfunctional Influences

The above assessment of the factors relevant to the change process is actually the first step in the most important single activity for combatting undesirable systematic influences: *comprehensive planning.* However, *comprehensive planning by itself will never result in more than the production of comprehensive plans.* Unless these plans are followed up systematically, there is very little likelihood that any significant change will take place. But comprehensive planning will help to make it clear to everyone concerned what has to be done to achieve some desired result. Frequently, it turns out that to achieve results in one specific subsystem, it is necessary to act on several different subsystems or on systems in the external environment.

Involvement of People. To determine what systems must be involved, however, requires a further step after some kind of assessment of the relevant systems and subsystems. At some point, every state or local education agency official—or other persons seriously concerned with bringing about a particular change—*must consult with the people who would be affected by the change.* This step is crucial for a number of reasons and the more remote the planning body is in relation to the target system, the more crucial it becomes.

In the first place, no amount of meditation can simulate the perspective of people actually involved in a situation. So, no matter how thorough any person's analysis of all relevant factors may be, he can be expected to overlook some of them. Moreover, certain aspects of a system, such as informal relationships, simply cannot be uncovered by a formal analysis, no matter how rigorous it may be. Consultation with those in the system should always provide a more accurate view of the environment in which the change will have to function than would otherwise be possible.

It is especially important for everyone to recognize that the people who are employed by or deeply involved in a particular system are an active component of that system. They will, therefore, exert some influence on the proposed change; they will not accept it passively. To assume that the population of a particular subsystem in which some particular change is desired will passively accept that change is to treat the members of that population as clay rather than people. It is also highly unrealistic.

It is, therefore, necessary to consult meaningfully with the people in the particular subsystem in which some change is intended or desired and to determine how they perceive their goals, needs, and envisioned solutions. Not only does this procedure help to prevent gross miscalculations, but the act of consulting the people involved is beneficial because it increases the likelihood of favorable attitudes toward the proposed change. *People invariably look more favorably upon projects in which they have been involved or helped to develop than on projects which have been "imposed" on them.* People also tend to support a given change in proportion to the degree to which they understand the need for that change.

Some words of caution are in order at this point, however. Consultation with the population of the subsystem in which some change is intended or desired must involve bona fide communication and participation. Unless the people are actually *listened to and understood*, there is no valid reason for the person or persons who are attemping to lead in bringing about the change under consideration to leave his (or their) office. Moreover, people are becoming increasingly sensitive to insincere efforts to solicit opinions. Unless people are convinced—and in this case, as in many others, the "feeling" is much more important than the reality— that they will have a definite voice in the decisions that are being made, the resulting alienation may well be fatal to the project.

It is also important to communicate with the populations of other systems and subsystems that will be affected by the change and would, therefore, themselves affect the change. Students, teachers, and parents must always be included since they will be affected, or at least should be, by almost every change in educational subsystems. Although these groups have had a relatively small role to date in determining educational outcomes, they have the potential to exert massive influence for or against changes they perceive as desirable or undesirable. As Adelson says:

> Getting parents (and later on, children) to understand (a) what operations are available now—that is, what schools are accessible, their differences in terms of offerings, quality of output, etc.—and the relation of the options to later consequences; and (b) what options could be made available under alternative arrangements—as with larger, or smaller school districts, bussing, educational allowances—could produce very different behavior on their part.[8]

Trend Involvement. By this stage in the change process, it should be obvious to those promoting the specific change what internal and external influences will be working for them, and what influences will be working against them. If a subsystem will have difficulty making a change because of attitudes in a supporting subsystem, it may be necessary to change attitudes in the support system even before starting activity in the system in which the ultimate change is desired or planned; or if the relationships between an individual school system and the state agency are so poor that the need for a desired change could not be adequately disseminated or understood in the school system, there may have to be a change in the relationships between the two groups before the change could take place. And so on. There are no simple answers as to how to offset or modify environmental influences. But, once they have been identified—and a program of comprehensive planning such as recommended here should lead to identification—there is no excuse for not acting on them. It should be obvious that few changes can be accomplished by treating a system in which some change is intended or planned as if it existed in a vacuum.

It should be clear not only that input into a single subsystem is not enough, but also that actualizing real change may take much more effort than previously envisioned. Within the context of the American educational experience, it may well take a greater expenditure of effort than educational agencies have been willing to give in the past in order to overcome the environmental trends generated by, among others, the sheer size and complexity of the school system. The danger during the coming decade is that change programs will be attempted without sufficient reference to the internal and external forces operating on the particular subsystem in which change is intended. The results may be new programs without any significant change and outcomes that are disastrous for all concerned.

CREATING NEW ENVIRONMENTS

Richard E. Farson has neatly phrased another alternative to dealing with change, one that may become the way of the future: "Instead of trying to improve people, improve environments."[9] To an extent, the discussion in this chapter has been suggesting the same concept. But only to an extent. Perhaps the time has come to expand the study of social systems to include the possibility of creating *new* or modified environments rather than attempting to work within the constraints of the old environment which may be insurmountable.

Earlier it was postulated that existing social systems will usually react to a change in such a way as to minimize the effect of the change. But, it is also true that the resistance will not be complete, and change will take place, whether or not it is planned. In fact, all available evidence indicates that for a variety of reasons change is now happening in many social systems at an ever-accelerating rate. The growing contradiction between social systems which resist change, and the necessity for social systems that adapt to change is becoming increasingly evident.

A second, and related, factor in the need for developing new environments results from the fact that the increasing rate of general social change dramatically multiplies the possibility of what Boulding calls a "system break," that is, an event, discovery, new trend, development which radically separates what comes after it from what came before it.[10] While there are degrees of systems breaks, and therefore precise quantification is arbitrary, it is safe to postulate that they have been occurring at an ever more frequent rate; likewise, it is safe to assume that the rate of these dramatic breaks will continue to increase: knowledge begets knowledge, technology begets techonology, and so on. Since the very nature of a system break adds an element of unpredictability to a social system, and therefore is not amenable to conventional planning techniques, it is necessary to design more flexible self-renewing social systems which will be able to make more rapid adjustments to unexpected and unpredictable social changes.

Nowhere is this need for a new kind of social system more evident than in the American educational system. And perhaps no subsystem within the entire education system has a better chance of helping to provide that new environment than the state education agencies. This is the case for two reasons: (1) they have a *de jure* leadership role that no other component of the educational system has; and (2) for a variety of reasons, they are in a strategic position to develop or help to develop a new set of internal subsystems.

Such change-accelerating subsystems would be marked by personnel attitudes favorable to change, adequate resources—including time and security for experimenting—flexible internal relationships, and a maximum number of relationships with other systems, both educational and otherwise.

Personnel attitudes favorable to change mean a great deal more than not being opposed to change. Rather, such attitudes imply that there are people who will go out of their way to actively encourage change.[11] This is particularly important in the upper echelons of management. Study after study[12] has shown that the singular most important factor in innovating change is competent and perceptive top management leadership.

Flexible relationships within an agency or department are necessary because rigidly defined relationships inhibit change; they tend to force the impact of all changes in other systems into previously established, and most often inadequate, channels. In this regard, it is encouraging to note that some state departments are increasing their utilization of *ad hoc* task forces to deal with specific problems. These task forces are created from a pool of experts within the department and from outside consultants. When the task is completed, the task force disbands.

While the task force probably will help to create a new internal equilibrium, which will tend to slow down the change process, the resistance is likely to be considerably weaker than the influences of an existing department. Any existing state or local agency or department is likely to have certain informal relationships which could easily breed certain parochial attitudes; it could have other projects which would be in competition with the new project; and its formal and informal relationships with other groups would be tightly established by rules and traditions. Not only does utilization of the task force approach create a more flexible organization that is better able to respond to emerging needs and dilemmas, but it also increases the potential for interactions with the environment that is external to the organization.

The latter type of benefit is vital, because interactions of this nature greatly facilitate the flow of information between systems, which in turn disturbs old attitudes, promotes new expertise, and challenges traditional use of resources. In short, these relationships make it possible for the change in one system to have a greater impact on other systems.

SUMMARY AND CONCLUSIONS

The social environment, or the social system, can be divided into many interrelated social systems. Most often this network of systems is so balanced that it acts to depress the impact of change in one system on other systems. As a result, it is necessary to consider any proposed change in light of the *several* systems which will have some influence on it. In other words, it is necessary to take a systems view of change. Acting in terms of a single system is not enough.

As the rate of change continues to increase, it is becoming necessary to develop environments which facilitate rather than inhibit change. This is particulary true in the educational system. Hopefully state and local education agencies will made the adjustments in their structure which will enable them at least to avoid being swamped in the flood of societal changes, and, at best, to provide positive leadership for the other components of the educational system.

Footnote References

[1]P. W. Hughes, "Educational Planning: Benefits and Danger," in *Sociology of Education*, F. M. Katz and R. K. Browne, eds. (Melbourne, Australia: Macmillian of Australia, 1970), p. 93.

[2]John I. Goodlad and M. Frances Klein, *Behind the Classroom Door* (Worthington, Ohio: Charles A. Jones Publishing Company, 1970).

[3]George C. Homans, *The Human Group* (New York: Harcourt, Brace & World, 1950), p. 422.

[4]Richard Colvard, "The Colleges and the 'Arkansas Purchase' Controversy," in *Innovation in Education*, Matthew B. Miles, ed. (New York: Teachers College, Columbia University, 1964), pp. 117-156.

[5]*Ibid.*, p. 155.

[6]George C. Homans, *op. cit.*, p. 303.

[7]William W. Cooper, Harold J. Leavitt and Maynard W. Shelly II, *New Perspectives in Organizational Research* (New York: John Wiley and Sons, Inc., 1964), p. 519.

[8]Marvin Adelson, "Decisions, Decisions, Decisions: Is Educational Planning Important Enough?", in *Planning for Effective Utilization of Technology in Education*, Edgar L. Morphet and David L. Jesser, eds. (Denver, Colorado: Designing Education for the Future, 1968), p. 245.

[9]Richard E. Farson, "How Could Anything That Feels So Bad Be So Good?", *Saturday Review*, Volume LII, Number 36, September 6, 1969, p. 21.

[10]Kenneth E. Boulding, "Expecting the Unexpected: The Uncertain Future of Knowledge and Technology," in *Prospective Changes in Society by 1980*, Edgar L. Morphet and Charles O. Ryan, eds. (Denver, Colorado: Designing Education for the Future, 1967), p. 203.

[11]For an insight into the difference between tolerated and encouraged change, see California State Committee on Public Education, *Citizens for the 21st Century* (Sacramento: California State Committee on Public Education, 1969), p. 21.

[12]See, for example, Charles C. Halbower, "Influencing Change in Education," in *Final Report: California Project Talent* (Sacramento: California State Department of Education, 1969), pp. 110-116.

Chapter 7

Forces and Factors That Influence
Educational Change

Because education is part of a complex social system, it is necessary to identify the forces and factors that impinge in various ways upon the whole social system, and then to attempt to determine their implications for education. Wtihout a clear idea of the major forces reshaping the larger society, it is impossible to assess trends with which proposed changes will have to interact before they can be accepted, or to propose changes which will be consonant with anticipated directions of the larger society. On the other hand, an equally clear idea about the factors that tend to minimize change is a requisite for designing change strategies which will help to counteract these factors.

FORCES ACCELERATING CHANGE

Many of the forces that influence change in the overall American society are discussed briefly elsewhere in this publication and in the volume, *Emerging State Responsibilities for Education.*[1]* In this section, these forces will be discussed more specifically as they relate to the process of implementing change and the implications for the role and procedures of state and local education agencies.

TECHNOLOGICAL DEVELOPMENTS AND INFORMATION EXPLOSION

Numerous studies have documented the fact that the knowledge explosion of the last several decades has had tremendous effects on American society. It has expanded the powers and possibilities of technologies, opened up new insights into various behavioral patterns, and spawned new kinds of human processes for achieving desired ends. Each of these areas has simultaneously raised new problems for people desirous of achieving certain changes in society and given them new tools for attempting to effect these changes.

New Technologies. In education, the primary impact of new technologies has been through the advances in the field of communication—

---

*Footnote references are given at end of the chapter.

including especially the computer. At first, these advances were welcomed enthusiastically. Many looked upon them as panaceas for this or that problem. But in recent years, there has been a much more restrained appraisal of these developments. For example, many people have blamed television for much of the violence in American society, while others criticize computers for increasing the impersonalizing and dehumanizing tendencies in many aspects of life.

The fact is that technology is neutral; the crux of the matter is how it is used. The essential message of Buckminster Fuller, John McHale, Donald Michael and others is that *technology is here to stay and it is now up to humanity to use it as constructively as possible.* Unfortunately, this concept has all too easily been turned into a glib truism that has been used by educators—and others—as a substitute for harnessing technology to humane enterprises. One of the potentials would be the restructuring of the existing educational system. While the role technology could play in that restructuring is immense, educators have only begun to understand and develop that role. For example, few educational organizations—state, local or federal—have even begun to utilize television as a conscious instrument for educational change. The potential of television for increasing citizen awareness and involvement in educational issues has been virtually untapped.

Likewise, the computer in education has been largely restricted to such mundane, but important, educational tasks as storing or analyzing information, making class schedules, controlling budgets, assigning grades and laying out bus routes. One of the most creative educational uses to which computers have been put involves limited applications to instructional purposes. But even these applications have not been very well developed in many school systems. The possibilities for using computers in planning simulations or to generate and analyze alternatives are just beginning to unfold.

The technological revolution has also significantly altered the process by which change can take place. For better or for worse, it seems that, thus far, new technologies have made it much more difficult for change to start at the base of any social system. In the first place, new technologies have made it possible for social systems to become much larger and much more complicated. The larger and more complicated a system becomes, the greater the perceived need for *standardization* within that system. This standardization tends to blot out initiative, especially in lower echelons of an organization, and deprive the individual of the feeling that he can have any important impact. Consider the problem confronting a teacher who wants to change his grading system but cannot do so because he is locked into a district-wide computerized reporting and filing system. When individuals or groups attempt to propose changes, they often learn or are advised that they "don't understand the total picture." Their ability to provide any meaningful input is thereby drastically curtailed. Many individuals and groups may have lost interest in educational involvement because the system seems almost impossible for them to comprehend, let alone help to change in any significant respect.

Some of these problems can be ameliorated by redesigning the educational system so that it is more flexible. But because flexibility inevitably implies decentralization in some decision making—which also tends to result in some decrease in quality *control,* though not necessarily in *quality*—it seems unrealistic to expect most educational systems to move dramatically toward much greater flexibility. The trend toward accountability, as accountability is presently conceived, underscores that fact. At least for the immediate future there apparently will be a tremendous burden on people in leadership positions who seek to take much initiative in instituting needed changes.

Increased technology has a second detrimental effect on the process of change: it considerably raises the costs of trying any new approach. Ziegler states, however:

> One powerful objective for educational technology and social intervention would be to reduce the size of financial, material, institutional and human investments in education so that the longer-term character of the investment is shortened.[2]

It is obvious that exactly the opposite is taking place. Theoretically, various technological and social innovations will eventually allow the educational system to come close to attaining this objective, but in the meantime these factors increase the obligation of educational leadership to plan adequately for proposed changes which involve the purchase of expensive technologies or technological services. The failure to do so in the past—which has contributed to a rash of aborted experiments and under-used hardware—is one of the factors involved in the current disenchantment with education in many school systems.

New Knowledge. In the past thirty years, as a result of advances in the disciplines of sociology, psychology, biology, and the whole spectrum of fields within these disciplines, there has been a significant increase in man's understanding of how his fellow man functions.[3] Most of these advances have been in highly specialized areas that many citizens only vaguely comprehend. On the other hand, much of this new knowledge has seeped into the conventional wisdom so easily that the average citizen usually does not realize how much more he knows about these human processes than his ancestors knew. In between these two poles, however, is a sizable body of information and theory that is potentially very helpful to those who are concerned with beneficial changes in education.

Much of the vast body of literature on the nature and process of change falls into the last category discussed above. Some of this material is very useful; some less so. The fact that many leaders, intellectual and practical, have turned part of their attention to the conscious study of change has resulted in the identification of many new potentials and resources. The major unresolved question is whether most people will accept these new insights and use them in an intelligent way, or whether they will continue to rely on their prejudices and intuitions.

One of the less intelligent uses of this new knowledge, however, has been the tendency of certain technicians to let it become a barrier between themselves and the general populace. Some of these "experts" seem to have assumed that because a person does not know a particular set of jargon, he cannot make any intelligent input into the improvement of the educational process. Another variant of the same problem comes from the professional change agents who parlay a little impressive-sounding knowledge into expensive contracts which may, or may not, produce results commensurate with the original knowledge. But neither of these problems should be allowed to detract from the overall potential of the recent advances in human knowledge.

New Processes. Among the outgrowths of new technology and new social knowledge are some new social processes. These processes are derived from the structures that have grown up to support and utilize other advances. They range from those which are heavily dependent on technology—such as Planning-Programming-Budgeting Systems (PPBS)—to those which are primarily dependent on social knowledge—such as the various programs developed by the National Training Laboratory (NTL). Some of these processes—such as the more sophisticated simulation models—are also dependent on the defensible use of technology and social understanding.

Generally speaking, the potential of these new processes for effecting change is much the same as the potential of other developments discussed above. It is possible that they will become meaningful and powerful tools for effecting and implementing needed changes. On the other hand, it is also possible that—through injudicious use—they could become obstacles to needed change. The latter could take place if particular processes become so rigid that they freeze movement within the educational system (as the more complex "information systems" tend to do), or if they become "the cause" of cultists who reject those outside their fold (as has already happened in some cases of specialists in sensitivity and encounter techniques).

If these processes are to be of maximum benefit to society, it will be necessary to develop a systematic method for linking their operation to the concerns of average citizens. In other words, these processes will be most important when they are used as direct means to reach the goals of citizens, rather than merely as means which simplify the tasks of administrators. Such a direct linking of new social processes and societal goals can be accomplished only when there is some bridge of mutual understanding, communication and good will between members of the general society and those who are utilizing these new processes. In functional terms, this means there must be provision for both some input into the process and some monitoring of the output of the process by the larger society. It should be emphasized, however, that: (1) this can happen only as a result of conscious and deliberate attempts on the part of those in power (it is virtually impossible for those out of power to take the initiative); and (2) the *existing* channels for communication can never accommodate a real two-way process. It will be necessary to devise whole new structures for communication and involvement because the existing structures will *never* be adequate. The chief reason for this inadequacy is that existing structures are only designed to publicize actions *after* rather than *before* the fact.

SOCIETAL EXPECTATIONS

The role the total society plays, or could play, in the process of educational change is quite muddled. Most books on educational change and planning have added to the confusion by simply asserting that citizen involvement is a good thing.[4] While, of course, that assertion is beyond debate, the statement is much more significant for what it does not say than for what it seems to imply. Most particularly, it does not make clear:

- What pressures the general society does or should exert on educational change processes; and

- What effect citizen involvement is or is not likely to have on the process.

The key to resolving these issues lies in an anlysis of two factors: society's expectations for and of education, and the relationship of these expectations to education. This task is more complicated than might seem to be the case at first glance because there is no single entity that can be described as *the society*. What exists, rather, is a series of diverse and often only casually related pressure and interest groups. Each group has, in degrees, different expectations and different ways of trying to force these expectations on the whole educational process. The problem is further complicated at the state level because comparatively few people are directly interested in the state education agency (SEA). By and large, the average citizen's vision of education extends no further than the neighborhood school, or, perhaps the local school board. Society, generally, is—and perhaps always will be—interested primarily in the *output* of the schools. The extent of its interest in input is primarily limited to concerns about the amount of tax money being used for education.

There are, however, two pervasive societal expectations that have a decided impact on educational change. These are the beliefs that our society can (1) end deprivation, and (2) provide a good life for all. Although these beliefs stem from the same source—the material affluence generated largely by technological processes—the importance attached to each expectation differs from group to group.

Minority Groups. The elimination of deprivation is a primary concern of most minority groups in the country. This concern, in turn, is translated into a specific expectation that the schools will provide their children with a sound basic education that will start them off on the road to college and material success. While the last five years have seen a growing diversity in minority expectations—an increased interest in ethnic studies, self-concept development and the like—most minority parents agree with Bayard Rustin, Kenneth Clark and others who insist that the greatest priority for minority children is basic skills. Consequently, attempts at educational change which support this expectation will, in most cases, be welcomed and supported by minority groups. In this case, the expectation is a force that would facilitate change. On the other hand, a proposed change that does not correspond with these expectations— playing down the role of achievement tests, for instance—is likely to be resisted in one way or another by minority groups.

Unfortunately, minority groups tend to be a much more potent negative force than a positive force. Because of their relative lack of sophistication in the bureaucratic skills necessary to effect changes in a school or a school district, their lack of awareness of alternatives and the plethora of past unkept promises, minority groups usually find it very difficult to get seriously involved in a positive way with the schools. Many parents who were once vitally interested in the schools have become so confused and disheartened by the maze of procedures which surround the educational process that they have reached a point where the only action they seem willing to take is a veto action—they attempt to shut down what they don't like. While minority groups may not be greatly interested in presenting their own suggestions and alternatives to the educational authorities, they often complain vigorously about something which does not meet their expectations. It is especially necessary, therefore, that any agency proposing a change relevant to minority groups take the extra steps needed to ensure that a real cross section of minority group representatives has been consulted. Otherwise, the result might be an educational Edsel.

Majority Groups. Ascertaining the expectations among majority groups is very difficult because of the fragmentation of those groups. Most people in the dominant group—parents and students—have vague, but traditional, expectations. They expect the schools to teach the students to read, write, add, subtract and generally get them ready for the next year of their schooling—until they eventually graduate from school or college and obtain a job or position for which their schooling has prepared them. These expectations are essentially the same in many respects as those of minority groups. But, because the expectations generally have been rather well fulfilled, they often have not been clearly defined; rather they constitute an amorphous set of assumptions that are largely taken for granted.

Other Groups. Contrasted with the expectations already described are those of a sizable and growing number of students and a smaller but also growing number of parents who have radically different notions about the schools. They insist that the job of the schools includes helping to develop the complete child—his emotions, his sense of self-worth, his use of freedom, and other qualities. Of the groups discussed, this group is most vocal in its criticism of the schools because it places a great deal of emphasis on the importance of education and therefore demands that the schools perform this task far better than they have in the past.

Implications of Conflicting Expectations. The fact that such different expectations about what comprises appropriate learning experiences exist simultaneously in almost every state greatly complicates the task of changing the learning environments and procedures. Almost any proposed change—if it is likely to affect substantial numbers of people—will not meet the expectations of many of them. As Donald Michael has observed:

> Resort to the political process of 'reconciling differences' will not solve the problem. . . . As presently practiced, it is one of the chief reasons we get so few well-articulated plans, so little significant evaluation, and so little done when it needs to be done. The resultant compromises usually mean the plan, such as it is, is gerry-rigged. . . .[5]

One does not need to agree with all implications of Michael's statement to recognize that direct inputs to planning from the general population will not necessarily result in clear mandates, but instead may help to bring to light the conflicting expectations. Any committee which is truly representative will probably encounter considerable difficulty in deciding on clear statements of goals and an appropriate plan of action.

The problems may even be more difficult at the state level—whether direct changes in learning environments or leadership attempts to facilitate changes at the local level are involved—primarily because the population that will be affected is much larger. Despite these difficulties, several states and local school systems have found ways to get a "working consensus" that has made it possible for them to effect some significant changes in the provisions for education. Every educational agency—state as well as local—needs to face directly up to the fact that it is not dealing with a single force of "citizen expectations" but with a plurality of forces, some of which may be pushing in opposite directions. Any proposed change in learning environments should therefore (1) be aimed at a specific group having homogeneous expectations, (2) be designed to promote a plurality of approaches, or (3) be prepared to help in developing new expectations.

NEW ROLES FOR EDUCATIONAL AGENCIES

In response to the pressures for change, educational structures at federal, state and local levels have undergone significant changes in the last decade. These developments should have important ramifications for potential innovators. The fact that each of these agencies is undergoing serious role redefinition means that many things are in a state of flux, or, in some cases, turmoil. Many agencies and institutions, therefore, tend to be more receptive to change than they were ten years ago, or perhaps than they might be some years later. Chomsky's comment about society in general—"There now exist opportunities for change that are not likely to recur"[6]—is especially applicable to education.

A second effect stems from the fact that, as each of these structures takes on new roles and responsibilities, the way in which each one relates to the other also changes. What was once an appropriate relationship between state and local education agencies may no longer be viable. Any proposed change, then, should be much more closely attuned to the developing relationships than to old relationships. In fact, one of the goals of some proposed changes should be to make the developing relationships more functional.

The Federal Agencies. In the past fifteen years, the federal government has played a much more direct and active role in education than it did prior to that period. Its most obvious influence has stemmed from the substantially increased amount of money it has provided for the overall educational system.

During the early days of increased federal involvement, the position of the state education agency (SEA) *vis a vis* local education agencies (LEAs) seems to have been weakened in some respects. Some districts— especially those in major urban centers—apparently felt that the U. S. Office of Education (USOE) was more sensitive to their needs than the SEAs, and consequently they turned to the former agency for help. During the last few years, however, this trend has shifted somewhat and the overall effect of federal involvement in education has probably served to strengthen the state education agencies. It has certainly served to strengthen their capacity to influence change by providing them with new monies that are presumed to be used for creating change. As long as the actual disbursement of these monies is carried out at the state level, the SEA is in a better position to encourage meaningful change than it would be if it were totally dependent upon a state legislature for the funds needed for the change.

The extent to which the new role of the federal government will prove to be a significant force for encouraging educational change will depend in large measure on how effectively the SEAs use the opportunities afforded them by increased federal funding. If they disburse federal monies without adequate planning or with the same lack of imagination, of equity and of provisions for accountability that has been characteristic of some SEAs, there is little likelihood that significant improvements will ensue. State education agencies, however, can and should use their leadership to ensure that the new federal involvement leads to significant change.

In addition to supplying funds to help states deal with certain problems, the new federal involvement has also provided a certain amount of leadership for constructive change which individual districts or states might have never been able to provide. One reason the federal government can do this is because it is sufficiently removed from the day to day workings of state and local educational systems that its view of the forest should not be obstructed by the trees. The desegregation effort, the first experiments with performance contracting, and the inter-state cooperative projects are examples of this kind of leadership. The net effect has been to create in the overall educational system a climate much more receptive to, and facilitating of, potentially useful changes. Again, how much of this kind of initiative actually gets implemented depends almost entirely upon the extent to which, and how, state and local education agencies carry their share of the burden. Yet, whether or not all state education agencies (SEAs) and local education agencies (LEAs) respond effectively, the recent role of the federal government in education has made— and is making—it easier to propose and implement change at all levels.

Local Educational Agencies. Recent changes in many local educational systems are much less clearly defined than the changes that have occurred at the federal level and in some states. On the one hand, local education agencies have begun to realize that they can no longer afford to be mere dispensers of uniform facilitating services to the various schools of the district. For the most part they recognize, and have begun to act upon, the need to become involved in organizing and preparing curriculums, programs, and teachers that are adapted to the special needs of many diverse groups; in providing some services formerly left to family, church or chance; and in providing positive leadership that deliberately fosters the identification and attainment of educational goals and a realistic appraisal of progress in each school and on a district-wide level.

On the other hand, LEAs have run into a bewildering array of obstacles—some of their own making—which have prevented some from fulfilling the new role which many would like to assume. Teacher militancy, drugs, taxpayers' revolts, racial issues, power struggles and top-heavy bureaucracies are typical of the problems confronting many LEAs. Moreover, at least a portion of the disagreements relating to such issues have been carried over into the curriculum and other areas directly related to the learning process. As a result, almost all educational problems at the local level have become so enmeshed with other policy issues that many LEAs find it difficult—if not impossible—to move at all.

Caught as they are in these various dilemmas, LEAs have been in the unenviable position of realizing that they should be doing something that is different from what they have been doing, but seem unable to move decisively in the direction they want to go—regardless of what direction that is. As a result, many LEAs have indulged in a series of superficial or piecemeal "changes" which have left the essential structures of both the schools and the school system unchanged, while everything around them is changing.

This situation urgently calls for competent leaders who can surmount, or deal effectively with, the challenges and obstacles that societal changes have created. It also has tremendous implications for SEAs. Some SEAs apparently would rather steer clear of involvement with these issues because they are controversial and so embroiled in local specifics that it is difficult to adopt a statewide approach to their resolution. The future, however, may well be a different story. If the SEAs, with the cooperation of institutions of higher learning and other appropriate groups, can provide leadership in developing realistic *and* systematic approaches for dealing with the complex problems with which they are confronted, they should find that their leadership will be accepted in a way previously unanticipated.

The State Education Agencies. Generally speaking, the emerging role of SEAs can be identified partly by a process of elimination. Many SEAs are not in a position to utilize financial incentives as a means of helping to bring about change, as the federal government is doing on a limited basis. Moreover, since they are not directly involved with teaching and learning, they cannot directly bring about changes in teaching and learning procedures—as is possible for local agencies. Finally, if they were required to continue to emphasize the establishment and enforcement of minimum standards that often fail to meet the needs of a changing society, they probably would tend to retard—or at least would not encourage —needed improvements in education. The chief role for the SEA in the future, therefore, should be to provide the leadership and services needed to plan and effect improvements in education, and to evaluate progress. It can influence change primarily to the extent that it can convince Congress and the U. S. Office of Education or the state legislature to support the projects which are deemed necessary and worthwhile, and persuade, encourage and assist local school systems in planning and providing for excellence in education.

The prospects that the SEA can and will assume this role are reasonably promising in several states. As indicated in preceding sections, the U.S. Office of Education is relatively open to suggestions and Congress has turned some of the responsibility for distributing federal funds over to SEAs. Local school districts currently recognize many of their needs and if the SEA poses its alternatives astutely it can have significant impact. The fact that the SEA can also provide appropriate support services to local systems enhances its bargaining position with local districts.

The crucial fact for the SEA is that it is in no position to mandate or dictate change; it can only help to effect changes by proposing them in such a way that other educational agencies are willing to consider and perhaps adopt them. It, therefore, is very important that state education agencies:

- Work closely with all other relevant agencies;

- Pose alternatives in a non-threatening manner;

- Keep lines of communication as open as possible; and

- Concentrate on unique support services which local districts actually want and need, and avoid any duplication of services.

FORCES INHIBITING CHANGE

In addition to the open-ended forces operating on society, there are some basically static factors which inhibit the spread of planned change in the educational system.

THE ORDEAL OF CHANGE

Eric Hoffer speaks of "the ordeal of change."[7] This is the ordeal which almost everyone undergoes as he struggles to adapt to a new way of doing things. In most cases, the adaptation is eventually made. But, for some people, the ordeal of change seems almost too painful to accept.

Adaptation to changes in the social environment tends to be more difficult than to changes in other environments for at least two reasons: (1) some of the results of changes in the physical or technical environment can readily be observed; and (2) social adaptation is more difficult because a major social change requires not merely that daily routines be altered, but that entire frames of reference be changed. For example, accepting the "new morality" demands a whole new way of looking at the concept of God, religion, and the relationship (or lack thereof) between each of these and man. Changing a frame of reference, in turn, makes it necessary for people to question the presuppositions and assumptions around which their lives have been built. Furthermore, many proposed social changes cannot be proven or even demonstrated to constitute a real improvement in the lot of man; they are much more often based on hopes and beliefs. It is small wonder, then, that many people find it easier to reject major social changes than to accept them. This explains, in part, why some people accept education "gimmicks" and reject more fundamental changes.

This natural inertia is a major impediment in instituting meaningful educational change. However, it also creates a secondary problem—a spinoff. The adoption of a major social change requires some degree of alteration in the adopter's entire frame of social reference—a framework which was formerly shared in some degree by his peer group. But the adoption of a given social change is not a uniform process; some people adopt it long before others are willing to consider it seriously. The short-term result is often that gross disparities emerge between the social perceptions of various segments of the population which once shared a common frame of reference. A good example of this is the way in which many children and their parents have developed different frames of reference. The most usual consequence is some kind of social conflict, because one group has a different frame of reference from that utilized by another group, and communication becomes difficult—often impossible. Each group interprets phenomena according to its own standards. A black militant, a liberal integrationist and a conservative school board member will each see the results of a particular development as "proving" his point. Each has different frames of social reference. In such situations, it is very difficult to appeal to any group on a rational basis because definitions of what is "rational" will differ from group to group. Failure to understand this aspect or phenomenon of change has resulted in the alienation of many citizens and students, and the consequent rejection of many proposals or programs that were designed to "educate" or "involve" them.

Furthermore, barring some unexpected developments, the near future seems to promise even more fragmentation. Change is inevitable, but at different rates.[8] As each social change alters an individual's or a group's frame of reference, it becomes more and more difficult for him to relate to others. As succeeding waves of change wash over the country, the disparities between social perceptions will tend to increase. Nor can they be "willed" away. Old procedures for consensus making may no longer be valid. The most appropriate response to this emergent situation seems to be (1) to recognize the perceptual disparities between groups, and (2) to develop methods and structures which allow those in leadership positions to deal with such disparities.

One further point should be made: the clash between social perceptions, although usually retarding change, is not always dysfunctional. Donald Klein makes this clear in an article which points out the valuable role played by people who resist change.[9] He suggests that the importance of this role stems from several considerations:

- Resisters are most likely to perceive and point out any real threats to the well-being of the system which may be unanticipated consequences of projected changes;

- They are especially likely to react against any change that might reduce the integrity of the system; and

- They are sensitive to any indication that those seeking to produce change fail to understand or identify with the core values of the system they seek to influence.

Those trying to bring about change, therefore, should clearly recognize and confront directly the issues resulting from differences in social perceptions. The overall effect may be beneficial to the entire system.

THE SIZE OF SOCIAL SYSTEMS

The gargantuan size to which many of this society's institutions have grown is another factor inhibiting change. The problem is particularly acute in education which has become the nation's largest single industry. Almost all important educational agencies—from the USOE and the SEAs to the LEAs in every large city—are simply too big or at least too bureaucratic. "Too big" is measured in a number of different ways. Most obvious is sheer size. After an organization grows beyond a certain point, increased size makes functioning more difficult. As Culbertson points out:

The large organization, which increasingly characterizes society, hampers change for a number of reasons. Chief among these are the fact that change, if effected, is so widespread and affects so many people, and that the larger organization increases the distance between the point of action and the point of decision-making; with the resultant increase in problems of understanding and communication. Thus, before any change is made, vastly greater effort must be devoted to the development of understanding, and even after the change is agreed upon, considerably greater resistance may be expected.[10]

"Too big" may also be a statement that applies to the complexity of structure within a given system. Any proposed change may be stymied if it must filter through a confusing labyrinth of committees, task forces, programs, institutions or systems. On the basis of these criteria, many state and local agencies may be too big and cumbersome for optimum facilitation of change.

Generally, the effects of structural "bigness" are the same as those resulting from bigness relating to sheer size. As a rule, the two occur together: more people and more functions create more complexity of structure; greater complexity of structure tends to create the illusion that it is able to accommodate more people and functions. But structural over-complexity adds a new dimension to the problem of change: if diffuses power. Each identifiable group within a system has some power—perhaps veto power, perhaps the power of delay, or perhaps merely the power of opinion. As the number of sub-groups multiplies, it becomes more difficult to make a change, even though, as in education, the various sub-groups are ostensibly working toward the same goal.

Consider the difficult course which some major educational changes must take. They may have to win approval, or at least acquiescence, from the relevant departments in the USOE, from the SEA, from professional education associations, from the various colleges and universities preparing the professionals to live with the change, and perhaps even from Congress and/or the state legislature before they even reach the local level. At the local level, every conceivable interest group can argue about the merits of the proposed change. First, there are the interest groups within education—especially the teachers' union or association, the administration, and the school board. Then, the PTA, the local newspapers, and so on may favor or resist the proposal. Ultimately, this diffusion of power tends to inhibit change by making the process both difficult and time consuming. But it also helps to ensure that proposed changes are not adopted without careful consideration by many who would be affected in one way or another.

PROVISIONS FOR RESOURCE DISTRIBUTION

Any society has only a certain amount of resources (not only money, but also competent and well trained people, facilities, materials, etc.) with which to conduct its affairs. The process of change is affected by the way those limited resources are distributed both within the whole society and to and within the educational system. The question is not solely one of quantity and quality—although that is often a central concern—but also one of the mode of distribution. Moreover, the extensive use of inflexible annual or biennial budgeting techniques makes long-range planning for change in education difficult or almost impossible in some cases.

As a matter of fact, just about every aspect of the patchwork arrangements utilized in this country to finance the educational system tends to inhibit change within that system. Heavy reliance on property tax for the support of elementary and secondary schools, inequitable distribution formulas, shifting responsibilities among various funding levels, and the gerrymandered boundaries of many school districts—all contribute to the tendency of the educational system to devote most of its funds to year-to-year operations, with far too little concern for systematically designing education for the future. Many modern industries, as Houser points out, often spend as much as five to ten percent of their annual budgets for research in order to keep competitive. Education below the university level devotes somewhat less than one percent of its annual budget to research.[12] Moreover, most of the money that is spent on research in education comes from the federal government. While this may be an efficient procedure in many cases, the distance of the funding agencies from practitioners at the state and local level has created a number of problems.[13]

Likewise, the amount of money devoted directly to change efforts in education is grossly inadequate. The money that is available—such as funds provided through Title III—is subjected to such a wide variety of influences and demands that it often is used less effectively than desirable. Sometimes it is spread too thin for the desired level of impact to be achieved; in other cases, the funds may be prematurely cut off or drastically curtailed because results are slow in coming, ideas have changed, or the federal government does not continue to support a program and other levels of government are unable or unwilling to assume the responsibility. And, since money for change-oriented programs is usually seen as something of a budgetary "fringe," the net effect of such funding patterns is to create considerable uncertainty and discontinuity in provisions for encouraging change. This situation not only results in disrupting many promising efforts before they have reached fruition, but also creates a climate in which the security necessary to undertake meaningful change is unfavorable.

Furthermore, while the government and/or the educational system allots too little money for the support of planned change, it continues to support old methods and practices because they appear to be a part of the "business as usual" routine—even when these practices are no longer defensible. For example, as the percentage of local budgets devoted to the salaries of people who are most responsible for effecting improvements in education and learning—or, according to some critics, for some of the problems—approaches or exceeds eighty percent of the total in some systems, it seems apparent that the statement of the California State Commission on Public Education about education in that state may be applicable in some other situations: "Education gives the appearance of a tradition-bound industry spending the bulk of its money on teachers' salaries and very little on books, materials and technical aids to instruction."[14]

STRUCTURAL RIGIDITY

Many of the existing legal and other provisions and arrangements relating to education clearly reflect what seems to be our general inability —or neglect—to keep educational structures subordinate to the functions and the functions subordinate to appropriate goals. The educational system often allows its functions to be governed by its structure and its goals to be determined by its functions. Constricting legal provisions for example, obviously impede change. In many states, some of the laws—although perhaps once functional—currently impede the achievement of meaningful educational goals. These restrictions range from unrealistic limitations on voting tax increases and bond issues to regulations which specify the number of square feet of window space a school must have.

The most glaring of these dysfunctional legal provisions, however, are in the area of school financing. Many states, for example, are still required by law to treat the cities as if they were among the wealthiest areas in the state, when, in fact, most large urban school systems are undergoing a major financial crisis. The result is to ensure grossly inadequate educational opportunities for children in many cities.[15]

In many states, before significant educational changes can be effected, it will be necessary for educators, legislators and other leading citizens to agree upon and insist on the adoption and implementation of an adequate plan to replace inadequate and outdated legal provisions. In almost every state, such a group almost certainly could reduce the obstacles to educational change.

There is, however, another aspect of structural rigidity which is much more subtle: it is the tendency for agencies and organizations to become so preoccupied with existing functions that it is difficult or virtually impossible for them to devote adequate attention or resources to planned change. This happens in SEAs which have so many regulatory and clerical responsibilities prescribed by law that they have neither the time nor the resources to assume leadership in planning and implementing needed changes. It also is found in many local school systems and institutions of higher learning and even in some professional organizations that are not seriously restricted by legal provisions.

At some point in time, it becomes necessary for an SEA or local school system, together with all others interested in the achievement of quality of education, to weed out the functions which are no longer necessary and assign a defensible priority to the remaining functions. As Drucker has said:

> The most difficult and most important decisions in respect to objectives are not what to do. They are, first, what to abandon as no longer worthwhile and, second, what to give priority to and what to concentrate on. . . . The decision about what to abandon is by far the most important and the most neglected.[16]

Until these steps are taken, this functional inertia is a major force which locks agencies and organizations into the present and makes it difficult or impossible for them to face the future realistically.

SUMMARY AND CONCLUSION

There are powerful forces reshaping the American social environment. While some people will undoubtedly insist that these forces are evil and others will argue that they are benign, it becomes increasingly clear that most of these forces fall into neither extreme. They represent, rather, the potential for either great good or great evil.

The way in which these tremendously powerful influences for social change affect the educational system is a case in point. Changes—such as increasing knowledge, rising societal expectations, changing concepts of education—are pushing the educational system in certain directions. Of themselves, these directions hold both promise and danger for education. The question is whether the educational system can control these forces and somehow help to direct them more toward the promises than toward the dangers.

But just as there are forces propelling the educational system in certain directions, regardless of the desirability of those directions, there are certain other forces and factors which resist change, regardless of the desirability of any given change. These forces result in problems not simply because they resist change, but largely because they resist change indiscriminately. To resist change indiscriminately is, in turn, counter-productive because it generates an intolerable amount of structural stress. There will be changes; the problem is to maximize the positive effects of functional changes and minimize the negative effects of dysfunctional changes.

It is necessary, then, for the educational system to do two things. It must first attempt to control the forces for change entering the educational system from the outside. Control, in this sense, does not imply that change forces should be minimized, but rather that these forces be channeled into constructive directions. Second, the educational system must bring itself into some degree of harmony with the outside social system so that it actually can prepare students for a creative life in that social system. State and local educational agencies, institutions of higher learning, and professional organizations urgently need to prepare to assume a dynamic and constructive role in this very important process.

Footnote References

[1]Edgar L. Morphet, David L. Jesser, and Arthur P. Ludka, eds., *Emerging State Responsibilities for Education* (Denver, Colorado: Improving State Leadership in Education, 1970).

[2]Warren L. Ziegler, *An Approach to the Futures-Perspective in American Education* (Syracuse, New York: Syracuse Educational Policy Research Center, 1969), p. 56.

[3]Karl W. Deutsch, John Platt, and Dieter Senghaas, "Conditions Favoring Major Advances in Social Science," *Science*, February 5, 1971, p. 450.

[4]Edgar L. Morphet et al, *op. cit.*, pp. 15, 59, 91, and 107-108.

[5]Donald Michael, *The Unprepared Society: Planning for a Precarious Future* (New York: Basic Books, Inc., 1968), p. 103.

[6]Cited in Willis W. Harman, "The Nature of Our Changing Society," prepared for the E.R.I.C. Clearinghouse on Educational Administration; Eugene, Oregon; October, 1969, p. 34.

[7]Eric Hoffer, *The Ordeal of Change* (New York: Harper and Row, 1967).

[8]Donald Michael, *op. cit.*, p. 53.

[9]Donald Klein, "The Dynamics of Resistance to Change," in *Change in School Systems*, Goodwin Watson, ed. (Washington, D.C.: Cooperative Project for Educational Development, 1967), p. 31.

[10]Jack A. Culbertson, Theodore L. Reller, and Paul B. Jacobson, *Administrative Relationships: A Casebook* (Englewood Cliffs; Prentice-Hall, Inc., 1960), p. 455.

[11]Warren L. Ziegler, *op. cit.*, p. 22ff.

[12]Cited in Maurice Rosenblatt, ed., *Light A Fire* (Washington, D.C.: National Committee for the Support of the Public Schools, 1963), p. 61.

[13]See Muriel Crosby, "Who Changes the Curriculum and How?" *Phi Delta Kappan*, March, 1970, p. 387.

[14]California State Committee on Public Education, *Citizens for the 21st Century: Long-Range Considerations for California Elementary and Secondary Education* (Sacramento: State Committee for Public Education, 1969), p. 55.

[15]Joel S. Berke, "The Impact of Present Patterns of Funding Education for Urban Schools," prepared for the National Conference on School Finance; San Francisco, California, April 6, 1970.

[16]Peter S. Drucker, *The Age of Discontinuity: Guidelines to Our Changing Society* (New York: Harper and Row, 1968), p. 192.

Chapter 8

Change Strategies: Some Alternatives

The urgent need for meaningful and responsive changes in the existing educational system has been well documented in this and other publications. Moreover, the necessity for more adequate and effective planning for urgently needed changes in education and for implementing these changes has also been well documented. However, even though these needs have been evident to many people and recognized by educational leaders for many years, concerned citizens—educators, legislators and lay citizens—are becoming increasingly aware of the fact that *relatively few meaningful and lasting changes have occurred in education.*

More students have been enrolled, more classroom units have been created, more teachers have been hired, more buildings have been built, and more curriculums have been added. These, of course, constitute certain kinds of changes. But relatively few *significant* changes have been made. Many of the needs that were clearly discernible a decade or two ago are still extant; and most of the problems that emanate from the unmet needs are still unresolved. *Moreover, these problems are becoming more acute with each passing month and year.*

The apparent inability of educators and other concerned citizens to effect, and somehow institutionalize, the changes that must be made to meet the needs of an ever-changing society constitutes a major problem that assumes even more serious dimensions when we recognize that: (1) more is known about change and the change process than ever before; and (2) more knowledge and expertise relating to planning are available than at any time in our history. In short, in an era in which there is literally an abundance of knowledge relating to change and the change processes, it becomes difficult to understand why so few meaningful and lasting changes result from the planning that has been accomplished in many states and local school systems.

IMPEDIMENTS TO CHANGE

Several of the apparent reasons for the failure of planning to bring about significant changes in education have been discussed in Chapter 6. The need for effective change strategies, however, should be more clearly

122

seen in perspective if some of the other probable reasons, noted below, for the failure of plans to result in meaningful changes are briefly considered.

● *Desire to Maintain the Status Quo*

There seems to be a tendency for many humans to want to preserve— and defend—the *status quo*. Unfortunately, this tendency appears to be especially evident within the ranks of the educational profession. In instances in which this tendency or desire is marked, it is highly probable that much of the planning that is accomplished, regardless of quality or specificity, will be of little value.

● *Implementation of a Specific Change*

At first glance the idea that the implementation of a change may be a barrier to change may seem illogical. The concept, however, is valid, and well may have been a prime factor in the failure of many "plans" to materialize into lasting and significant changes. In the first place, the implementation of a particular change may require the utilization of all available human and other resources. If resources are not available because of prior commitments, planning for other needed changes will result only in the development of plans. The logical end product of planning— an identified and desired change—simply will not materialize.

In a similar, yet slightly different context, the implementation of a particular change may well create an organizational structure that is not conducive to any further change. The implementation of a new or different instructional technique, for example, may result in a new or different instructional hierarchy that is—or rapidly becomes—self serving. If and when this situation exists, the results of planning for any future desired change the likely to be less than satisfactory.

● *Exceeding an Acceptable Rate of Change*

As Adelson has pointed out, communities tend to be characterized by a maximum rate at which they are willing to accept changes.[1*] It seems equally valid to assume that—because they are at one and the same time reflections of community attitudes as well as unique social entities— schools and school systems have similar characteristics. Each school and school system has a rate at which changes can be introduced and accepted, and will tend to reject changes that are in excess of that rate. To attempt to implement changes when the maximum acceptable rate has been attained is apt to be futile.

Thus, it should be evident that there are many possible—and probable —reasons why so many well intentioned plans have failed to result in lasting and meaningful change. But whatever the reason, and regardless of specific variations, there would appear to be at least one overriding and

*Footnote references are given at end of the chapter.

all-encompassing factor: *Many educational planners have neither considered nor developed viable change strategies that are based on sound principles relating to the change process.*

RELATIONSHIPS BETWEEN PLANNING AND CHANGE

If the processes of planning and change are to be effective and meaningful, the relationships between the two processes must be carefully considered. Each process can function independently of the other, and when this happens, the results are often vague, haphazard, and intangible. All too often the "planner" clearly sees the reason for planning, and the "change-agent" similarly is able to see the reason for a desired change—but neither clearly understands or accepts the reasons of the other.

Each process—planning and change—may have separate and even discrete purposes or reasons. This should not be interpreted to mean, however, that each function can exist or operate separate and apart from the other. To be effective, *planning must relate to a desired and identifiable change. Change,* to be effective, *must relate to and be the result of a well-conceived and carefully considered plan.* Duhl has emphasized the essential kind of relationship between planning and change:

> The planner is an agent of change, and any agent of change is a planner. It does not matter whether he is a politician, a producer, a businessman, an administrator, or an educator. There are many kinds of planners, each performing different functions and fulfilling different roles, depending upon the specific problem or situation with which he must deal. *What is essential to his definition as a planner is that he be concerned with instituting change in an orderly fashion, so that tomorrow something will be different from what it is today.* (Italics supplied)[2]

Educational leaders who are responsible for planning need to recognize to a greater degree than ever before the forces and factors that facilitate or inhibit change. They will also need to develop a much broader understanding of the change process, if their planning is to be effective—that is, result in needed changes. But at the same time, educational leaders who perceive themselves as change-agents will have to understand that there is a clearly defined *process* of planning, and that *only when the process is properly utilized will effective change be possible.*

STRATEGIES FOR EFFECTING NEEDED CHANGE

In Chapter 2, it was suggested that educational change is bound to happen, but that planned educational change must be *made* to happen. The distinction between *change* and *planned change* should be obvious, but for many who will be vitally affected by changes in education the distinction apparently is not clearly understood. Some educators seem to assume that, because change is inevitable, their task is one of "riding with the current"—of simply letting changes take place. In other words, some educators are quite willing to be *influenced by change,* but are unwilling or unable to engage in the process of *influencing change.* Within recent years, however, there has been a growing concern among educators about ways of influencing change. Concepts such as *planned change, strategies of change, strategies for improvement, change processes, change-agents, power structures* and *dynamics of change* provide some indications of that concern.

Emergent thinking clearly points to the desirability—if not the sheer necessity—of *planned educational change* as opposed to merely reacting to those changes which "are bound to happen." However, mere recognition of the desirability or necessity does not constitute either a solution or a method for effectively bringing about those *educational changes* that are needed. Recognition should, however, cause many questions to be raised—questions to which adequate consideration must be given before educational leaders and others can actually ensure that planned educational change will take place. Some of these questions are:

● How may planned educational change be made to happen?

● Who (agency, institution, organization or person) should be responsible for *making* planned educational change happen?

● What criteria (bases) should be used to determine which changes should be "planned for"?

● What are the likely or probable consequences of *"allowing* educational change to happen," rather than *"making* planned educational change happen"?

Questions such as these are illustrative of what must be considered when strategies for *making* planned educational change happen are developed. More important, however, is the fact that each question implies that there is more than one way to consider planned educational change, and that there are at least several "right" ways of making it happen.

As concerned leaders seriously consider alternative procedures for bringing about needed changes, they must constantly keep in mind the *kind* of changes that are necessary in education. LeBaron[3] has perceptively observed that there are three such kinds of changes: (1) changes in people; (2) changes in the institutions or organizations; and (3) changes in program or process. He has also suggested that personnel responsible for effecting needed changes should proceed in the order given—that is, from people to organization to program. Unfortunately, in too many instances, educators attempt to implement change in terms of the institution or program, with little or no attention given to *people.* Such a procedure, obviously, will be relatively ineffectual.

Finally, those who are concerned with effecting planned changes in education must consider *alternative procedures* by which planned change can probably be brought about, and determine for themselves which alternative is best in terms of factors such as goal attainment, time span, and the environment. Only when such considerations are recognized and acted upon will it be possible to develop effective strategies for change.

SOME IMPORTANT CONSIDERATIONS

Goodlad has perceptively observed:

> We are finding that effecting change is enormously difficult. Teachers and principals do not abandon long-standing practices because they read about innovations or attend an inspiring lecture.[4]

If, as Goodlad suggests, teachers and principals do not abandon long-standing practices as a result of an inspiring article, book, or lecture, what are some methods or strategies that can be employed to bring about the changes that are perceived to be needed? Are there viable change strategies that will enable educators to "leave the static ways and static guidelines which have dominated the history of schooling and adopt the *process ways* which must become the educator's ways if the school is to survive?" (Italics supplied)[5]

The professional literature relating to change includes numerous proposals relating to change strategies, and many have been carefully described.[6] One such strategy implies the utilization of role definition, social interaction, problem solving, and linkage.[7] Others include concepts such as mutuality of goal setting, non-mutuality of goal setting, power ratios, emulative change, and coercive change.[8] However, as Howsam so aptly stated, "There is much semantic looseness among educators where change is concerned."[9]

In one attempt to focus on the problem of semantic looseness, Chin[10] has suggested that there are three basic strategies for effecting deliberate or planned change: (1) rational-empirical; (2) normative-reeducative; and (3) power-coercive.

The first strategy (rational-empirical) is one in which attempts to effect change are based on reason and demonstration. In this approach the need is made clearly visible and understandable, and the value of the suggested change is demonstrated. The second strategy (normative-reeducative) is one in which deliberate efforts are made to help people who will be affected by a proposed change to modify or change their attitudes. In the third strategy (power-coercive) a desired change is brought about through the imposition of power. Each of these strategies is illustrative of an alternative way in which meaningful change might be brought about. Inherent in the three strategies are the following concepts relating to change:

- Overall effectiveness in attaining established goals or changes is closely related to the understanding of the need for, together with acceptance of, the established goal or goals.

- Educational change is "people-oriented" rather than "thing-oriented" and people have to be considered and involved.

• Change can be achieved through the imposition or application of power or pressure.

Educators and others who are concerned with the planning of educational change need to be familiar with and understand the concepts noted above. Additionally, they must be able to evaluate each in terms of the probability that it will *effectively bring about needed changes*. When this understanding exists, those responsible for effecting needed changes will be better prepared to accomplish their task—that is, to bring a needed change from the *idea* stage to an *operational* stage. These concepts, together with some apparent advantages and disadvantages of each, are discussed in a somewhat different context in the ensuing paragraphs.

EFFECTING CHANGE THROUGH A DIFFUSION PROCESS

• *When it is possible to demonstrate effectively that a new or different practice will provide a reasonable solution for an identified problem area in education, wider acceptance of the practice may be gained and change is thus encouraged.*

The concept that it is possible to bring about change through a diffusion process contains elements of change strategies that have been described by Chin[11] and Guba.[12] As Chin has described the rational-empirical approach, the need must be made clearly evident, and demonstrable evidence of the effectiveness of the specific change presented. In the model of the change process developed by Guba, diffusion (telling, showing, helping, involving, training, intervention) must take place before adoption of a suggested change will take place. Each element described would appear to complement the other in the overall alternative suggested above.

In some respects this concept, or alternative method for effecting change, represents the original intent of Title III of the Elementary and Secondary Education Act of 1965 which provided funds for the establishment of "demonstration projects." In a somewhat similar manner, the concept is embodied in the original philosophy of "demonstration schools" on campuses of teacher training institutions. In fact, it is to be found in the basic principles of the education process itself.

But while the concept has occupied a prominent role in "change efforts," questions are being raised with regard to its effectiveness as a means of achieving change. Those responsible for effecting change in education will need to raise similar questions.

Some Possible Advantages

Acceptance. Through an approach such as suggested here, it is possible to obtain a greater degree of acceptance of the proposed change than might be possible through other approaches. If those concerned can be made aware of the need, and can see tangible evidence that the change will probably bring about the desired results, they are likely to accept it. Wider acceptance of the proposed change, therefore, is one perceived advantage.

Commonality of Purpose. Closely related to the above is the advantage of achieving clarity and commonality of goals or purposes. If the need is clearly set forth and understood, a mutuality of purpose is possible.

Some Possible Disadvantages

Lack of Relevance. Efforts with some demonstration projects in the past have proven to be ineffective in bringing about change on a wide scale. There is an apparent tendency for people to say, in effect, that "the practice of innovation may work in *that* situation, but *my* situation is different." Lack of effectiveness, in terms of limited spread of the practice, may be perceived as a disadvantage. The goals established by or for the demonstration effort may not concur with the perceived goals of the "clients" and, as a consequence, the demonstration efforts may have little perceived relevance.

Creation of Unreal Limitations. When diffusion or demonstration is used as a technique to effect change, there may be a tendency for the intended "clients" to perceive that which is being attempted in a narrow or literal sense. Limitations made necessary by factors in the demonstration situation may be perceived by the "clients" as necessary in any similar situation, even though there will undoubtedly be different factors in differing situations. If limitations are perceived in any such literal fashion, the alternative strategy described here will not be effective.

EFFECTING CHANGE THROUGH ATTITUDE MODIFICATION

 • *Resistance to a given change will be lessened if those who are likely to be affected by the change understand and accept the need for the change. It is possible to achieve such understanding through a deliberate educative or reeducative process.*

To people involved in the educative process, the merits of this strategy should be obvious because it is consistent with one of the basic concepts upon which the entire educational program (for students) is predicated. At the same time, however, *educators who work primarily with other educators tend to lose sight of the place and value of education in the change process.*

The concept, as used here, is much broader in nature than the term *education* typically denotes. It includes by implication other types of educational experiences such as participation in planning and decision making, sensitivity training and the T-group process. This concept has been expressed in varying ways by Chin, Howsam, Kimbrough, and others in the *Designing Education for the Future* series.[13]

As with any alternative procedure, the strategy of effecting change through educative or reeducative efforts has apparent advantages and disadvantages. The degree to which these are relevant in a particular situation undoubtedly will have a bearing on the acceptance or non-acceptance of the strategy.

Some Possible Advantages

Favorable Climate for Change. When a process of education is utilized in efforts to bring about a given educational change, there will likely be a better understanding among the public or publics involved of the need for the change. At the same time, through a process of education it is possible to help people to prepare for change. In either event, a more favorable climate for implementation of needed change is likely to be created.

Effectiveness. When people affected by a proposed change clearly understand the rationale behind the proposal, they are likely to support the change. Such support in turn will probably result in an *effective change process,* and in *effective implementation* of the change itself.

Greater Degree of Involvement. Closely related to the perceived advantages of climate and effectiveness is the advantage of *involvement.* It is through involvement that both (favorable climate and effectiveness) are gained. At the same time, it must be recognized that an educative process, properly utilized, facilitates such involvement. In this vein, this concept or alternative is advantageous.

Some Possible Disadvantages

Substantial Expenditure of Time. Perhaps in the minds of some people the most obvious disadvantage relating to the concept of utilizing the educative, or normative-reeducative, strategy as a means of effecting change is to be found in the length of time usually involved. The various processes which might be employed are likely to require a greater expenditure of time than may be perceived as being available, and as such, may not be considered to be realistic.

Possible Rejection. Another potential disadvantage of this alternative relates to the possibility of rejection, on the part of those affected, of "newer" types of educative processes. Such rejection may result from a lack of understanding of the process itself, a gross misuse of the process involved, or even from a sense of contentment with "things as they are." Whatever the cause, if and when such rejection occurs, much of the impetus (and understanding of the need) for change may be lost.

EFFECTING NEEDED CHANGES THROUGH IMPOSITION OF POWER

- *When sufficient power or pressure is applied in a given situation, people within that situation will react to the power or pressure in either a positive or negative manner. In either event, change, as a result of power or pressure, is possible.*

The concept of inducing or causing change by an imposition of power or authority is neither new nor unique. Throughout history absolute rulers have utilized the concept to bring about changes which they deemed to be desirable; it was embodied in the concepts of governance developed by Machiavelli; and it is to be found in many modern day organizations. It is, however, more commonly practiced within the military establishment than perhaps in any other type of organization.

While the concept as such may be repugnant to those who would consider *humaneness* a desirable feature in any change process, it nevertheless does offer some apparent or perceived advantages.

Some Possible Advantages

Some of the perceived advantages of using power or authority to effect needed changes are discussed in the paragraphs below:

Short-Range Efficiency. The use of power as a means of bringing about change implies that the decision-making authority rests either in a single person or agency, or in a small group of "elite." In such instances, no other human resources are needed to make the decision. A decision relating to change, having been made in a unilateral fashion, can be transmitted and implemented in rapid fashion.

Expediency. When a decision concerning a needed change has been made, the most expedient manner of implementation may be the process of communicating the decision from a superordinate to a subordinate. When the power of the decision maker is clearly established, the subordinate will be expected to attempt to implement the decision in a rapid and unquestioning manner.

Some Possible Disadvantages

Long-Range Inefficiency. Unless there is genuine acceptance of the identified change, it is doubtful that, in this country, changes brought about through imposition of power alone will be lasting in nature. Instead, such changes are likely to be ephemeral and almost entirely dependent upon the perceived motives of the person or persons in the power position at a given moment.

Ineffectiveness. Perhaps the more obvious disadvantage to be found in the concept of utilizing power or authority to effect a given change has already been implied: the concept is repugnant to people who realize they must work and associate *with* other people. If the process or method is not perceived as being desirable by those who are affected by it, there are likely to be varying degrees of resistance throughout the organization. Such resistance, however great or small, will result in a lessening of efficiency.

ANALYSIS OF ALTERNATIVE STRATEGIES

Three alternative strategies that might be employed to effect needed change have been presented and discussed. Some apparent advantages and disadvantages of each have been suggested for consideration by those who are, or will be, responsible for developing strategies for bringing about needed changes. The alternative strategies suggested do not constitute the total array of alternatives that are or may be available. Because of the obvious overlapping areas, there may be some necessity for strategies that are, in effect, combinations of those described. At the same time, totally different alternative strategies may be necessary, and will possibly emerge. It is imperative, therefore, that those responsible for implementing or effecting needed changes identify as many reasonable alternatives as possible, and that they consider each in terms of basic intent and probable effectiveness.

In the case of the alternative strategies presented here, the one based on power has some obvious advantages. The apparent advantages, however, are of a short-range as opposed to a long-range nature. If the objectives are related to expediency, and if there is no concern about the long-range effect, one might elect to use this alternative strategy. However, because significant educational changes are rarely without long-range effects, consideration must be given to identifying ways in which most lasting and beneficial effects may be obtained. With this in mind, the use of power as a means to effect meaningful educational change would seem in most situations to be an undesirable strategy.

The strategy of effecting desirable and needed change through participatory educative or reeducative efforts would appear to some people to counter the disadvantages noted in regard to the use of power. In terms of a long-range perspective, it is likely to be the most effective of the three alternative strategies. In terms of involvement, it offers more potential than the other two. Additionally, and more importantly, it would appear to facilitate the creation of a climate or environment that would be conducive to needed changes. The apparent advantages of this strategy would seem to greatly outweight the perceived disadvantages, and—in terms of overall effectiveness—it probably is the best of the three strategies presented.

The other strategy suggested—diffusion and demonstration—offers the potential advantage of gaining a greater degree of acceptance of change, but at the same time presents the decided disadvantage of "unreal" limitations. The potential disadvantages could have the effect of compounding, rather than minimizing, problems associated with effecting change. For this reason, it should be considered as being more desirable than the power or coercion strategy, but less desirable than the educative strategy.

IMPLICATIONS FOR EDUCATIONAL AGENCIES AND INSTITUTIONS

The overall objective of educational *planning* in, or sponsored by, any educational agency or institution is—or should be—that of enabling the agency or institution to arrive at, or at least move positively in the direction of, some pre-determined improvements in the educational program. The needed improvements, or goals, must be realistic in nature, and should be based on demonstrable *needs*. The needs—or at least an awareness of the needs—must be established before the overall goals are set. To proceed otherwise would result in meaningless—and often unattainable—goals.

Once the needs have been demonstrated and the goals defined, it is necessary that an orderly process or mechanism (an adequate or appropriate organization and procedures) be developed that will ensure expeditious attainment of the goals. State and local educational agencies, if they are to be successful in leadership efforts relating to effecting needed changes in education, must be organized in a manner that will facilitate the implementation of *planned* changes. Such an organizational pattern would require at least three fundamental components: (1) there must be provisions for analyzing the existing situation—the "what is"—and for identifying the discrepancies between "what is" and "what should be"; (2) the organization must provide for actual planning—designing procedures—that may reasonably be expected to reduce the apparent discrepancies; and (3) the organization must include provisions for implementing—and determining the value of—the plans or designs that have been formulated.

But while the components noted above are essential to successful planning *within* the organizational structure of an education agency, they are not the *only* considerations. As Wright and Furse[14] suggest in a recent monograph, the state education agency must include organizational provisions for:

- Developing internal planning mechanisms;
- Coordinating statewide educational planning; and
- Assisting others to develop comprehensive planning.

Unless a state or local education agency carefully considers and includes provisions for the essential components and relationships within its organizational framework, the results of any planning effort are likely to be ineffectual, and the needed changes will not be forthcoming. Education agencies may guard against such eventualities, however, if special attention is given to concepts such as the following.

• *Awareness of Need*

Howsam[15] has suggested that an educational institution or agency should include, in its staffing pattern, a position for at least one "educational heretic." According to Howsam, "the assigned task [would be] that of helping others in the organization to perceive things as they really are and thereby inducing efforts at improving conditions." The Chief State School Officer of Nevada made a similar observation:

> I think most legislators agree now that state departments of education certainly need to be agents of change and perhaps each one of these state departments of education should have within its component organization one set of individuals whose duty it is primarily, perhaps, to work for change and to afflict the comfortable to accomplish it.[16]

While a person in such a position—that is, an "educational heretic"—probably would not have responsibility for actually effecting a given or needed change, he would have, as a basic responsibility, the function of helping the people involved to understand, or develop an awareness of, the need for the change. *Unless provisions are made to accommodate this function, those who are likely to be most affected by a proposed change may not work actively toward its attainment.* To the contrary, they will probably work actively against it.

• *Collection and Analysis of Data*

Closely related to an awareness of need—if not an essential ingredient —is the necessity of a sound procedural arrangement for the orderly and systematic collection—and analysis—of information relative to the problem at hand. *Unless provisions for such a procedure are incorporated and utilized, there can be no rational bases for the myriad number of decisions that must be made within the state education agency.*

• *Determination of Defensible Alternative Procedures*

A state education agency that is concerned with planning for needed changes must include, or provide for, the capability of identifying reasonable or defensible alternatives (changes) that will likely lead toward the desired goal or goals. At the same time, however, the structure of the agency should include provisions for the determination of ways in which sound judgments relating to the identified alternatives may be made.

• *Development and Testing of Plans*

The state education agency—as well as other educational institutions —must have the capability of developing of plans, but at the same time it must also have the capability of testing—or determining the validity— of any plan. This should not imply that every plan developed within the agency, for example, must be tested *within* the agency. The organizational structure of the agency must, however, contain provisions whereby the necessary testing can be accomplished.

● *Dissemination of Worthwhile Practices*

If a plan has been developed for the purpose of bringing about a needed change, and if the testing of the plan has demonstrated that it does—or is likely to—produce the proposed change and that the change would be beneficial, there should be, within the agency, a mechanism through which the plan might be implemented where similar needs are determined to exist.

Some educational leaders refer to this process (or mechanism) as diffusion. Still others use the phrase, "spread of practice." However it is described, the basic purpose, in reality, is that of helping others who face similar problems to become aware of the potentiality and availability. Too often, the "wheel is re-invented" merely because of a difference in geographical locale. Methods of avoiding "re-invention of the wheel" must be found; the agency or organization must include provisions for effective dissemination or diffusion practices if the complete cycle of planning for needed changes is to occur.

SUMMARY AND CONCLUSIONS

As has already been implied, there are numerous ways in which an organization, agency or institution may plan for a needed change. The most desirable way—or strategy—is the one which brings about the needed change in the most effective and meaningful manner. In order to accomplish this purpose, the organization must have the capability to identify, develop and utilize reasonable strategies that will facilitate accomplishment or attainment of the task or goals.

In developing appropriate strategies for change, considerable emphasis must be given to the processes of—and to the interrelationships between —planning and change. In addition to the need for an understanding of the interrelationships, however, there is an equally important concept that must be considered—*the relationship of the environment to change.* Every change will occur in some type of environment. Should the environment be *conducive* to a needed change, ways should be found to utilize favorable environmental factors as *facilitating forces.* On the other hand, should the environment be *resistant* to a needed change, strategies will have to be designed that will tend to decrease the resistance or factors which contribute to the resistance. It is imperative that educational leaders, as they attempt to develop appropriate strategies designed to implement needed change, consider all of these factors and relationships.

State and local education agency personnel with the responsibility for leadership in planning and implementing needed improvements in education will have to look upon planning as only a means to an end; not merely an end in and of itself. At the same time, if planning is properly perceived as being only a *means,* it is essential that personnel who have been given primary responsibility for this type of planning clearly understand the *relationships that exist between planning—the means—and the needed change—the end.*

The relationships between the necessary processes must be clearly understood by all concerned. Unless this understanding exists, and unless educational leaders deliberately strive to create mechanisms in which the processes can be interwoven and function in concert with each other, planning undoubtedly will continue to be a professed "good." It will be actively sought and supported. However, planning efforts that do not recognize the close interrelationship between planning and change are not likely to result in tangible or significant improvements.

Footnote References

[1]Marvin Adelson, *Educational Ends and Innovative Means* (Santa Monica, California: System Development Corporation, 1967), p. 25.

[2]Adapted from unpublished paper prepared for the project, *Improving State Leadership in Education,* by Walt LeBaron.

[3]Leonard J. Duhl, "Planning and Predicting," *Daedalus,* Summer 1967, p. 780.

[4]John I. Goodlad, "Studying and Effecting Educational Change," *Changing Schools* (UCLA), March 1971, p. 3.

[5]*Ibid.,* p. 2.

[6]See for example, R. Havelock, *Planning for Innovation* (Ann Arbor, Michigan: University of Michigan, 1969).

[7]Adapted from an unpublished paper prepared for the project, *Improving State Leadership in Education,* by Charles Jung.

[8]Warren G. Bennis, "A Typology of Change Processes," in *The Planning of Change,* Warren G. Bennis, Kenneth D. Benne, and Robert Chin, eds. (Holt, Rhinehart and Winston, Inc., New York, N.Y., 1961), p. 154.

[9]Robert B. Howsam, "Effecting Needed Changes in Education," in *Planning and Effecting Needed Changes in Education,* Edgar L. Morphet and Charles O. Ryan, eds. (Denver, Colorado: Designing Education for the Future, 1967), p. 71. Reprinted by Citation Press, Scholastic Magazines, Inc., New York, N.Y.

[10]Robert Chin, "Basic Strategies and Procedures in Effecting Change," in *Planning and Effecting Needed Changes in Education, op. cit.,* p. 43ff.

[11]*Ibid.,* p. 43ff.

[12]Egon G. Guba, *The Basis for Educational Improvement* (Bloomington, Indiana: The National Institute for the Study of Educational Change, 1967), p. 2.

[13]See especially *Planning and Effecting Needed Changes in Education, op. cit.*

[14]Lyle O. Wright and Bernarr S. Furse, eds., *Developing Comprehensive Planning Capabilities in State Education Agencies* (Salt Lake City, Utah: Utah State Board of Education, 1969).

[15]Robert B. Howsam, "Effecting Needed Changes in Education," in *Planning and Effecting Needed Changes in Education, op. cit.,* p. 76.

[16]Burnell Larson, in *Report of the First Annual Conference on PPBES in Education* (Chicago: Research Corporation of Association of School Business Officials, 1969), p. 75.

PART FOUR

STATE ROLE IN IMPROVING MAJOR ASPECTS OF EDUCATION

Chapter 9

The Facilitation of Relevant Learning

John Gardner has noted that "Most human societies have been beautifully organized to keep good men down" and that, while some individuals have found a way through the barriers, on the whole these societies "have severely and successfully limited the realization of individual promise."[1]* Probably in no society was this concept stated as a policy. Instead it was implemented by establishing hereditary privileges and developing other devices and attitudes that made the full realization of individual potential impossible for substantial numbers of people.

In societies and nations in which the concept of special privileges for favored groups has prevailed, most of the "leaders" saw no need to provide much formal education for the masses. They believed that even a little learning of the kind encouraged for the ruling classes could become "a dangerous thing"—and would constitute a threat to these groups. A few people in this country apparently continue to hold that point of view. For example, one speaker was quoted in a recent interview as saying: "We are in danger of producing an educated proletariat. That's dynamite!"

The industrial revolution that required the leadership and services of competent persons regardless of their status in a stratified society, the evolution of religious and social concepts that recognized the dignity and potential worth of every individual, and many other related developments began to undermine and discredit the tradition of hereditary privileges— especially in some of the nations in Western Europe. Many of those who came to settle along the eastern coast of this continent were in revolt against "the establishment"—or at least against the tradition of providing special privileges for those who controlled the governments and even the religious and industrial organizations. When these settlers created a new nation following the revolution, they generally agreed that it should be a

---

*Footnote references are given at end of the chapter.

137

democracy—a government of, by and for the people. Many of the leaders were convinced that some education should be provided for every citizen partly because they believed that the kind of government and nation they envisioned could not be expected to develop satisfactorily if only a small proportion of the people had an opportunity for any kind of education.

But, as this society has become more complex and the nation more prosperous, major problems relating to education have continued and, in some respects, have became increasingly acute. These include:

- The provisions for the organization and operation of education and the procedures for facilitating instruction and learning have changed too slowly to meet the needs of the nation—partly because urgently needed changes often have been resisted not only by some educators and educational organizations but also by many lay citizens and political leaders.

- Some people apparently are neither willing to accord a high priority to the need for modernizing education, nor to support financially or otherwise significant efforts to achieve excellence in all aspects of education.

- A substantial number of students and other young people do not currently seem to attach a high value to formal education—perhaps partly because of the attitudes of their parents or peers or because the present provisions and procedures do not sufficiently challenge them or meet their needs.

- Some people apparently do not believe in much education for minority or other disadvantaged groups, and seek in various ways to perpetuate their own special privileges and prerogatives even though these may severely limit the realization of individual promise for others.

Since, in this country, the citizens of each state are primarily responsible for the appropriateness and adequacy of the provisions for the education of the people who live in the state, major attention in this chapter is devoted to the roles, responsibilities and relations of the states and state education agencies in planning and effecting improvements in learning opportunities and procedures and in evaluating progress.

PURPOSES AND GOALS OF EDUCATION

In traditional or static societies the major purpose of education is to transmit the social and cultural heritage. In free dynamic societies, this purpose must be modified and expanded not only in the statements made about education but in the minds and hearts of all citizens. *The major purpose of education in these societies should be to help each and every member to develop fully his capacity and talents and to learn to utilize them creatively and continuously to improve himself and society* by:

- Helping to identify and discard elements of the social and cultural heritage that are no longer relevant to the changing needs and may handicap or prevent needed changes. (Examples include racial, religious and class prejudices, and the traditions and attitudes that perpetuate inequalities in educational and economic opportunities);

- Cooperating in a continuous search for new and constructive solutions or appropriate ways of resolving present and emerging problems. (Examples include environmental pollution, the continuing threat of war, stultifying bureaucratic policies and procedures, and ineffective or handicapping educational policies and practices); and

- Seeking continuously to create a favorable environment for learning, and to provide for and help to encourage excellence through appropriate provisions in all aspects and levels of education for every individual.

The members of every society, directly or indirectly, determine the scope, kind and quality of education that is to be provided, who is to participate and to what extent. *If the citizens of any nation agree on the importance of high quality in education and in other aspects of life in the society and have competent and creative leadership, they can at least closely approach the goal of excellence.* On the other hand if they are willing to tolerate inept leadership, inefficient organizational policies and procedures, and low standards in instruction and learning—or in the political, industrial and economic realms of society—that is exactly what they will have. They can never expect excellence to be attained except perhaps in a few communities and areas, and even these may be in danger of having to yield to the lower standards and expectations of the majority.

The purposes and goals of a society and of its educational institutions tend to be interrelated. A society that demands excellence in government, in business and in industries will insist on excellence in its schools, colleges and other provisions for education. *The best hope for progress in a society that has tolerated low standards in some aspects of life is for the people to demand and attempt to provide for excellence in all aspects of education.* Eventually high quality education for everyone can help to raise the standards and expectations throughout the society.

GOALS FOR EXCELLENCE IN EDUCATION

The previous statements concerning the major purpose of education express an ideal, a hope and, in fact, a necessity under modern conditions. The tough question is: How can this hope be implemented in a society in which many people readily subscribe verbally to most statements about ideals but do little to help to attain them? *Many of our current difficulties have arisen because of the wide gaps between what many people say they believe and what they actually do in every day life.* There is an urgent need to find ways to narrow and, as promptly as possible, to eliminate these dangerous gaps not only in education but also in other aspects of society.

Some of the urgently needed steps are:

- To find appropriate ways of helping at least a majority of the citizens to reach agreement on the national, state and local goals that must be attained if the major purposes of education are to be achieved;

- To state the goals and objectives clearly, and to identify the strategies and procedures that are most appropriate for the attainment of each; and

- To find optimum ways of helping every individual to make a deep and abiding commitment to the attainment of each goal and of the major purposes of every aspect of education and of society. Without such commitment there is little probability that the purposes and goals will ever be attained.

One of the first steps in planning for excellence in education should be to obtain the cooperation of representatives of all groups that should be concerned in attempting to reach agreement on appropriate purposes and goals of education—on the qualities future citizens should possess—and on ways of getting commitment to their attainment. For years there have been numerous statements about purposes and goals, but apparently only limited commitment by substantial numbers of people to many of them. The present situation seems to be somewhat like that described by Aristotle more than two thousand years ago:

> All people do not agree on those things a child should be taught, both with respect to improvement in virtue and a happy life; nor is it clear whether the object of it should be to improve the reason or rectify the morals.

There must be goals for individuals as well as goals for society. Bebell has suggested these should include: intellectual or the commonly accepted "academic" goals; practical goals concerned with meaningful living in a highly complex society; personal goals in areas of achievement that are uniquely valuable to the individual; and moral or ethical goals.[2]

Gibson has proposed that *all goals be concerned with the dimensions of human quality:* the quality of the person as a human being; the quality of the skills he needs; the quality of his knowledge, including the bodies of information about man and society; the quality of learning, perceiving and thinking; and civic quality concerned with what is needed for him to become an effective citizen.[3]

ROLE OF STATE EDUCATION AGENCIES

The determination of the major purposes, goals and objectives of education cannot safely be left entirely to the people in the thousands of communities or local school systems throughout the nation. If this were done, the quality of education would tend to be diluted by the limited perceptions and perspectives of people in areas in which there is little or no real insight into what is needed to ensure excellence in education for everyone.

The major national purposes, goals and priorities are proposed in general terms by national leaders and committees, but those that are accepted must be supported by a majority of the citizens if they are to be implemented. Moreover, many of the national goals are not likely to be attained without state and local initiative and action. *A major responsibility of every state education agency should be to devise procedures that are designed not only to ensure agreement on and help to implement national purposes and goals pertaining to education, but also to obtain agreement on and lead in implementing appropriate state goals and to assist local school systems to develop and implement any other supplementary goals they consider desirable.* This seems to be an essential procedure if we are to move vigorously toward the attainment of excellence in education throughout the nation.

More specifically, each state, and especially the state education agency, has an obligation and should be prepared to:

- Arrange for appropriate committees or task forces to study current and prospective changes in society, and to assist them to ascertain the implications for educational goals and procedures;

- Encourage and help the citizens and officials of the state to agree upon appropriate national goals and priorities for education and to join with the citizens of other states in insisting that the federal government take the steps, including the provision of funds, needed to facilitate implementation;

- Provide for a competent representative committee or committees to develop and propose pertinent and meaningful goals and objectives for education in the state, suggest periodic revisions as deemed necessary, and cooperate in ensuring the acceptance and implementation of those agreed upon as essential; and

- Assist local school systems and colleges of education to develop and implement their own supplementary statements of goals and objectives.

The development and acceptance of pertinent and meaningful statements of goals and objectives is one of the basic steps that must be taken if excellence in education is to be achieved in every community and state and throughout the nation. Unless these goals and objectives are relevant to the needs of a changing society they will soon have little meaning for many people. Moreover, unless they are clearly stated it will be impossible to determine what progress is being made. And unless they are accepted by most of the students and staff of each school system and the citizens in every community they will have little impact on, or few implications for, the society they should benefit.

THE ENVIRONMENT FOR LEARNING

Some of the problems and challenges in modern society arise from the fact that the purposes and goals of education (which tend to reflect national purposes) in certain nations differ considerably from those in others. Some of these differences are stimulating rather than harmful, but others contribute to international and sometimes even to internal tensions and conflicts.

Many of the problems in nations that seek to foster a free dynamic society stem from the fact that the citizens often differ so greatly in perspectives and points of view that it is difficult to obtain majority agreement on and commitment to a realistic, well balanced and meaningful statement of appropriate goals. The establishment of priorities often presents even more difficult problems. Bebell, after noting that most goal statements represent generalizations and that many of these are viewed by some people as threatening, observed:

> Educational goals include emotional as well as intellectual areas, but their implementation is so difficult, especially in the emotional areas, as to create almost insurmountable difficulties.[4]

This confused and confusing situation is part of the environment in which education must function in this country. But, in addition to the mixed attitudes and expectations regarding education found to some extent in all communities and states, there are other important physical, socio-economic and intellectual-emotional factors, some of which have almost been ignored in planning and conducting educational programs.[5] In many school systems the personnel seem to have naively assumed that by being diligent and conscientious they can "educate" all students for which they are responsible, regardless of the environmental factors and conditions that may make their best efforts almost meaningless.

While the schools cannot directly control unfavorable *external* environmental conditions—in the homes, in the neighborhoods, on the streets, in organizations or even in governmental agencies—they cannot afford to ignore them. *If learning is to be significantly improved for many students, those who are involved in education must be sufficiently creative to find ways of working effectively with parents, with peer groups and with various organizations and agencies to improve the standards, expectations and conditions in the community.* If they fail to do so, their efforts to facilitate meaningful learning opportunities and experiences for substantial numbers of students will be all but wasted.

The school systems and schools are in a position to control within reasonable limits many of the *internal* environmental conditions that affect learning and should make every effort to ensure that they are as favorable as possible. School systems should: employ and encourage teachers who not only are skilled and effective facilitators of learning but also are deeply interested in all students regardless of their racial origin, economic circumstance or ability; provide a supporting staff comprised of competent professionals who are interested in helping teachers and students rather than in perpetuating bureaucratic traditions and policies; and provide the kind of facilities, equipment and supplies that are needed to facilitate learning and help the staff and students learn how to utilize them effectively. In fact, they can and should constantly seek and encourage in many innovative ways to create a more favorable environment for the achievement of excellence in all aspects of education for everyone concerned.

The citizens in every local school system can also help to improve the internal environment for education by selecting for service on the school board only competent people who are genuinely interested in improving education and insisting that they adopt appropriate policies, select competent staff members, provide modern facilities, attempt to provide adequate financial support, and take other steps that are essential to improve learning opportunities for all students. When necessary, the citizens should also insist that the legislature not only remove (or avoid) restrictions that prevent or retard needed improvements but also make available sufficient funds from state non-property tax sources to enable the system to provide adequate housing, programs and services without an excessive or unreasonable local tax effort.

State Role in Improving the Environment

Because favorable environmental factors and conditions throughout the state are essential if optimum learning opportunities are to be provided for all students—and unfavorable conditions tend to persist in many communities—it seems essential that all state education agencies make every reasonable effort to help to effect improvements, especially in the significant social factors and forces. The steps and procedures in most states probably should include:

1. Selecting a competent and representative task force or committee to (a) identify the external and internal environmental forces and conditions that tend to restrict or deny meaningful learning opportunities for students, (b) develop and propose a comprehensive plan that includes alternative ways of minimizing or eliminating these conditions, and (c) suggest steps and procedures for implementing the plan— that is, for creating a more favorable environment for learning throughout the state;

2. Seriously seeking to obtain the cooperation of, and to find ways of cooperating with, appropriate state and other agencies and groups in improving various aspects of the environment; and

3. Finding and utilizing more effective ways of cooperating with and providing services to local school systems in conducting studies and de-

veloping procedures that will assist them in improving the environment for learning.

The Curriculum, Instruction and Learning

The curriculum, instructional procedures and learning are closely related in many ways. Both the curriculum and the instructional procedures should be designed and utilized to facilitate and optimize meaningful learning for all kinds of students at all levels. Both must be modified and improved continuously as new insights are gained from experience or research findings, or as conditions and needs change. Fortunately the fact that the educational program must be dynamic and relevant to changing needs has been clearly recognized by many people and some significant improvements have been made during recent years.

The Curriculum

The traditional curriculum, even in the elementary and secondary schools, has been rather closely related to the disciplines developed by scholars in the generally recognized fields or subjects of study. Curriculum development (planning) for many years consisted primarily of a series of segmented operations based largely upon the subjects to be "taught"—with relatively little attention devoted to the totality (the meaningful relationships among the several segmented parts)[6]. Moreover the curriculum at all levels has been primarily a result of the continuation of many long established traditions (some of which are no longer defensible), and of a series of decisions made in a context of conflicting sets of values and interests and in the presence of a multiplicity of competing demands and concerns.

Curriculum revision should have two major purposes: (1) facilitating the attainment of pertinent statements of the purposes, goals and objectives of education; and (2) ensuring that appropriate provisions are made for learning experiences designed to meet the needs of *each* student and of the changing society in which he will live. *Curricular changes must therefore be systematically planned*—not made merely on the basis of isolated revisions in segments of the educational program—and designed to meet emerging as well as present needs.

Tumin has perceptively commented:

There is one major question to ask when choosing curriculum: What do we want our children to become? If we translate this question into somewhat more operational questions, these would include: What do we want our children to come to *value?* What do we want them to be able to *feel and see and hear and smell and touch?* From what do we want them to learn to get pleasure? What do we want them to *understand* about *themselves and the world of nature and man?* How do we want them to *behave* toward *other human beings?* To what do we want them to be inclined to *commit themselves?* What technical *abilities* do we wish to *cultivate* in them?[7]

Parker and McGuire included the following among the concepts they consider to be crucial to all decisions concerning the appropriateness and totality of any curriculum plans:

- Some things are more important than others—that is, more relevant to the learning needs of individuals; moreover, some are more difficult and complex and take much longer to learn than others.

- Individuals differ in many respects; success and achievement are the most effective motivators with the possible exception of "acceptance."

- How people learn to relate to each other is basic to progress toward the solutions of our problems of living together.

- In any efforts to plan improvements in the curriculum there must be more consideration of and emphasis upon *the present* as a basis for giving appropriate attention to *the emerging future.*

- Most situations are problem oriented and choices among alternatives must be made; *the generation, creation, and development of new or different alternatives* (ideas) *may be the most crucial dimension of the future.*

- Curriculum planning for the future must include provisions for educating people to deal constructively with change.

- The curriculum should help students learn to accept freedom and responsibility and to make rational and defensible decisions.[8]

Bebell has commented that many changes, including the following, should be made in the curriculum if it is to meet emerging needs:

- The future will demand citizens who have been trained to *think* rather than primarily to remember. (Increasingly the information available to an individual while he is in school will become outmoded, irrelevant or superseded before his working life is over.)

- The curriculum should be based *more upon process* than it has been in the past.

- There should be an increasing focus and emphasis on the development of high quality in elementary education; secondary-school curriculums should be less oriented toward traditional academic fields and increasingly toward other areas.

- Both teachers and students should have greater flexibility in curricular planning; there should be greater independence on the part of each learner in building his own program.

- There should be greater emphasis on developing a curriculum that will recognize and meet all important human needs and facilitate international understanding.[9]

Modernizing the curriculum is a difficult and complex but exceedingly important undertaking. Vested interest groups undoubtedly will resist some of the needed changes but substantial numbers of people are convinced that major improvements are essential at all levels. *A dynamic society cannot afford a static and increasingly obsolete curriculum for the education of its youth,* many of whom will help to determine the destiny of the nation not only during the remainder of the present century but also during the early part of the next century.

Many local school systems have already made important changes, and national committees and groups have proposed other modifications, some of which are being implemented. But progress will be slow, piecemeal and poorly coordinated in many school systems unless state education agencies, with the cooperation of representatives from institutions of higher learning and other appropriate groups and consultants, provide the leadership and services needed to ensure that the curriculum throughout the state is planned systematically in an effort to make certain that all aspects contribute maximally to the attainment of appropriate goals for education, and is relevant to the needs of students who are living in a dynamic society.

INSTRUCTION AND LEARNING

On the basis of a recent study sponsored by the Carnegie Corporation, Silberman concluded that most schools are so preoccupied with order and discipline that they neglect *real* education. He stated:

> It is not possible to spend any prolonged period visiting public school classrooms without being appalled by the . . . mutilation of spontaneity, of joy in learning, of pleasure in creating, of sense of self. . . . Because adults take the schools so much for granted, they fail to appreciate what grim, joyless places most American schools are . . . what contempt they unconsciously display for children as children.[10]

These observations are intended to apply to an organization that in many unfortunate respects has tended to become tradition-bound and bureaucratic, and to those members of the organization who go through the accustomed rituals associated with learning but fail to consider many of the human factors involved in attempting to stimulate and challenge individuals who differ in many subtle ways. Moreover, they serve as an indictment of those members of a rapidly changing society who are eager to benefit personally from promising discoveries and inventions but are skeptical about, and may even discourage, promising changes in educational policies and practices.

For many generations, the classroom has provided a controlled setting for the presentation of information from a single source (the teacher) to multiple receivers (the students), with the kind of feedback and criteria for success in learning determined primarily by that single source. The traditional concept of "teaching"—that is, one who "knows" telling those who do not know, then commending the few who remember most of what nas been said—is still widely accepted by many people including a substantial number of elementary and secondary school teachers and university professors. Yet, in most instances, there are far better and more effective ways of facilitating learning. Some educators (as well as many others) apparently never bother to think seriously about whether what they are doing actually is being done in the most effective and meaningful way. To paraphrase Silberman, what is mostly wrong with many schools and colleges is "mindlessness—a failure to think seriously about purposes or consequences."

All normal children are eager to learn and, with appropriate help and encouragement, will continue to expand their range of interests and their joy in learning. As Tumin has observed, instead of relying on traditional procedures and notions of fixed, uni-dimensional ability, we should think instead "of the interaction between a child, the teacher and the experiences called the curriculum as *a process of the continuous creation and recreation of new domains and dimensions of capacity.*"[11]

There are many constructive ways of facilitating learning. Some are more appropriate for certain kinds and conditions of learning and for certain students or groups of students (minorities or other culturally disadvantaged, for example) than others. Unfortunately some counter-productive ways of attempting to prod students into more active learning—such as nagging, ridicule and threats of punishment—are still rather commonly used and often result in antagonisms and even withdrawal from the formal education process. It should not be considered surprising that some of the younger students learn to dislike schools and that many older students rebel against "the system," or drop out of school as soon as possible.

The citizens in every community should insist that the board and school officials encourage, support and assist instructional personnel to find and utilize all feasible ways of helping every student to progress in meaningful learning. These should include, as appropriate, the carefully planned utilization of differentiated staffing, paraprofessionals, teaching and student assistants, parents, team teaching, computer-assisted instruction, a wide range of interesting reading, audio and visual materials, skilled counselors, in-service preparation and upgrading programs—in fact, every feasible way of helping every student to become interested and make satisfactory progress in learning. A school system that neglects these basic obligations should be recognized as failing to meet its responsibilities not only to its students but also to the public it should serve.

The goals in and for learning are now recognized in most schools as including not only cognitive learning, but also many other aspects of learning. The failure to find ways of helping all students with learning in the non-cognitive or affective domain—with the development and evaluation of personal goals, of moral and ethical values, of appropriate habits and emotional and intellectual attitudes, of wholesome interpersonal relations—still constitutes a major and unfortunate weakness in many school systems. In earlier societies and during previous generations in this society, it was possible for the churches, homes and schools—by a process of indoctrination or persuasion—to impose traditionally sanctioned and accepted moral and ethical values on most members of the younger generation. In modern pluralistic societies this procedure often is no longer effective. *There is currently a dangerous and apparently growing gap between the verbal expressions and the actual behavior of many people that threatens the stability of society and the well-being of its members.*

The schools, in cooperation with parents and other groups, have a major obligation to help to find effective ways of assisting every student to develop a value system that is compatible with his own needs and aspirations and with those of the society in which he will live. Some other implications for instruction and learning include:

- Making adequate provisions for early childhood and kindergarten education as a means of helping to avoid later learning problems;

- Providing for increasing amounts of meaningful student participation and activity in the learning process including greater use of the "discovery" method, student selected projects, independent study, group work, class discussions of important issues, field experiences and so on;

- Helping students and teachers to learn how to raise and attempt to find answers to appropriate questions;

- Providing for much more individualization of instruction;

- Helping teachers to re-examine and improve their teaching styles;

- Helping students to develop a constructive self-image;

- Placing much greater and more realistic emphasis on non-cognitive learning;

- Encouraging teachers to emphasize goals that have the highest priority without neglecting the others;

- Devoting much greater attention to appropriate instructional processes and conditions, and giving less emphasis to the formal qualifications of teachers; and

- Giving more attention to a well-balanced and appropriate program of continuous learning and placing less emphasis, especially in the secondary schools and in adult and higher education, on a narrow academic disciplinary approach. Toynbee, after discussing the emphasis on specialization in higher education, cautioned that "the price of specialization is a myopic and distorted view of the Universe. An effective specialist makes, all too often, a defective citizen and an inadequate human being."[12]

ROLE OF STATE EDUCATION AGENCIES

Improving the curriculum, instruction and learning procedures must be clearly recognized as a *vital, continuous and cooperative process* in every state. This process has many facets, and each must be carefully designed to facilitate to the maximum extent possible the achievement of the purposes and goals of education that are relevant to the needs of a pluralistic society.

Each state, therefore, will need to develop, deliberately and systematically, appropriate and carefully coordinated plans for effecting continuous improvements in these areas. The state education agency in every state should be in a position to provide the leadership and services needed to develop these plans and ensure that they are revised, as necessary, to take into consideration new developments and insights. It should also be in a position to assist not only local school systems but also colleges and universities to improve their own programs and procedures.

Among the important responsibilities of state education agencies in this context are the following:

- Include on the staff especially competent and recognized leaders who are familiar with significant programs and developments throughout the nation and can help universities, local school systems and committees to identify needs and to plan and effect improvements;

- Select, on the basis of appropriate criteria, competent and representative committees to advise on, or assist in, developing policies and programs;

- With the cooperation of college and university and local school personnel, identify and develop, or adapt as necessary, a variety of audio-visual and other curricular and instructional materials and procedures and facilitate their use throughout the state;

- With the cooperation of appropriate groups, develop criteria for identifying especially promising instructional and learning procedures, and encourage school personnel to become familiar with and utilize these procedures;

- Assist local school personnel to learn how to identify and utilize community resources, including parents and students, in improving the educational program; and

- Encourage in every way possible the development of promising innovative procedures for improving learning and making it more meaningful for all students.

THE PREPARATION AND CERTIFICATION OF EDUCATORS

The programs and procedures utilized in preparing educators can handicap or facilitate the provision of adequate learning opportunities for students during coming years. In fact, some of the current problems and difficulties in effecting improvements in learning result from inappropriate policies and practices in preparing and certifying educators that are still continued in some states and institutions. Reorienting educators to modern needs, concepts and procedures through in-service programs is a slow and difficult process.

One of the basic difficulties arises from the commonly recognized fact that programs for preparing educators have had a low priority in many institutions of higher learning, and often have not been considered very "respectable" by many university officials and professors in other disciplines. Fawcett and Corbally have commented:

> The recognition that it may be possible to 'prepare educators' is honored by the creation of colleges of 'Education' but ignored in preparing educators to teach at the college level. . . . In general, the relationships between the university professor of education and the educationist in the field have either been strained or nonexistent.[13]

Some schools and colleges of education have what seems to many to be a "hodgepodge" of courses and credits including a number that, if completed satisfactorily, will enable a prospective educator to be certificated to teach certain subjects or at certain levels, or to perform some other kind of professional service in education. Under these circumstances it should not be surprising that many people who meet the requirements for teaching seem to be more interested in teaching "subject matter" to promising students in their own areas of specialization than in facilitating meaningful learning for all students. Moreover, few education faculties seem to have developed a realistic plan for obtaining systematic feedback concerning the performance of their graduates as facilitators of learning in various kinds of situations.

What should be the purposes and goals of programs and procedures for the preparation of educators? How should these be related to the purposes and goals for elementary and secondary schools and for other aspects of education? How can the effectiveness of programs and procedures be determined unless the goals have been agreed upon and clearly stated?

Some schools and colleges of education are attempting to deal realistically with issues such as these as a basis for planning systematically for improvements in their own programs and for determining the adequacy and effectiveness of these provisions. Moreover, they are recognizing that an "ivory tower" approach to the solution of these problems is neither appropriate nor realistic. They are seeking the cooperation and assistance of representatives from state education agencies, people serving in local school systems, and other appropriate groups.

Some of the other promising procedures include:

• **Cooperating** with state education agencies, local school systems and other groups in planning and conducting realistic studies dealing with problems relating to current and emerging needs and alternative ways of meeting them, with learning problems encountered in various kinds of situations, and with many other pertinent matters;

- Devoting much more attention to major issues and their interrelationship and implications for education than to the study of historical developments except as a means of providing background and perspectives;

- Providing, with the cooperation of local school systems and other groups, practical experience and guidance for their students in various kinds of situations, and relating these experiences intimately to their programs and courses in the institutions of higher learning;

- Helping their students to become informed about, determine the implications of, and utilize various kinds of multimedia and technological devices and materials in different learning situations; and

- Providing opportunities for prospective educators and others to serve as members of a team in dealing with practical situations, to work with paraprofessionals, parents, administrators, counselors and others, and to become involved in individualized instruction.

Certification or credentialing of educators in a number of states has been largely a routine matter of checking on required courses taken and the accumulated hours of credit for those who have met the requirements of the institutions they attended. There seems to have been little or no attempt made in those states or institutions to determine whether these people are prepared emotionally, professionally or otherwise to assume the responsibility for serving directly or indirectly as facilitators of learning over a period of years for substantial numbers of students.

Some state education agencies, institutions of higher learning, local school systems and professional organizations have cooperated during the past few years in an attempt to develop a new plan and procedures for certification. There seems to be substantial agreement that both teacher preparation and certification programs should be primarily concerned with finding valid ways of determining the individual's *ability to perform effectively* as a teacher, or in some other professional capacity, instead of merely stating the experiences he has had or should have. A few states have been engaged in a serious effort to develop criteria and procedures to be utilized in performance-based teacher certification.[14] The Washington State Board of Education, for example, has recently approved guidelines for certification based upon performance objectives and behavioral outcomes. These standards are unique in several respects including: (1) they are *process-oriented;* (2) they emphasize and encourage appropriate changes; and (3) they place evaluation in its proper perspective as an integral part of the feedback process within preparation. They also include, by implication, a new design for in-service preparation that provides for state education agency-institutional-local school system and professional organization cooperation, and for state collaboration in providing financial support.

ROLE OF STATE EDUCATION AGENCIES

Among its many important responsibilities in this area, the state education agency in every state should be expected especially to provide the leadership and services needed to:

- Obtain the cooperation of knowledge representatives from local school systems in encouraging and assisting all institutions of higher learning to modernize and give high priority to their programs for the preparation of educators, including paraprofessionals and various kinds of specialists;

- Revise and modernize provisions for the certification of educators to place appropriate emphasis on evaluation of competencies based on valid performance criteria, and far less on courses and credits; and

- Help local school systems to find appropriate ways of giving special encouragement and assistance to teachers and other professional employees—especially during their first few years of service—and to obtain guidance and assistance in developing appropriate in-service programs.

EVALUATION AND ACCOUNTABILITY

Most attention until recently has been devoted to the evaluation of students on the basis of their scores on various kinds of tests and examinations and an appraisal of their class contributions and conduct. Thus, students have been graded or "labeled," often quite early in their school careers, and unfortunately the original classifications have tended to persist. Customarily, students have been primarily responsible or accountable for their own successes or failures. Most authorities agree that this procedure is neither reasonable nor defensible in the light of what is now known about conditions that affect learning—that it is simply an indefensible tradition that has been established and perpetuated without adequate consideration of the rationale or implications.

Actually the citizens of a state and members of the legislature are responsible and should be held accountable for providing—or failing to provide—adequate arrangements or sufficient resources to make possible a relevant and reasonably adequate program of education and appropriate opportunities for all students regardless of their handicaps. The citizens of a local school system, the board of education and the school officials should be held accountable for policies and practices that recognize—or fail to recognize—or meet special needs. Teachers and counselors should be held accountable for finding—or failing to find—ways of maximizing learning opportunities and progress for the students they are expected to serve. And students should be accountable for cooperation in self-evaluation, for reasonable commitments to make progress in appropriate aspects of learning, and for meeting these commitments.

Evaluation should, therefore, be concerned with: (1) the arrangements and provisions for education nationally, in each state, in each institution that prepares educators, in each school system, and in each school; (2) the contributions of each teacher and staff member; and (3) the progress of each student in attaining goals and objectives that are agreed upon. As Tumin has observed, *"evaluation must include not only a determination of the end product of a process but also an understanding and appreciation of what elements and facets of the process have contributed to what aspects of the outcome."*[15]

Thus, *evaluation must be concerned with the process as a basis for appraising the product.* The ultimate criterion of educational accomplishment is the later life of each individual. In the meantime, however, appropriate procedures must be devised and utilized to measure and evaluate (1) the progress of each student day by day, month by month and year by year in every aspect of learning, and (2) the contributions (strengths and weaknesses) of the provisions and procedures utilized in education in terms of the progress made in attaining pertinent goals. A necessary condition for accountability is that the responsibility for organizational and individual goal achievement be agreed upon and assigned as appropriate to students, members of the organization and others who are in a position to contribute. Thus, *accountability is "an assignable, measurable responsibility to be fulfilled under certain conditions and within certain constraints."*[16]

ROLE OF STATE EDUCATION AGENCIES

Every state education agency, institution of higher learning, local school system and school should be held responsible for planning and providing adequate and effective learning opportunities and procedures for all students. This responsibility must be met as promptly and realistically as possible. In this important effort, state education agencies should be prepared to provide the necessary leadership and services, but will need the cooperation and assistance of many other groups and must be in a position to provide guidance and assistance to all local school systems in the state. Dyer[17] has proposed that the major purposes of such programs should be to:

- Provide basic information for helping every student in the state assess his own progress through the educational system of the state so that he can become increasingly mature in understanding himself, his educational needs, and his future possibilities.

- Provide the teachers and administrators in every school system with basic information for assessing the effectiveness of all the principal phases of their educational programs in sufficient detail to indicate the specific steps required for continually strengthening those programs.

- Provide the state education agency with the basic information needed for allocating state funds and professional services in a manner best calculated to equalize educational opportunities for all children in all school systems of the state.

- Provide research agencies at both the state and local levels with data for generating and testing hypotheses concerning the improvement of all aspects of the educational process.

- Provide every school system with strong incentives to experiment, under controlled conditions, with new and promising educational programs, materials, devices, and organizational arrangements.

- Periodically provide the state legislature and the general public with readily interpretable information concerning the progress of the state system of education as a whole and of each local school system.

THE CHANGING STATE ROLE AND FUNCTIONS

One major function of state education agencies is to lead in developing defensible goals and policies and, at the same time, in providing for needed diversity in education. Each state agency can and should become a major force within the state to encourage the development of promising alternative and diverse approaches to education. From its position of leadership it can encourage the planning of improved curricular and instructional procedures even when these may require changes in the nature of educational institutions. If the state education agency is to achieve this aim, it will need to be restructured in most states on the basis of its major functions and the problems with which it should deal. The "old line" bureaucratic organization is no longer viable and should be considered obsolete when it interferes with the self-actualization of creative educational planning leaders, technicians and policymakers (in somewhat the same manner that the traditional classroom procedures may tend to interfere with the self-actualization of students). Consequently, most state education agencies, in meeting their obligations for leadership and services in planning diverse and relevant programs, will find themselves radically changed. Moreover, they will find their boundaries less definite as they cooperate with other state and federal agencies and with such educational-political synthesizing organizations as the Education Commission of the States in a bona fide effort to coordinate the political processes needed to ensure adequate education for all students.

A second important function of state education agencies will be to make needs analyses and resource-allocation decisions. These agencies will necessarily continue to function as the major educational data collection organizations within the states. The procedures for monitoring this information can and should be organized in such a way that these agencies can not only analyze and evaluate it realistically, but also identify, clearly state and *emphasize the critical educational needs within the states as an important means of helping to convince state legislatures and the federal government that it is necessary for them to provide the resources required to meet these needs.* The needs analyses and the resource-allocation decisions must be related to basic education processes rather than to the maintenance of traditional institutions. Again, significant changes will be required within the structure of these agencies.

A third role might be considered as toleration-building—helping to create a climate that tends to encourage and support needed changes in education. State education agencies, contrary to their traditional institutional roles, can become major forces for gaining public acceptance for alternative programs of education. Through their potential for influencing the control and allocation of resources, these agencies can encourage new educational formats and the development of programs outside traditional school structures. In the same manner that they can encourage change within the schools, the states can also, through the effective use of resources, encourage appropriate provisions for a broader spectrum of the school's population especially for slow learners and minority groups, and a broader perspective for determining educational success. The process of toleration-building should include helping members of the legislature to understand the need for variations in educational structures and levels of support. It should also include supporting new designs for educational structures that are necessary to encourage and support promising new programs. Present policies and structures of some state education agencies are not very supportive of—in fact may even work against—this form of toleration building.

Most employees of state education agencies have been former teachers and district administrators, and their socialization and acculturation have been based on the values of the traditional institutions. The problem, thus, becomes one of "freeing," preparing and encouraging the planning experts, decision makers and other personnel to meet the emerging needs of educational programs that will be relevant for the future.

A fourth major role or function of state education agencies becomes one of providing leadership in developing appropriate procedures for the evaluation of teachers, programs, students and cost-effective operations. Evaluation should be based on carefully defined competency expectations in the same manner that the design of relevant curriculums should be based on provisions for the development of necessary student competencies. The task for each state agency, then, becomes one of providing or developing the leadership needed to establish significant competency definitions and expectations for students at various levels of education, and to encourage a program for achieving these competencies. It is no longer adequate to certify educational achievement in terms of the number of courses or the number of years of education completed. Both student and teacher achievement must be based on the ability to perform effectively the expected competencies that are related to learning and the process of instruction.

In a similar manner, the effectiveness of an educational institution should be judged on the basis of its ability to provide and support programs that produce effectively these competencies within appropriate cost-effective and resource-use parameters. The development of a competency-based system of education within a state may be difficult, partly because present political and popular sentiment may oppose many aspects of such a program. There is general agreement that the concept of cost-effectiveness should be applicable, within reasonable limits, to education, but *there is not always a willingness to invest in and spend for education at the necessary funding levels to make appropriate achievement possible for all students.*

Teachers have traditionally been opposed to any form of evaluation of their activities—for merit pay or other purposes—largely because of the "feeling" that teaching is a subjective activity. Students have found themselves evaluated on the basis of their performance on examinations which usually test their knowledge consumption (and sometimes, their problem-solving ability), but rarely their ability to perform creatively or to change as persons. All of these areas will require the development and insightful utilization of appropriate competency criterion measures to ensure that the competencies are being developed. The task is formidable, but it is important enough to require the emphasis which it can and should receive from each state education agency and local school system in a state. These concepts, among others, appear to provide sound bases for the operations of state education agencies through the 1970's.

IN SUMMARY

The major and continuing purpose of all federal and state legal provisions relating to education and of all federal, state and local educational agencies, institutions and organizations should be to ensure, insofar as practicable, adequate and relevant learning opportunities for all who can benefit from education. That concept should guide all planning activities, constitute the basis for all changes that are proposed, and provide the rationale for all designs for evaluating—and all efforts to evaluate—organizations, programs and progress.

While state planning for the improvement of education is essential, the best and most defensible state plans, as such, cannot ensure optimum provisions for education or adequate learning opportunities in local school systems or schools that have been assigned the responsibility for conducting the educational programs. State education agencies, therefore, must always be in a position to assist these systems and other educational institutions to plan for and provide appropriate learning opportunities and to evaluate their programs and provisions.

All aspects of society and of education should be expected, and designed insofar as practicable, to contribute maximally to the learning process. This is not the case at present. Learning must be relevant to the needs of each individual and of the society in which he will live. Learning programs and procedures in all instances must be carefully planned in light of the best information and insights available and be continuously revised to meet the needs of a changing society and of students who differ greatly in aptitudes and abilities. Provisions should, therefore, be made for a variety of programs and approaches. Standardized procedures will not meet the needs.

In brief summary, each state education agency must be in position to provide, and should provide, the leadership and services needed to:

- Develop, obtain agreement on, and implement meaningful statements of educational purposes and goals;

- Create a favorable external and internal environment for learning;

- Plan, implement and revise as necessary curricula that will meet both present and emerging needs;

- Obtain the cooperation of, and cooperate effectively with, other appropriate agencies and groups in ensuring adequate and relevant learning opportunities and procedures for all who should be educated at every stage of their development;

- Encourage and support creative self-actualizing behavior for all educators and students;

- Ensure that the provisions for the preparation, certification and evaluation of educators are appropriate in terms of modern insights and will facilitate the attainment of all goals;

- Ensure, insofar as practicable, that the resources of the state are utilized to improve learning, rather than to perpetuate existing organizational and institutional practices that are no longer appropriate;

- Plan and implement provisions for continuous evaluation of student progress and of organizational, administrative and instructional effectiveness to the end that bona fide accountability can be achieved for both the processes and the products of education; and

- Ensure continuous progress in the quest for excellence in all aspects of education and for everyone who can benefit from education.

Footnote References

[1]John W. Gardner, *Excellence—Can We Be Equal and Excellent Too?* (New York: Harper & Brothers, Publishers, 1961), p. 3.

[2]Clifford F. S. Bebell, "The Educational Program," Chapter 1 in *Emerging Designs for Education,* Edgar L. Morphet and David L. Jesser, eds. (Denver, Colorado: Designing Education for the Future, 1968), pp. 8-9. Republished by Citation Press, Scholastic Magazines, Inc., New York, N.Y.

[3]John S. Gibson, "On Quality in Education" (Unpublished paper prepared for the Committee on Public Education, Colorado General Assembly, April 1970), p. 1

[4]Clifford F. S. Bebell, "The Educational Program," *op. cit.,* p. 19.

[5]See, for example, discussion in *Emerging State Responsibilities for Education,* Edgar L. Morphet, David L. Jesser and Arthur P. Ludka, eds. (Denver, Colorado: Improving State Leadership in Education), pp. 86-88.

[6]J. Cecil Parker and Raymond A. McGuire in *Emerging Designs for Education, op. cit.,* pp. 59-60.

[7]Melvin Tumin, "Teaching in America," *Saturday Review,* October 21, 1970.

[8]Adapted from Parker and McGuire, *op. cit.,* pp. 61-64.

[9]Adapted from Clifford F. S. Bebell, *op. cit.,* pp. 20-26.

[10]Charles Silberman, *Crisis in the Classroom: The Remaking of American Education* (New York, N.Y.: Random House, 1970), p. 10.

[11]Melvin M. Tumin, "Ability, Motivation and Evaluation: Urgent Dimensions in the Preparation of Educators," in *Preparing Educators to Meet Emerging Needs,* Edgar L. Morphet and David L. Jesser, eds. (Denver, Colorado: Designing Education for the Future, 1969), p. 5. Republished by Citation Press, Scholastic Magazines, Inc., New York, N.Y.

[12]Arnold J. Toynbee, *Higher Education in a Time of Accelerating Change* (New York, N. Y.: Academy for Educational Development, 1968), Paper No. 3, p. 7.

[13]Novice G. Fawcett and John E. Corbally, Jr., "The Emerging Role of Higher Education," in *Preparing Educators to Meet Emerging Needs, op. cit.,* p. 33.

[14]Based on a paper by Marshall L. Frinks, *Planning and Effecting Improvements in the Preparation and Certification of Educators,* prepared for and published by the project. See also Theodore Andrews, *"New Directions in Certification."* Report of a study sponsored by the Washington State Education Agency and Improving State Leadership in Education (Denver, Colorado: Improving State Leadership in Education, 1970).

[15]Melvin M. Tumin in *Preparing Educators to Meet Emerging Needs, op. cit.,* p. 12.

[16]Russell B. Vlaanderen and Arthur P. Ludka, "Evaluating Education in a Changing Society," in *Emerging State Responsibilities for Education, op. cit.,* p. 145.

[17]Henry S. Dyer, "Statewide Evaluation—What Are the Priorities?", *Phi Delta Kappan,* Vol. LI, No. 10 (June 1970), p. 558.

Chapter 10

Modernizing Provisions for the Organization, Operation and Support of Education

Excellence in education cannot be attained in any community, state or nation merely by adopting and implementing a few promising innovations. These steps may help, but the continuation of outmoded policies or practices will tend to limit or nullify many of the potential gains. Education is a complex social system including many subsystems or components that are interrelated in many ways. *If this system is to function effectively, each subsystem and all related factors and conditions must be designed to contribute maximally to the achievement of the purposes of education.*

In every state, efforts to achieve excellence in education have been handicapped by the perpetuation of traditional provisions and practices relating to the organization, administration and operation of education, by ineffective provisions for cooperative and supporting services, by obsolete or inadequate physical facilities and equipment, or by provisions for financial support that are conflicting, unrealistic in the light of recent economic trends, or do not meet the needs of modern education in other respects. It would be no less than tragic for this society if the efforts of many eager students and dedicated teachers were to continue to be frustrated because of inappropriate policies and practices in any aspect of education.

The relevance and adequacy of existing educational provisions and practices in each state should be judged by the extent to which they contribute effectively to—and avoid handicapping in any way—the facilitation of relevant learning for everyone who can benefit from education.

POLITICAL PROCESSES AND LEGAL PROVISIONS

In authoritarian nations in which the political and perhaps even the religious beliefs are prescribed and enforced by the government, no publicly expressed differences of opinion about the purposes and goals of government, of education, and of closely related agencies or organizations are condoned. On the other hand, in free pluralistic societies differences of opinion are expected and even encouraged in most nations—at least in areas where the evidence available is not adequate to justify defensible conclusions. In these nations the society expresses—usually in vague and conflicting ways

> its wishes about the desirable ends of education in terms of the kinds of persons it wishes its members to become and of the knowledge, skills, attitudes, values, beliefs and so on that they should, by the process, assimilate from our culture. But these vague directives provide the educators with no more than broad energizing ideals to guide them in their task.[1]*

The social purposes of free pluralistic societies and their institutions—including those established for education—are expressed, reinforced and implemented primarily through a variety of political processes. Thus, as should be expected, *the purposes, major policies and many of the goals of education* (and often some of the procedures) *are determined politically,* at least in a general sense, and hopefully primarily on a nonpartisan basis. They can be influenced by educators but, in most instances, are not determined by them in isolation from the political process.

Developing Educational Policies

Educational policies are general guides for action and presumably are designed to facilitate the attainment of the purposes and goals of education. In a changing society, policies must be made and remade continuously as conditions and needs are modified. Bowles has pointed out that:

> It is not easy to discover how educational policy is made. . . . Sometimes it is made sharply and clearly as part of a general plan for . . . development. Sometimes it is the result of emergency, on-the-spot decisions. . . . But however policy is made, it controls the structure and organization of the educational system and the flow of students through the system. And its effects go beyond the educational establishment to affect the lives of individuals and even the structure of society.[2]

Bowles has also noted that when the problems of education (for example, those relating to instructional procedures and accountability) are not solved within the system, they are appealed to the public and the decision is ultimately in favor of the majority. In other words, *if educators do not change education in the directions desired by the public, the elected representatives or political leaders will do so through the established political processes.* The policies established for education should provide considerable opportunity for the local and individual initiative and creativity that are so essential in a dynamic society.

In this country, the basic policies are determined—hopefully after careful study and public discussion—by governmental agencies. Kimbrough has cautioned, however:

> In order to assure that the public schools will serve purposes consistent with a democratic society, control over basic educational policy should be kept close to the people. Elected representatives of the people have authority for the determination of policies. Educators should continue to develop and use procedures which emphasize a broad representation of the public in the development of educational policy.[3]

---

*Footnote references are given at end of the chapter.

Educational policies should be clearly stated but are sometimes merely implied or assumed, or may not even be made known to the general public. They should be internally consistent, but sometimes are conflicting. For example, until about two decades ago one section of the Kentucky Constitution directed the legislature to provide a uniform and effective system of education throughout the state, but another section required that all funds for schools be distributed on a school census basis, and thus made it impossible for good schools to be provided in some areas.

It is generally agreed that, in a dynamic society, most policies should be stated positively (for example, tuition-free public education is to be provided through the secondary school level), but a number of negatively stated and limiting policies are found in some states (for example, funds from public tax sources may not be used to support kindergartens).

Federal educational policies are established by the Congress, by U.S. Court decisions and, to a lesser extent, by directives of government officials. Most of the basic policies relating to education in each state are found in constitutional provisions, laws and court decisions. But state and local boards, within limits prescribed or implied by law, are also policy-making bodies. The responsibilities of state education agencies for educational policies include:

- Assembling, analyzing and making available pertinent information that should be utilized in considering needs and developing policies;

- Encouraging and helping to provide for widespread participation in the development of proposals for new educational policies and revisions in current policies;

- Developing and explaining proposals for policies that should be considered for approval by the state board of education;

- Obtaining the cooperation of local school systems, members of the legislature and other groups in developing policies that should be incorporated into law and in effecting modification of policies that are obsolete or restrictive; and

- Assisting local school systems to develop appropriate supplementary policies or revise existing policies.

DEVELOPING APPROPRIATE GOALS

The goals for education (discussed in Chapter 9) are closely related to policies but are much more specific because they state what is expected to be accomplished through education. They not only provide a framework for developing the curriculum and instructional procedures but also, if properly prepared and supplemented by appropriate statements of objectives, provide a basis for measuring progress and determining the adequacy and effectiveness of the procedures utilized. The goals should be expected to be reasonably consistent with the policies, but as goals are modified or supplemented to meet changing conditions and needs they tend to go beyond and call for changes in existing policies.

Educators at all levels should be expected (and should expect) to assume a major responsibility for developing or proposing clear and meaningful statements of goals and objectives including those that apply to each level or aspect of education. The development of objectives, in particular, is primarily a technical responsibility because each statement should be concerned with expected outcomes (that can be expressed insofar as feasible in behavioral or performance terms) and used as a basis for determining the progress of each student and ensuring accountability in terms of the contributions of teachers and the provisions for education.

The goals for education and some of the objectives, however, are or should be recognized as matters for deep public interest and concern. State education agencies, therefore, need to find meaningful ways to encourage and provide for representative educators and lay citizens including members of the legislature to study, react to, and suggest changes in statements concerning proposed statewide goals, some of the most important of which should be reflected in legal provisions. Local school systems should be encouraged to follow a similar policy. *There must be general public understanding and acceptance of all goals because public cooperation and support will be essential if they are to be attained.*

IMPROVING LEGAL PROVISIONS FOR EDUCATION

Most people now believe that changes in education should be carefully and systematically planned—not made on the basis of impulse, temporary pressures, or without considering the implications or consequences for learning, costs and other factors. *There is as much reason and need for planning systematically for changes in the legislation relating to education as for planning improvements in various aspects of education.* Laws greatly influence and often determine what can or cannot be done in and through education: they may stimulate and even require improvements in various aspects of education, or may perpetuate inefficient policies and practices as a result of provisions made for the organization, operation and support of schools.

In practically every state, there are some obsolete legal provisions that perpetuate inequities and inequalities. For example, in a number of states the laws require, or at least condone, segregation of students on the basis of the boundaries and wealth of the district in which they reside, and perpetuate inequities for taxpayers and inequalities in opportunities for students by indefensible provisions for financing schools. These provisions often guarantee that the most wealthy districts will have available, on the basis of the same local tax effort, two or more times the amount per pupil as the least wealthy. Some states as well as the U.S. Congress have tended to discourage meaningful long-range planning in education by making it necessary for the schools and state education agencies to depend on uncertain and often delayed annual or biennial appropriations, instead of providing, as several states do, for a contiuing basic appropriation and allocation. A detailed listing of the legal provisions that tend to result in handicaps and constraints should be developed in each state as one basis for planning and effecting changes.

In every state, *the laws relating to education should be designed to facilitate the development and implementation of policies and procedures that will contribute maximally to the attainment of defensible purposes and goals for education—and especially to the improvement of learning environments, opportunities and procedures for all students.* This criterion should be utilized as a basis for determining the relevance and adequacy of all existing legislation as well as of proposed laws.

Zeigler has noted that planning for the future will require:

> . . . the reformulation of current ideas, not only about educational planning per se, but also about the activities of policy making, and the politics of education. . . . The traditional political process for setting new or maintaining old educational policies is no longer an adequate basis for the generation and assessment of policy options. In short, the political process must be transformed. It must facilitate policies which, in the very least, do not constrain options for the future to be lived by the adults whom we are now educating as children.[4]

Zeigler also emphasized the importance of *participatory planning*— seriously involving educators and lay citizens in the process of learning about the means and ends of education, and noted that "the politics of education might be conceived as an educative process wherein policy-planning for alternative futures—and thus alternative 'presents'—becomes the instrument for . . . enactment."[5]

During the past half century, a number of states have codified their laws relating to education and, in some cases, eliminated provisions that were considered to be obsolete. More recently, several states have sponsored or conducted studies that were designed to provide a basis for effecting improvements in education. Some of these studies have resulted in rather systematic changes (supported by legislators and others who had been involved) in some laws or sections of the laws. Within the past couple of decades, legislative councils, research bureaus or similar agencies have been established in a number of states to study proposals for legislation and provide suggestions designed to effect more systematic and defensible approaches to changes in laws. In these and other ways improvements are being made in most states.

In nearly every state some influential groups or members of established power structures have been organized to oppose certain changes in education or to promote legislation in areas in which they have special concerns. Such groups may serve useful purposes but often complicate the problem of planning systematically and comprehensively for the improvement of legislation. As members of these groups participate in studies and help to develop recommendations, however, they usually begin to recognize the need for changes and frequently support constructive proposals. Kimbrough has stated: "The very future of democratic society depends upon developing democratic power structures that can cope successfully with the changing environment."[6]

Some of the educational problems in many states result from conditions such as the following: (1) few people involved in elementary education are concerned about legislation relating primarily to secondary or post-secondary schools and the reverse; (2) few teachers are concerned about legislation relating to the state or local school systems unless it obviously would affect them; (3) few university educators or board members seem to have much interest in legislation relating to elementary and secondary schools or to state education agencies; and, (4) in most states, neither local nor state education agency personnel have given much attention to legislative proposals relating to colleges and universities. Because most educators apparently have not seriously considered education as a social system in which all levels and aspects are interrelated, legislators unfortunately often have had to weigh the demands and expectations of one subgroup or level against those of others as well as against other demands and expectations. In many cases, as a result, *far too little attention has been given to the basic educational issues involved or to optimum ways for resolving them.*

Because education is primarily a state responsibility, it seems essential that state education agencies be prepared to assume a major responsibility for leadership in planning, coordinating and submitting proposals for legislation relating to all levels and aspects of education and for devising procedures for evaluating existing legislation on the basis of criteria similar to those proposed above. Voluntary educational and other related organizations, as well as local school systems and institutions of higher learning, can and should help with this process in each state but seldom are in a position to provide the coordination and overall perspectives that are essential.

On a broader basis, the Education Commission of the States has the potential for helping to synthesize the political and educational perspectives in all states, as well as for helping the citizens of each state to distinguish between alternative proposals or approaches that are more defensible than others. This potential should be clearly recognized and supported by everyone concerned with improving the provisions for education throughout the nation.

PROVISIONS FOR ORGANIZATION AND OPERATION

The legal provisions relating to the organization, operation and support of education in a state or nation cannot, merely as laws, ensure excellence. When even a few of the many factors and conditions that affect education are unfavorable, progress is slow, difficult and uneven. When many conditions—and especially some of the most significant—are unfavorable, the concept of excellence becomes little more than a lingering mirage that results in disillusionment, frustration and resentment for many parents, students and educators.

Excellence in education in a state or nation can be closely approached when:

- A substantial majority of the people have a clear understanding of the goals and components of education and their interrelationships —of what education means—and insist that every effort be made to ensure that continuous progress is made on all fronts;

- A realistic comprehensive plan is developed, implemented and modified as necessary to meet changing or newly recognized needs;

- The provisions for all aspects of organization and support and the operating procedures are designed and revised as needed to contribute maximally to the attainment of the goals; and

- Progress in every aspect of education is carefully and continuously monitored at state and local levels in order to obtain pertinent information that is used to identify problems and as a basis for revising provisions or practices that are not contributing effectively to excellence.

When this nation was established, those who drafted and approved the Constitution, by implication, assigned the basic responsibility for providing education to the component states. Few people in this country question the wisdom of that decision. Even though the people in some states have made more realistic and effective provisions for education than those in others, most citizens seem to be convinced that this arrangement provides for more flexibility and offers greater promise of meeting changing needs than would be possible under a national system.

STATE POLICIES AND LEGISLATION

In most parts of this country, education developed primarily as a family and community obligation rather than as a state responsibility. But the states soon began to find it necessary to assume some responsibility for elementary education, and later for secondary and post-secondary education. During these early years, there was no comprehensive plan for education, but legislation relating to one aspect or another was enacted when the need was recognized by a substantial portion of the residents. In fact, only a few states established any agency for elementary and secondary education until nearly three-quarters of a century had elapsed. Thus, for many years education was only nominally recognized as a state responsibility.

Since the beginning of the present century, however, hundreds of laws relating to education have been enacted in most states. As previously noted, some of these perpetuate provisions and practices that have become outmoded in the light of modern developments and insights. If the citizens in each state and their representatives in the legislature could forget the laws, policies and practices to which they have became accustomed and undertake to create a system of education that is designed to meet present and emerging needs, there undoubtedly would be many important differences in most states because the people involved would be in a position to devise a coordinated plan that would be relatively free from conflicts and inconsistencies. Even under these conditions, there would probably be serious disagreements about some elements and the plan, as adopted, might be inadequate in some respects. Moreover, even the best plan that could be devised under present conditions would need to be modified from time to time as conditions change or new information becomes available.

The citizens of every state urgently need to examine carefully all existing legal and other provisions for education as a basis for identifying and retaining those which seem to be appropriate in terms of a defensible "conceptual design" for education, and revising or replacing any that are no longer appropriate. Handicapping or inefficient policies and practices should no longer be tolerated in any state.

How can the people in a state proceed to meet this challenge—to effect improvements that are considered essential? There are several possibilities, including: (1) depend on the customary political processes to effect changes on the basis of demands and pressures; (2) urge the legislature to appoint a committee to consider the problems and issues and develop proposals for their solution; (3) contract with a consulting firm or a group of "experts" to make the studies and prepare a report; or (4) establish, with the authorization or support of the governor and the legislature, a competent representative committee that is charged with the responsibility for developing plans, obtaining the services of appropriate consultants to assist or conduct pertinent studies, and preparing recommendations after considering the advantages and disadvantages of feasible alternatives. As explained in Chapter 4, each of these procedures has some potential advantages and disadvantages but, in most situations, the fourth alternative seems to hold more promise than any of the others as evidenced by developments in a number of states during recent decades including Florida, Kentucky, Ohio, Texas and Utah.

The development of defensible proposals and plans is not likely to be possible unless:

1. Adequate human, technological and financial resources are available;

2. Valid criteria that can be used to determine the strengths and weaknesses of present provisions are agreed upon;

3. Feasible alternatives are clearly identified;

4. Pertinent information is assembled and analyzed in a manner that will make it possible to ascertain not only the appropriateness and adequacy of existing provisions but also the probable implications—advantages and disadvantages—of each feasible alternative in view of prospective changes in society; and

5. A serious effort is made to ensure that all proposals are interrelated and that each contributes effectively to the achievement of excellence in education.

STATE ROLE, ORGANIZATION AND RESPONSIBILITIES

In some states, the people seem to have assumed that if the state would provide limited funds for public elementary and secondary schools and establish a weak agency that would be primarily responsible for establishing and checking on compliance with minimum standards and for gathering and reporting certain kinds of information, the major responsibility for these schools would be met. This was a naive assumption even a few decades ago and is clearly unrealistic at present. Many of the current problems relating to educational deficiences for substantial numbers of people in the nation can be traced in part to this assumption which still affects policies in many states. In fact, some federal officials and even some members of Congress have insisted from time to time that, because of inadequate state provisions and policies, federal funds for certain educational purposes should be made available directly to local school districts—and that the states should be bypassed.

This situation has changed rather rapidly in several states during the past decade. Some states have developed and are in the process of implementing long-range plans for improving education, but others have done little more than make a few gestures in that direction. Fortunately, federal funds have been made available through the Elementary and Secondary Act of 1965 to assist state education agencies to provide leadership and services in planning and effecting changes and in evaluating progress. Moreover state education agencies are being encouraged to assist school districts, individually or in cooperation with others, in developing proposals for Title III and other federally funded projects and in appraising developments. Thus, these funds have helped greatly to strengthen certain aspects of the role of the states in improving education, but state support and laws relating to this purpose have changed only to a limited extent in a number of states.

The factors and conditions that underlie the reluctance or failure of some states to assume much bona fide responsibility for education differ somewhat from state to state, but usually include one or more of those discussed briefly in the paragraphs that follow.

State-Local Relations. The concept of *local control* of education—a necessity during pioneering days—has sometimes become an emotionally charged political slogan that is used to confuse issues or to serve as an excuse for failing to face present-day realities in education. It would be much more appropriate and helpful for the people in all states to focus attention on the basic issue that needs to be resolved in every state: How can bona fide *local responsibility* for education best be increased and made more meaningful under modern conditions? Many people have become convinced that any move toward increased state responsibility for education would deprive them of some of their traditional rights and responsibilities. But, as several authorities have pointed out, *an increase in the ability of one level of government to deal with certain educational problems need not reduce—in fact, should increase—the ability of another level of government to deal with those problems.*[7] Both lay citizens and educators in local school systems need to understand that, instead of opposing improvements in state leadership and services for education, they should strongly support them as a means of enhancing local responsibility for education and increasing the opportunity to improve their own provisions and programs.

Separate Boards. Many states have established separate boards and agencies for elementary and secondary schools, for institutions of higher learning and, in some cases, even for junior colleges and for vocational-technical education. Some of the advantages and disadvantages of various kinds of provisions for state organization of education are discussed in Chapter 3 of *Emerging State Responsibilities for Education.*[8] In states in which there is no legal provision even for the coordination of planning, the emphasis tends to be on competition for funds and power rather than on cooperation in effecting improvements in all aspects of education. Appropriate provisions for encouraging cooperation and coordination within education seem to be urgently needed in every state.

Ineffective State Education Agencies. Because, in many states, the agency for elementary and secondary education traditionally has been relatively weak and ineffective, neither the governor nor the legislature has held it in high regard and few of the urban and other large school systems have relied on that agency for much assistance. As previously noted, the provision of federal funds for planning and coordination is helping state education agencies to develop a more meaningful role and improve their services. But this is a slow process in many states largely because of the cross currents and traditional attitudes that are difficult to change. The retarding factors include:

1. The state board of education in some states does not include many especially competent people who are seriously concerned about education, and has relatively low prestige.

2. In 20 states the chief state school officer still is elected by popular vote, often on a partisan ballot. In some of these, the person elected to that position often has had little understanding of state and national educational problems and needs, and has seemed to be more interested in selecting a staff that can help him to be re-elected than in providing the

leadership and services needed to plan and effect improvements in education throughout the state.

3. Some governors insist that they can do little to help to improve education unless they can appoint the chief state school officer. Yet studies of states in the Northeast by Bailey and others have identified a number in which the leadership of members of the legislature and of a governor who does not appoint the chief state school officer has been significant in helping to effect major improvements in provisions for school support. They also noted that "The quality of leadership of state commissioners of education has often proved crucial to the success of state aid programs."[9] There seems to be no convincing evidence to indicate that more progress has been made in improving education in the four states in which the chief state school officer is appointed by the governor than in most of the 26 in which he is appointed by the state board of education.

4. Some legislators seem to be convinced that they should determine the basic policies for education in the state by preparing and sponsoring legislation relating to education without consulting with, or considering recommendations made by, the state education agency. Since legislation may facilitate or retard needed improvements in education, it would seem that legislators should be interested in obtaining and considering all pertinent information before proposing or acting on legislation relating to education. The state education agency can and should help with this process.

Attitudes and Expectations of Citizens. The importance the citizens of a state attach to education has many implications for the provisions made for the organization and operation of education and their willingness to consider changes in existing provisions. If they value education highly, they are likely to insist on the best and most effective provisions that can be devised. Many people, however, may be relatively complacent about some of the constraints or inadequate provisions to which they have long been accustomed (such as inefficiently organized school districts, or a weak state agency for education) unless the disadvantages are readily apparent.

Decisions relating to the kinds of provisions that should be made in a state for the organization and operation of education are complicated by the lack of pertinent information and the wide range of opinions based partly on the values held by people concerning such issues as:

- What should the schools and educational institutions be expected to accomplish?

- What and how should students be "taught" in the schools and colleges?

- For how many years and for whom should education be provided at public expense?

- How much should be invested in (spent on) education and how should these funds be provided?

- Who should be held responsible for any shortcomings or weaknesses in education?

- At what levels (local, state and national) should various kinds of decisions be made about education and by whom?

The issue concerning the level or levels at which the basic policy decisions should be made about education is one of the most important, pervasive and controversial. The way it is resolved has some implications for many other issues and especially for the provisions relating to·organization and operation of education. One of the urgent needs in every state is to identify and obtain agreement on the many aspects concerning which decisions can best be made at the local level as well as on those that can best be made at the state level, and on procedures for ensuring that the implied responsibilities are accepted and implemented at each level.

It seems apparent that the *decisions regarding major policies that have implications for education throughout a state must be made at the state level on the basis of widespread and meaningful participation and discussion.* If the people in a state decide, as in Hawaii, that all responsibility for the organization and operation of education should be assumed by the state (with limited provision for local decision making on certain matters), they will need to develop a state organization that is designed to meet these needs. If on the other hand—as will probably be the case in most states—they decide after careful study that certain responsibilities should be assigned on a rational basis to local school systems and others to the state, they will obviously need to develop a different organizational plan.

The citizens of every state should recognize that only a properly organized and competently staffed state education agency can provide or facilitate many of the necessary linkages in the state between local school systems and institutions of higher learning, on one hand, and between local school systems and the political decision-making processes at state and federal levels, on the other.

THE STATE EDUCATION AGENCY

A new and challenging role is emerging for state education agencies. Some have already begun to assume that role in a meaningful way— that is, *to provide the leadership and services needed to plan and effect improvements in all aspects of education and to evaluate progress.* This statement should not be interpreted to mean that these agencies should do the planning or neglect their other responsibilities, but rather that they should assume the initiative and provide the necessary guidance, coordination and services. It also means that *the legislature in every state should make clear by appropriate legislation that a major responsibility of the state agency is to provide the leadership and services needed to ensure that this goal is attained.* At present, many state agencies are handicapped by lack of an appropriate legislative mandate, by line-item budgets that do not provide adequate resources for planning, and by a traditional pattern of organization that is not adapted to modern needs.

Haskew[10] has pointed out that leadership in planning means: (a) to have ideas for change; (b) to proffer those ideas in a form with which others can and do identify; (c) to provide implementing nurture for those ideas until their promise is apparent to potential followers; and (d) to attract intelligent followership. He has also noted that *planning must become a way of life for the state education agency and all who are concerned with improvements in education,* and that merely establishing a new structure, such as an office of planning, will not meet the needs.

It will be difficult for some state education agencies to prepare to assume this new role because: (1) they must continue but reorient many of their traditional responsibilities and relationships; (2) appropriate policies and guidelines will need to be developed and approved by the state board of education; (3) an appropriate new organizational structure for the department of education will probably have to be designed; (4) many members of the staff will have to be reoriented and retrained in order to develop the necessary insights, competencies and skills; and (5) special safeguards will need to be established in an effort to ensure that technicians do not assume that they are to make the basic policy decisions, or that the department staff does not assume that its role (always tempting and heady) is to do the planning rather than to provide the necessary leadership and services.

On the basis of a special study of recent developments in several states, Nix concluded:

> Most state education agencies now are vigorously concerned with long-range planning. Many have established special planning units to provide leadership, technical assistance, and continuing emphasis upon the process of planning. Most of this emphasis, however, has been given to planning for the educational provisions and programs for local schools. Only to a limited extent has the discipline of planning been focused internally upon the state department's own development as an institution. A number of states have developed carefully articulated statements of goals for the statewide educational system. Moreover, efforts are being made to identify needs of some state agencies, as well as those of students and schools.

> Several states are striving to connect the program-planning process more directly with the budgeting process—in some cases using advanced program budgeting techniques. Attention is being given to the inconsistencies among the *state plans* that state agencies prepare as a requirement for participation in certain state- and federally assisted programs, and efforts are underway to make these state plans more meaningful and consistent. Formal reorganization plans are being developed in several states, based upon new directions to be taken by the state agency, and projected for implementation over a period of time. Staff development programs are being conducted on the plan-making process. State agency personnel are becoming more familiar with the concepts, language, and techniques of planning, and they are gaining skill and interest in using these techniques.

Obviously, long-range planning for the development of the state education agency has value only as it ultimately serves to improve the quality of the programs in the schools of the state. The state agency can provide the needed leadership only if it can develop sound plans for the use of its own resources to perform well-selected, relevant roles in the total system.[11]

One of the major problems in every state education agency is to avoid the tendency to develop a bureaucracy that establishes and perpetuates a rigid system which may be comforting to those involved but ignores emerging needs and resists change. All bureaucracies tend to disregard clear signals from without the organization that changes are needed and to become more or less isolated from the aspects of society they are expected to serve. Communication across the boundaries of an organization is more difficult than communication within the boundaries. *State education agencies need to make a special and continuing effort to communicate effectively with, and to obtain the cooperation of, everyone who is concerned about education.* They should, at least periodically, seek the assistance of competent outsiders on many policy matters, including the evaluation of the organization, services and procedures of the agency itself. The basic criterion to be used in planning and evaluating the role and services of every state education agency should be: *Does every function and service contribute maximally to the improvement of the learning environments, opportunities and procedures for everyone in the state who should benefit from education?*

Local Organization and Responsibility

Numerous studies have documented the fact that many school districts in a substantial number of states are too small to provide adequate educational opportunities at a reasonable cost and that an increasing number have become so large and bureaucratic that they apparently can neither adjust to modern needs nor utilize the available funds and other resources effectively. Although substantial progress has been made in eliminating small districts and reorganizing others during the past four decades, most of this reorganization has been accomplished on an unsatisfactory patchwork basis in many of the states. The states and the nation can no longer afford the inefficiencies and handicaps to learning progress resulting from the present archaic situation found in many areas. The people in most states urgently need to begin systematically to devise a new kind of local structure and procedures that will make it possible to achieve excellence in education for all students at a reasonable cost. Expedient cutting, patching and gerrymandering will no longer suffice in any state.

As Hooker and Mueller[12] along with others have noted: (1) at least three-fourths of the districts in the nation have fewer than 2,000 students; (2) a substantial number of districts in several states (and all districts in Arizona) are legally organized to provide only elementary or secondary education—that is, cannot provide for education through the twelfth grade in a unified school system; (3) some states continue to provide special subsidies that make it profitable for the taxpayers to maintain

small non-operating school districts; (4) the artificially established boundaries of districts in metropolitan as well as in rural areas often protect
islands of privilege and wealth and segregate pockets of poverty; (5) even
in states in which a county-unit school system has been established, the
population in some counties is too small to provide an effective school
system and many of the boundaries are unrealistic; (6) constraints established by the state often make it impossible for much meaningful local
responsibility to be exercised; and (7) state education agencies often
have to devote an unreasonable proportion of their time and attention to
the needs of the smaller school districts.

If the state and federal governments provide most of the funds needed
for the support of education—as seems both necessary and desirable during coming years—appropriately organized local school systems should
be in a much better position than at present to devote major attention to
planning and providing more adequate provisions for education and to
devising and utilizing appropriate procedures for measuring and reporting on the learning progress of students. In other words, *they can and
should be expected to be in a position to assume bona fide local responsibility for education.*

Only the citizens of each state can assume the basic responsibility for
developing a modern plan for the organization of local school systems
or districts. The design and details probably should be developed under
the sponsorship of a special committee or group authorized by the legislature, and the basic policies will need to be approved by that body. The
state education agency, however, should be deeply involved in the process which should include appropriate provisions for the decentralization
of large school systems and for the organization of area service units as
found necessary. As reorganization is accomplished, the state education
agency should be in an increasingly better position to assume one of its
major and most meaningful roles: *To assist local school systems to plan
and effect needed improvements in the provisions for education and in
procedures for determining and reporting on learning progress.*

PROVISIONS FOR SERVICES AND FACILITIES

All provisions for education are, or should be, interrelated. Unless
the state provisions are the best that can be devised and are free from
handicapping limitations; unless the leadership and services are adequate
and of high quality; and unless there is effective long-range planning to
meet changing needs, education throughout the state will be handicapped
and progress in effecting improvements will be limited. The achievement
of excellence in education throughout the state becomes impossible when:
some local school systems are too large or too small, or are not organized
to function effectively; the board or administration is inept; influential citizens oppose needed changes; personnel policies result in the selection or
retention of ineffective teachers and other employees; the school facilities

are obsolete or poorly planned; supporting services are inadequate; the financial support is too limited; there is no realistic planning except for the current fiscal year; or when other handicapping provisions and practices exist. Moreover, inappropriate or unrealistic provisions for federal funding and relations inevitably result in serious frustrations and handicaps for both state and local school systems.

THE BOARD AND ADMINISTRATION

The local board of education not only selects the superintendent and appoints the staff but also determines policies for the school system subject to limitations and procedures established by state legal provisions. Inadequate or restrictive state provisions (especially those relating to financial support or personnel policies) may make it impossible even for an especially competent board in a logically organized school district to plan or provide for an adequate program of education.

Thus, in some states, the state itself must be held accountable for some of the major defects or weaknesses in locally operated and administered programs. *A major objective in every state should be to make it possible for every local school system to provide adequate educational opportunities beginning with early childhood education and extending at least through the secondary schools, then to hold each such system accountable for the kind and quality of program provided.*

But, as explained in *Emerging State Responsibilities for Education,*[13] only the citizens in each local school system (or the city or other officials in school systems in which the board is appointed by them) can determine whether or not the school board will be composed of especially competent members who are seriously concerned about excellence in education. *Enlightened community involvement* (that can be encouraged or discouraged by state and local policies and traditions) *should be considered essential in every local school system.* Such participation should be carefully planned—not left to chance developments. The plan should include continuing provisions for the citizens to become well informed about modern educational problems, progress and needs, and to agree upon the purposes and goals as well as upon basic policies and procedures. Major differences in perspectives and expectations usually lead to fruitless controversies that tend to result in inadequate or ineffective provisions for education.

The areas of critical behavior on the part of the board and the administration about which everyone in a school system should be continuously concerned include: (1) setting appropriate goals; (2) developing defensible policies and priorities; (3) determining roles and functions; (4) appraising the effectiveness of the provisions, programs and procedures; (5) coordinating administrative functions and structure; (6) working with community leadership to promote improvements in education; (7) utilizing effectively the educational resources of the community; (8) involving people meaningfully in appropriate ways; and (9) communicating honestly and effectively with everyone potentially concerned.[14] In fact, the last two areas listed should be considered basic for satisfactory progress in each of the others.

One of the important, but often neglected, responsibilities of state education agencies is to find effective ways of helping local school systems to assume meaningful local responsibility for education by planning and effecting improvements in all areas of critical behavior.

SUPPORTING SERVICES

The facilitation of learning has many interrelated facets. Central to the process is an interested and eager student and a competent and understanding "teacher" who is in a position to serve effectively as a learning facilitator. But, under modern conditions, both teachers and students will be seriously handicapped unless all conditions are reasonably favorable. As pointed out in Chapter 9, the schools cannot control many of the home and community factors but can and should seek to find ways to help to ensure that they are as favorable as possible.

Each school system, with the support of the citizens of the community, can and should identify and help to modify or eliminate constraints imposed by the state, including inappropriate policies and serious limitations on resources. Almost everyone knows that learning can be handicapped by poor health or inadequate nutrition. Yet few states or communities have adequate arrangements for such services unless they can be afforded or are provided by the parents. Most states now make some provisions for the transportation of students, but the local school systems in many states are still required to provide and finance the buildings in which most of the learning sponsored by the schools is expected to take place. Many of them cannot afford, or at least do not provide, adequate housing. Moreover, the many kinds of supplies and equipment required for a modern educational program are often too limited or inappropriate to meet the needs.

Few citizens in most communities, and sometimes even school boards and staff members, have more than a vague idea about the wide variety of special services that are essential to assist teachers and students in the facilitation of learning. If some of these services are not available, are assigned to inadequately prepared people, or are not effectively coordinated, the progress of many students is almost certain to be handicapped.

Modern education requires a carefully planned and coordinated *team approach* to the improvement of learning—rather than an emphasis on "prima donnas" who seem to be primarily concerned with credit for their own isolated contributions or with increasing the size and prestige of the division in which they function. The bureaucratic kind of organization that has become traditional in many state and local school systems will not suffice to meet current needs. The organizational structure must constantly be redesigned to serve changing conditions and needs.

Important emerging responsibilities of state education agencies in terms of supporting services include:

- Helping local school systems to identify their needs and to devise and implement the kind of organization and provisions for operation that will best meet these needs;

- Developing an adequate management information system and a compatible state communications network that will enable every local school system, including staff and students, to have ready access to pertinent information; and

- Locating, analyzing and making available to local systems appropriate evidence and findings from research studies relating to the facilitation of learning and helping them to utilize this information effectively.

FACILITIES

In many school systems, the teachers, students and other personnel are likely to be handicapped for many years by school buildings that were designed to accommodate traditional programs. Some of these can be remodeled to serve present-day needs, but many cannot. Some state laws still include obsolete building codes and standards that provide serious handicaps. Important responsibilities of state education agencies in this area include: helping to modernize state school building laws and standards; helping local school systems to develop appropriate educational specifications (decide upon their detailed educational needs) as a basis for altering old structures or designing a new educational plant; encouraging local school systems and architects to design structures with maximum flexibility so the interior can be modified at minimum expense to meet changing conditions and needs; and encouraging the legislature to provide state funds needed to ensure adequate educational facilities throughout the state.

PROVISIONS FOR FINANCIAL SUPPORT

The citizens of this country have made, and are continuing to make, a substantial investment in education primarily because they believe it is essential for the welfare and progress of the nation and its citizens. That point of view has been supported by the findings of economists who have concluded that the investment in the development of human capital has yielded a higher rate of return than most other kinds of investments, and has contributed significantly to the economic growth of the nation.[15]

These observations, however, should not be interpreted to mean that all expenditures for education make significant contributions to productivity or to other aspects of progress under modern conditions. In fact, some expenditures yield limited, or perhaps even negative, returns because the procedures used in inadequate schools discourage meaningful learning or may even result in the development of antisocial attitudes; some school systems are too small and others too large and bureaucratic to operate efficiently; and obsolete laws and traditions make needed changes impracticable in some state and local school systems.

Some speakers and writers have observed that many people seem to be losing confidence in the public schools or in many current educational procedures, and note the sharp criticisms and the tendency of citizens in many states and communities to refuse to approve increases in appropriations or local tax levies, or to support proposals for bond issues. *It would seem more accurate to conclude that most people have become convinced that inequities for taxpayers, inequalities in opportunities for students, inefficient and uneconomical practices, and outdated educational provisions and procedures should no longer be tolerated—that they want the investment in education to yield maximum returns to individuals and society.*

Perhaps many people are saying, in effect, that they have lost confidence in the ability or willingness of the legislature to replace obsolete and sometimes inequitable laws with appropriate modern legal provisions, in the kind of leadership and services provided by regulation-oriented state education agencies, in colleges and universities that fail to meet modern needs, and in schools and school systems that ignore the needs of, and fail to challenge, many students—that *they want to find a meaningful way to help to modernize all aspects of education as a means of helping to ensure that their investment will yield optimum returns.*

In many states, the existing legal provisions for financial support for elementary and secondary schools constitute an inequitable and confusing hodgepodge, rather than a carefully developed and balanced plan. Many state and federal appropriations are narrowly categorical in nature, provide more adequately for some aspects of education than for others (some aspects may be ignored), and make it difficult or impossible for school districts to plan for the future or even to develop annual budgets that meet their needs. Some state financial provisions reward small uneconomical districts for continuing to operate; others penalize urban and other school districts that have a large proportion of disadvantaged students who require special and often more expensive provisions if they are to benefit fully from education. Many reward districts in areas where the ratio between the assessed and actual value of property is low and penalize those where a higher ratio is maintained. The provisions in many states ensure that the most wealthy districts will always have proportionately more funds per student for education that the least wealthy. Only a relatively small proportion of the states provide any substantial support for capital outlay and debt service, and consequently handicap the least wealthy school systems.

In several states, the citizens have cooperated in devising a plan for financial support that has largely eliminated many of these and other inequitable and unrealistic provisions. It seems strange that in others they have not done so. It also seems strange that some teacher organizations have attempted to blame, and even to discredit, the board and administration for local financial deficiencies that result primarily from inadequacies or inequities in state provisions. Obviously inadequate information, or misunderstanding of the situation that actually exists, often tends to result in enough confusion that some of the basic problems are ignored or overlooked.

Fortunately the National Educational Finance Project, financed primarily by funds provided through Title V, Section 505 of the Elementary and Secondary Education Act of 1965, has made a series of studies that not only document inequities and inadequacies such as those discussed above, but also identify and explain the implications or consequences of alternative ways of attempting to resolve some of the current problems of school support.[16] On the basis of the detailed information provided through these studies, it should be evident that many of the existing provisions in a number of states are far from defensible, contribute significantly to much of the present confusion, inequities and criticisms, and that carefully planned improvements are urgently needed.

It should also be apparent that: (1) part of the funds for education provided in some states are not being used effectively and that the needs of many students are not being met because of inadequate or inappropriate provisions; (2) the needs for certain kinds or aspects of education (for example, early childhood, continuation and adult education, special provisions for the disadvantaged, programs during the summer months, and so on) far exceed the current provisions; and (3) only by careful and systematic long-range planning in each state can these needs be met and existing inadequacies be eliminated.

In the past, efforts to effect changes in provisions for school support have often been based on attempts to: (1) obtain additional funds from federal, state or local sources for schools or for certain aspects of education; (2) reduce certain appropriations or services in order to balance the budget based on existing revenues; or (3) adjust some obvious imbalances or inequities. These efforts constitute only expedient actions and have little or no relationship to systematic planning. The primary purpose of all planning for school support should be to determine what is essential to ensure reasonably adequate learning opportunities and procedures for all who can benefit from education—then to determine and provide the financial and other resources that are necessary to attain this goal as effectively and economically as feasible. *Planning for financial support should always begin with, and be based upon, planning for improvements in the educational program, services and organization*—for excellence in all aspects of education. Thus far, only a few states have made any serious attempt to utilize this procedure which should be considered essential in every state and local school system.

But in planning improvements in provisions for financial support of schools, many factors and conditions must be carefully considered. Three of the most important are: (1) the program that is developed should be well balanced—that is, provide equitably and adequately for all needs; (2) the organization and arrangements should be designed to ensure that optimum educational benefits are attained from the funds invested in education; and (3) the sources of income for school support should be related to the sources of income of the people who provide the support. In few states have these criteria received adequate consideration.

There is grave danger that the confusion and frustrations resulting from existing inequities and inefficiencies may result in failure to provide the support that is needed to ensure excellence in many aspects of education. In view of the fact that more than 50 percent of the funds for support of elementary and secondary schools still come from property taxes (and a much larger percent in some states), while less than 10 percent of the income of the people nationally is received from property, many authorities now advocate that the percent of funds for school support from state and federal non-property tax sources be substantially increased. *A significant shift from the present heavy reliance on property taxes seems essential in many states, but the changes need to be carefully planned if handicapping state controls are to be avoided.*

John Shannon,[17] Assistant Director of the Advisory Commission on Intergovernmental Relations, has pointed out that substantial state support: (1) would represent a giant step toward equalization of educational opportunity; (2) is necessary in order to fix political accountability where it belongs—at the doorstep of the governor and state legislature; (3) will hurry history along with respect to the measurement of student achievement; (4) is necessary because the combined demands of education and local government are placing too great a burden on the property tax base in general and on low income householders in particular; and (5) by lifting most of the school financing burden off the local tax base, the state would undercut much of the fiscal logic that now supports exclusionary zoning practices in many suburban jurisdictions. Shannon also stated: "The federal government should use its resources so as to reduce fiscal disparities between the states and to stimulate action in certain critical areas."

Many people are convinced that if the state provides practically all of the funds for school support, state operation and control will be inevitable—that there would be little or no opportunity for local initiative or responsibility. *That could happen* (perhaps with disastrous long-range consequences in some states) *but it does not need to happen.* In fact, *if the citizens of a state are willing to make the effort to develop and implement appropriate plans, they can: (1) increase local responsibility, initiative and accountability; (2) decrease the burden on the property tax and ensure greater equity for taxpayers; and (3) provide more adequate, relevant and equitable opportunities for students at all levels.*

Let us suppose, for example, that the citizens of a state would insist that the legislature provide for the development and implementation of a plan that would: (1) make the foundation program more equitable and, in some states, increase the current level of support from state funds; (2) eliminate by appropriate reorganization all districts that are too small to provide economically an adequate and effective educational program; and (3) make available annually to all local school systems on a defensible and equitable basis funds from state non-property tax sources that are at least equivalent to those currently derived from required property tax levies—provided each school system (a) develops, in accordance with criteria established by the state, a long-range plan for the improvement of instruction and learning, (b) establishes priorities and procedures for implementing the plan, and (c) provides for annual evaluation of progress and for necessary revision in the plans. Would not this or some similar plan constitute one appropriate way to increase local responsibility and accountability and, at the same time, facilitate improvements in education throughout the state?

At least two states (Florida and New Jersey)[18] have developed and begun to implement plans somewhat along these lines. There seems to be no valid reason why the citizens in other states should not develop similar or even better plans for resolving some of the most serious problems facing education throughout the nation.

The state education agency should be in a better position than any other agency or organization to provide the leadership and services needed to identify and dramatize existing inequities and inadequacies and to plan and help to effect needed improvements in provisions for the support of education. In this process, the state agency needs to obtain the cooperation and support not only of local school systems but also of other appropriate organizations and groups. Moreover, it is essential that the state board, chief state school officer and members of his staff find effective ways of cooperating continuously with the legislature and the governor in appraising developments and determining the advantages and disadvantages of alternative proposals for changes.

It seems apparent that many changes in provisions for the support of education will be urgently needed during the coming years. Many traditional practices will have to be carefully examined and challenging new possibilities explored from every point of view. However, *new proposals should be adopted only when the evidence shows that they are superior to present practices*—and never simply because they have strong supporters. For example, there are currently many vigorous advocates of performance contracting, the voucher plan, and of state support for non-public schools. Yet there seems to be no valid evidence available that would justify their *general adoption* under present conditions. Several authorities have noted that carefully prepared performance contracts may be appropriate for the development of specific skills of some students in certain areas; that the best use of vouchers may be to make them available for possible utilization by dropouts at some future time; and that providing general state or federal support for nonpublic schools might tend to handicap or prevent needed improvements in the public schools.

The state education agencies in all states not only should seek the cooperation of local school systems and other groups in exploring carefully all such proposals and providing pertinent information, but also should encourage the federal government to develop provisions for support that would help the states to develop better coordinated and integrated provisions for financial support for schools.

ACCOUNTABILITY IN EDUCATION

Fundamentally, accountability in education is the essential, but all too often neglected, process of planning and explaining the utilization of resources in terms of their contributions to the attainment of desired outcomes or results. If it is to be meaningful, accountability must be based on a clear statement of appropriate objectives that are agreed upon and a valid procedure for measuring the progress in attaining these objectives. State and local school systems have become accustomed to accounting in detail for all funds received and expended, but only in a general way for the utilization of the human resources involved in education and for the progress of students.

Presumably, all societies—and especially all modern technological societies—should be child- and youth-oriented because the future of the society depends so heavily on the full development of the potential of each new generation. But the evidence shows clearly that in every state there are thousands of children who are handicapped as a result of inadequate or inappropriate education. Lessinger has observed:

> For each child . . . failed by his school, all of us pay a price in taxes and in social unrest, and the child himself is deprived of his chance to develop his potential.[19]

Many schools have tended to function primarily as *closed systems* that seem to resist promising new procedures; all should become *open systems* in which challenging new ideas and approaches can flourish. As Lessinger has pointed out, *there is a need in every state and local school system for "development capital" that can be utilized to encourage and try out promising new approaches to learning and to devise appropriate ways of measuring the output of schools in terms of learning accomplished*—instead of in terms of the amount of teaching done—*so the stage can be set and procedures devised to ensure bona fide accountability*. He states that accountability requires three important steps in each school system and school: (1) develop performance criteria for each program; (2) provide for an independent educational accomplishment audit to measure the actual performance against these criteria; and (3) provide for a public report of the findings of the accomplishment audit.[20]

A recent publication notes that the development of technology could result in the isolation of the learner but, if properly utilized on the basis of carefully developed plans, should: (1) force re-examination of the goals of education; (2) automate some learning, with a more orderly sequence of some elements; (3) help to individualize some types of learning; (4) make it possible to do some things that are not feasible in any other way; (5) strengthen research; (6) help in the management of instructional details; (7) have an important impact on educational counseling; and (8) enhance the opportunities for bona fide accountability.[21]

Every state education agency has an obligation to lead in planning, developing and utilizing appropriate criteria and procedures for the kind of state and local accountability that will be meaningful under modern conditions—that will help to focus attention on and facilitate optimum progress for all students. These plans should be designed to assist the agency and local school systems in developing and reporting to the public on the procedures utilized and the progress made.

IN SUMMARY

The provisions for the organization, operation and support of education in each state are based on political decisions that can be significantly influenced by educators, but actually are made by the citizens and the representatives they select to serve in the legislature or as state officials. These provisions may facilitate or even prevent the attainment of excellence in education throughout the state.

All laws relating to education, as well as the goals, programs and procedures, should be systematically planned and designed to facilitate the development and implementation of policies that will contribute maximally to the improvement of learning environments, opportunities and procedures for all students. They should seldom, if ever, be based on expedient decisions and actions designed primarily to appease powerful pressure groups or to alleviate special problem situations. Unfortunately some laws actually retard rather than facilitate progress. But considerable progress is being made in a number of states in decreasing inequities for taxpayers, inequalities in opportunities for students, and modernizing other provisions for education.

In every state, the state education agency must continuously seek the cooperation and support of competent lay citizens and educators in planning and submitting proposals for improving provisions for the organization, operation and support of education, and should be expected to provide the leadership and services needed to help local school systems to plan and account to the public for bona fide progress in learning by all students.

In order to provide the leadership and services needed to plan and effect improvements in education throughout the state, every state education agency needs to develop and implement plans for modernizing its own role, functions and relations. Only by demonstrating its ability to meet changing needs will this agency become a viable and effective organization that can provide competent and consistent leadership in improving the state system of education.

During the years ahead, each state education agency will need, especially, to provide dynamic and constructive leadership and services in helping the citizens of the state to:

- Understand the importance of planning and effecting improvements in all levels and aspects of education;

- Agree on appropriate policies, goals and priorities for education and cooperate in ensuring that they are implemented and attained;

- Seek effective ways to assist in improving provisions for the organization and operation of education and in developing bona fide local leadership and responsibility;

- Assist in ensuring that the provisions for financial support are adequate, realistic, equitable for taxpayers, and encourage appropriate arrangements for optimum learning opportunities and procedures for all students; and

- Cooperate in developing and implementing realistic provisions and procedures for evaluating and reporting not only on the learning progress of students but also on the forces, factors and conditions that contribute to, or limit, satisfactory progress—that is, in ensuring accountability for all aspects of education.

The citizens, including educators, in every community and state throughout the nation urgently need to understand that the concept of excellence in education can be closely approached or perhaps attained only when they find optimum ways of cooperating to ensure that all forces, factors and conditions affecting education are favorable—that is, when the achievement of excellence in education is accepted by every citizen as one of his top priorities.

Footnote References

[1]T. B. Weaver, *Unity and Diversity in Education* (London: Department of Education and Science, 1970), p. 5.

[2]Frank Bowles, *Educational Opportunity and Political Reality* (New York, N. Y.: Academy for Educational Development, Inc. Paper No. 2, 1965), pp. 2 and 11.

[3]Ralph B. Kimbrough, *Political Power and Educational Decision-Making* (Chicago: Rand McNally & Company, 1964), p. 271.

[4]Warren L. Ziegler in *Notes on the Future of Education* (Syracuse University: Educational Policy Research Center, Vol. 1, Issue 3, Summer, 1970), pp. 14 and 16.

[5]*Ibid.*, p. 18.

[6]Ralph B. Kimbrough, "Power Structures and Educational Change" in *Planning and Effecting Needed Changes in Education,* Edgar L. Morphet and Charles O. Ryan, eds. (Denver, Colorado: Designing Education for the Future, 1967), p. 136. Republished by Citation Press, Scholastic Magazines, Inc., New York, N. Y.

[7]See, for example, R. L. Johns in *Implications for Education of Prospective Changes in Society,* Edgar L. Morphet and Charles O. Ryan, eds. (Denver, Colorado: Designing Education for the Future, 1967), p. 263. Republished by Citation Press, Scholastic Magazines, Inc., New York, N. Y.

[8]Published by *Improving State Leadership in Education* (Denver, Colorado: 1970)

[9]Stephen K. Bailey *et al, Schoolmen and Politics: A Study of State Aid to Education in the North East* (Syracuse: Syracuse University Press, 1962), p. 107.

[10]Laurence D. Haskew, "Implications for Leadership Performance" in *The Evolution of Planning in the Texas Education Agency,* Edgar L. Morphet and Arthur P. Ludka, eds. (Denver, Colorado: Improving State Leadership in Education, 1970), p. 18.

[11]Charles W. Nix, "Internal Planning by State Education Agencies." Summary of a report of a special study sponsored by the project, *Improving State Leadership in Education.*

[12]Clifford P. Hooker and Van D. Mueller, *Patterns of School District Organization.* Part I of a study of *The Relationship of School District Reorganization to State Air Distribution Systems* (Minneapolis: The University of Minnesota, 1970).

[13]Rowan C. Stutz and Edgar L. Morphet, "Improving the Organization, Operation and Support of Education," in *Emerging State Responsibilities for Education,* Edgar L. Morphet *et al,* eds. (Denver, Colorado: Improving State Leadership in Education, 1970), pp. 100-106.

[14]Adapted from John A. Ramseyer *et al, Factors Affecting Educational Administration,* Monograph No. 3, (Columbus: College of Education, The Ohio State University, 1955), p. 20.

[15]*Economic Factors Affecting the Financing of Education,* R. L. Johns *et al,* eds. (Gainesville, Florida: National Educational Finance Project, 1971).

[16]See especially the publications entitled *Status and Impact of Educational Finance Programs* (1971) and *Alternative Programs for the Financing of Education* (1971).

[17]"Equalizing Educational Opportunity—The State and Federal Roles." Statement before the Senate Select Committee on Equal Educational Opportunity, October 6, 1970.

[18]See, for example, Lynn P. Cleary, *The Florida Education Improvement Expense Program* (Denver, Colorado: Improving State Leadership in Education, 1970); and "Recommended Criteria for Implementation of Chapter 234, Laws of 1970" (Trenton, New Jersey: New Jersey State Department of Education, 1971).

[19]Leon M. Lessinger, *Every Kid a Winner: Accountability in Education* (New York, N. Y.: Simon and Schuster, 1970), p. 3.

[20]*Ibid.,* p. 32.

[21]*Educational Technology and Administration* (Washington, D. C.: American Association of School Administrators, 1970), pp. 27-28.